S0-BBF-591

*f*P

Also by Cathy Day

*The Circus in Winter*

# Comeback Season

How I Learned to Play
the Game of Love

Cathy Day

Free Press

New York  London  Toronto  Sydney

Note to Readers

The names and other identifying characteristics of the persons included in this memoir have been changed, and several e-mails and online postings were edited to remove identifying information. A few individuals depicted herein are composites of people I met and corresponded with during this time, and therefore several of the e-mails and online postings are composite representations of e-mails or postings I received.

Free Press
A Division of Simon & Schuster, Inc.
1230 Avenue of the Americas
New York, NY 10020

First Free Press hardcover edition February 2008

FREE PRESS and colophon are trademarks of Simon & Schuster, Inc.

For information about special discounts for bulk purchases,
please contact Simon & Schuster Special Sales at
1-800-456-6798 or business@simonandschuster.com

Book design by Ellen R. Sasahara

Manufactured in the United States of America

1   3   5   7   9   10   8   6   4   2

Library of Congress Cataloging-in-Publication Data

Day, Cathy.
Comeback season : how I learned to play the game of love / by Cathy Day.
p.    cm.
1. Day, Cathy.   2. Single women—United States—Biography.
3. Football fans—United States—Biography.   I. Title.
HQ800.2.D39   2008
306.81'53092—dc22
[B]                                                          2007041941
ISBN-13: 978-1-4165-5710-4
ISBN-10:     1-4165-5710-5

*For all the lonely people*

# Schedule

---

## Preseason

## The Season

## Push to the Playoffs

# SCHEDULE

## Postseason

# Preseason

The last thing he said to me, "Rock," he said,
"sometime, when the team is up against it, and the
breaks are beating the boys, tell them to go out there
with all they got and win just one for the Gipper."

*—Knute Rockne All American*

---

# THE 2005 SEASON

## OR

# Don't Stop Believin'

---

W hen I was a little girl, I told myself a story about the kind of life I
wanted to live someday. I didn't know how to tell a story back
then, so I looked around for a blueprint, a story whose plot I could modify for my own purposes. It needed to be about how to live an extraordinary life—an escape story. So I read lots of books, of course. Pittsburgh's
Andrew Carnegie built the public library in my hometown. Even though
I haven't set foot in that library in over twenty years, I can tell you exactly
where the sports biographies were shelved when I was a kid. My parents
thought it was a little strange: their chunky, bookish daughter who really
didn't enjoy *playing* sports devouring biographies of Satchel Paige,
Johnny Bench, Lou Gehrig, and Jackie Robinson.

The sports story provided me a straightforward formula, my own version of the Horatio Alger story. Replace "wants to go the distance with
Apollo Creed" or "desires to win Olympic gold medal" with "wants to be
an author." Replace "must face bias and an unsupportive father" or "fights
fear, fatigue, and a Russian adversary" with . . . well, I don't think I knew
who or what I was up against, but I knew it had something to do with
being a girl instead of a boy. I knew it had something to do with being

from a town in the middle of nowhere Indiana. I knew it had something to do with growing up in a family that rarely read books, let alone thought about writing them. If playing football is a guy's ticket out of "Life in the Steel Mills" or "Life as a Neighborhood Bum," then writing was my ticket out of "Life as a Small-Town Girl." I wanted to take the midnight train and go anywhere.

And I did. My story came true.

That's where *this* story begins. I've just moved to Pittsburgh to start my dream job teaching fiction writing at the University of Pittsburgh. My office is in a stately building called the Cathedral of Learning. My first book is out and doing pretty well. I've moved to the Steel City from New Jersey so that I can live closer—but not too close—to my family in Indiana. I may be thirty-seven but, as my grandma says, I still have my figure. I have finally achieved my professional goals and am ready to focus on my personal life.

If this was a movie, then this would be the part where, after pounding a lot of frozen meat with my fists and running down dirty, narrow streets, I reach the top step of the Philadelphia Art Museum. Triumphantly, I jump around in slow motion, framed by the pink, rising sun. But later, when I'm in the ring and call out "Adrian! Adrian!" nobody answers.

The night of the November 28, 2005, regular-season matchup between the Colts and Steelers, I brazenly make a bet with my fiction workshop at the University of Pittsburgh: if the Steelers manage to beat my home-state Colts, I'll give the class extra time to turn in their final exam. There's good-natured razzing all around as we pack up to go home. It's half an hour before kickoff when my bus, the 71C, lets me off in a strangely deserted Shadyside. When I moved to Pittsburgh a few months ago, I got the same advice over and over: the best time to drive anywhere is during game time. Everyone is either packed into Heinz Field (though still waxing nostalgic about Three Rivers Stadium) or holed up in front of a large-screen television. As my bus pulls away, I know that my body is walking down Ellsworth Avenue in Pittsburgh, but the rest of me is back home in Indiana with Colts fans: walking in downtown Indy toward that white, domed spaceship on the horizon; sitting in a sports bar in a big-box shopping center; descending into a finished basement decorated with up-turned horseshoes. I wonder what it would be like to fly over Indiana this Monday night, if all those TV sets, all those living-room picture windows blinking a flickery blue light would look like a million stars scattered across the cold, black earth.

At the door to my apartment building, I see two guys wearing yellow and black holding pizzas and beers. Because I am a nice girl from Indiana, I hold the door for them, but in the elevator I can't keep my silence.

"Going to watch the game?" I ask.

"You bet!" they say.

This is how a Hoosier trash-talks: I say sweetly, "Well, I hate to say it, but I'll be rooting for the Colts." They look at me like I'm insane. "I can't help it," I say. "I was born in Indiana."

They shake their heads like this is the most idiotic thing they've ever heard.

I try a more rational appeal. "Look, if you had to move to, say, Kansas City, you wouldn't all of a sudden become a Chiefs fan. You'd still be a Steelers fan, right?"

"Shit yeah," they say in unison.

"Well . . . that's what I'm saying." A stiff silence follows as we wait for the elevator doors to open. I get off first, and as I'm walking away, one of them yells, "Go Steelers!"

So what's a nice girl like me doing in a place like this?

I left Indiana—probably for good—fifteen years ago. When I was eighteen, my parents moved from Peru, Indiana, a small town two hours north of Indianapolis, to Aurora, Indiana, an exurb of Cincinnati, which is where I saw my first major-league baseball game and understood what Susan Sarandon meant in *Bull Durham:* "I believe in the Church of Base-ball." I went to graduate school at the University of Alabama and became a Tide fan. My academic career took me first to Mankato, Minnesota, training camp for the Vikings, where I was introduced to ice hockey and the Twins. Then I moved to Baltimore and went to Camden Yards to watch the Orioles and Cal Ripken. After that, I taught in New Jersey, a state of diffuse loyalties and identities. Was I supposed to follow the Eagles or Giants or Jets? And now I live in Pittsburgh, where I'm learning the cultural importance of Mario Lemieux and the Terrible Towel.

Twenty years of moving and making new friends and learning new jobs and moving and starting all over again—following sports, following a team, was how I made each new place home. But my fandom has always been fleeting. When I move, so do my loyalties. I have no idea whether Alabama beat Auburn last year or how the Orioles are doing. However, one thing has never changed: no matter where I'm living, I still love Indiana sports.

By the way, "Indiana sports," when you grow up in the northern half of the state, includes Chicago (unless they're playing an Indiana team, of course).

On January 26, 1986, four generations of the Day family gathered in our living room to watch Super Bowl XX. The Chicago Bears cremated New England 46–10. In the photograph commemorating this event, my thirteen-year-old brother brandishes his first beer, my dad and my grandpa sport Bears jerseys, and my eighty-seven-year-old great-grandfather holds a VHS cassette of "The Super Bowl Shuffle." A year later, I sat in my college dorm's TV room, watching mournfully as Walter Payton played his last game. The Bears lost that day. Afterwards, Sweetness sat on the bench with his head in hands, and my heart broke a little, so I called my dad to see how he was doing.

You need to know this: my father has read two books since he graduated from high school: my story collection and *Never Die Easy: The Autobiography of Walter Payton.*

In 1998, when the Bulls and Pacers were battling for the conference championship, my long-term boyfriend Alex (a native of Chicago) and I got so vicious we couldn't watch the games together. When the Pacers lost to the Lakers two years later in the 2000 NBA finals, my heart broke—as it had for Walter Payton—as Larry Bird's three-year coaching stint in his home state ended with a loss. When I heard that IU beat Duke in the 2002 NCAA tournament, my heart swelled for Mike Davis as he tried to escape the shadow of Bobby Knight. The week of Indiana's championship game against Maryland, I got a little hysterical. I was teaching in New Jersey at this point, and I wore cream and crimson every day and hummed the IU fight song (which is also my high school fight song) at the Xerox machine.

That night in 2002, I sat down to watch the IU game alone. After seven years together, Alex and I had broken up the year before, and I realized that since then I had neither watched nor attended a single sporting event. See, all those games I mentioned—in Alabama, Minnesota, Baltimore—I went to with him. I'd moved to New Jersey for two reasons: to be closer to him and to keep myself in the kind of teaching job that gave me time to write my book. The book was almost finished, but the relationship was kaput, and I realized that I was in a place where I knew almost no one. When the game started, I wondered how it had come to this: I was a single woman in her thirties sitting alone watching television. At halftime, I called my dad on the landline and my brother on my cell phone and we "watched the game together." Sort of. And IU lost.

Here's a funny story: Shortly after the breakup, I went to Boston to spend Thanksgiving with an old college buddy and her husband. There, I experienced my first Fix-Up. They invited a friend (that rare commodity, the Straight Single Man in His Thirties) to join us for dinner. He asked me what I did for a living. I told him the truth: I'm a college professor and a writer. After dinner, Straight Single Man kept touching my ass and talking about a book he'd just read. Later, he confessed he really hadn't read it; he just figured that's what I'd want to talk about. Later, he told my friend he wasn't interested in me because I probably wasn't the kind of girl who'd watch football with him on Sundays.

*Monday Night Football.* Colts versus Steelers. The elevator door closes on the cry of those Steelers fans. My cat greets me at the door to my apartment. I open my mail—bills. Check my messages—none. I put on my pajamas and turn on the TV. Munching popcorn, I watch Peyton Manning throw an 80-yard touchdown to Marvin Harrison on the first snap. Then the phone rings, and I must track two games at once: the football game on TV and the pseudo–dating game I've been playing with the man on the phone. I met him at my faculty orientation meeting, and we've been hanging out for three months. He's smart. He laughs at my jokes. We talk on the phone for hours sometimes. He took me to my first Penguins hockey game. When he picks me up to see a movie or eat dinner, he touches my knee and says, "You look really nice tonight." I haven't heard words like this in five years so, of course, I'm crazy about him.

Wait. We're coming to the agony-of-defeat-skier-plummeting-down-the-mountain-Favre-picking-Vicodin-out-of-the-toilet part of the story. Did I mention he has a girlfriend who lives in New York City? Did I mention that he's been mentioning her less and less lately? I can't stand the tension anymore.

"Look," I tell him, trying to follow the Colts versus Steelers game. "It's fourth-and-four. What are you gonna do? Are you gonna go for it? Or are you gonna punt?"

He says, "What, do you mean I've been flirting with you? No I haven't." An hour later, he admits that yes, he has, but no, he's not leaving his girlfriend. An hour after that, I tell the Punter goodnight and hang up. The Colts have beaten the Steelers on *Monday Night Football*, but I'm not celebrating. I've just said good-bye to my only friend in Pittsburgh. It's late, and Shadyside is quiet and dark. Another love-life postseason has begun.

You need to know this: in the game of love, my team has always lost in spectacular fashion. As with the Colts, some seasons begin with great promise, but something goes awry in the playoffs. Afterward, I sit on the bench with my head in my hands and my heart in my stomach. I walk to the locker room, where a teammate gives me that postgame pep talk. "There is a Super Bowl ring in your future! I just know it, Cathy! Now you're a free agent, and some team is going to snatch you up!" I know I must believe this. I know there's always next year. As Tim Robbins says in *Bull Durham*, it's a very simple game once you learn your interview clichés. Sometimes you win, sometimes you lose, and sometimes it rains.

A reporter sticks a microphone in my face.

**Reporter:** Cathy, what went wrong?
**Me:** Well, I'm disappointed. I put myself in good position, no question. But he had home-field advantage. He just wasn't able to take that next step, and that's disappointing. It is hard to swallow.
**Reporter:** Are saying it's not your fault?

**Me:** Well, he knew my offensive line had problems, but I know I didn't protect myself like I should have.

**Reporter:** Cathy, you're coming off a tough loss. You're thirty-seven years old, you've never been married. This season began with such high hopes. Everyone—especially your mother—really thought this was the year. How do you feel right now?

**Me:** Are you kidding me? How do I feel?

**Reporter:** Yes, how does a player pick up the pieces, year after year, come back and try again?

**Me:** I used to know the answer to that question. It was: *You just do.* But I honestly don't know if I have it in me to go through this again.

**Reporter:** Are you planning to retire? They say you still have a few good years left to play.

**Me:** Look, right now I just want to get drunk and sleep for two days, okay?

**Reporter:** This is Suzy Hightop reporting live. Back to you, Bob.

The Colts' amazing thirteen-game winning streak ends on December 18 against San Diego. I drive from Pittsburgh to Indiana for Christmas, but I'm in no mood for the holidays. I put on a red sweater and try to enjoy the day, but I can't shake my recent loss in the game of love. Over and over in my head, I replay my relationship with the Punter, trying to calculate what went wrong. Was it my offense or my defense? Did I have my head in the game? Or did I overthink? Was it me or him? Am I cursed?

My sister Andrea finds me alone on the back porch. "I want you to come inside," she says. "You need to stop thinking about him. You need to stop dwelling."

I look up at her. "How do you do that?" I really want to know the answer.

"You just do it. You think about something else. You snap out of it."

"I've never been very good at that," I say.

"I know," she says softly, then gives me a hug.

Later Andrea, her husband John, and their son Clay drive home to their house in Harrison, Ohio. My brother Scott and his wife Sara drive home to their house in Batesville, Indiana. Me, I have no house—not even in Pittsburgh. My parents' house is the closest thing I have to a home. I feel like I'm nineteen—not thirty-seven—and home for the holidays like a college girl.

All my life I've been a believer. I believed I would become a writer. I believed I would fall in love. I believed that *this* was the year the Colts would win the Super Bowl. But I can feel my faith in those things slipping away.

To prepare for the Colts versus Steelers playoff game on January 15, 2006, I replicate most—but not all—of the conditions of their first matchup. I'm in Pittsburgh, alone in my apartment, eating popcorn in my pajamas with my cat. But this time I don't make a bet with my students, brag on the elevator, or talk to the Punter. Later, I'll learn that 74 percent of TV sets in the Indianapolis viewing area are tuned to this game. I'm sharing the experience with three quarters of the population of central Indiana. I'm in Pittsburgh, I'm in Indiana. I'm in both places, I'm in neither. It's like waking in a dark hotel room, those "Where am I?" seconds when you're momentarily placeless. And isn't this the story of my life?

I'm in Pittsburgh, but in the RCA Dome the Colts are struggling. During the fourth quarter I call my family. Briefly I wonder if calling them is a good idea, since I wasn't talking to them—but rather the Punter—during the last Colts versus Steelers game. The Punter and I aren't talking anymore, but should I call anyway, for the sake of the team? *No!* I decide, *I should not!* Just then Steelers' running back, Jerome Bettis, a.k.a. "The Bus," loses the ball at the goal line. All around me I can hear Pittsburghers scream. At Cupka's Bar on the South Side, the heart of a die-hard Steelers fan literally stops beating, and he falls from his barstool. He misses what happens next: Nick Harper, whose wife had stabbed him twenty-four hours earlier, swoops up the ball and runs downfield. On the phone, my family shrieks "Goooooooooooo!" Everyone in the state of Indiana is on their feet yelling "Yessssss!" and everyone in western Pennsylvania is on their feet yelling "Nooooooooo!"

Then Steelers quarterback Ben Roethlisberger appears, trying to get in position to stop Nick Harper. Ben lunges and falls to the turf but manages to get his hand on Harper's kneecap. Later, sports commentators will refer to this desperate, backpedaling dive as the "Immaculate Tackle" in honor of another legendary Steelers' game-saving play: Franco Harris's "Immaculate Reception." The tackle is hardly "immaculate." It's a fluke! But it's enough to bring down Harper, who—if it hadn't been for Bearded Big Ben—would have run the ball for a touchdown. Later the heart-attack guy will say from his hospital bed, "It hurt me more to see [Bettis] fumble the ball, and to perhaps end his Pittsburgh career that way, than us losing the game. It was more than my heart could bear." On the sidelines, Bettis's coach and teammates reassure him. "That will *not* be your last carry in the NFL!" But why not? Did Walter Payton win the last game of his NFL career? No. Did Larry Bird end his coaching career with a win for the Pacers? No. Why should Jerome Bettis get what they didn't?

But there's still hope, Colts fans! Because all we need to tie the game and send it into overtime is for ace kicker Mike Vanderjagt to nail a 46-yard field goal. And unbelievably, Vanderjagt chokes. Wide right. The walls of my apartment building vibrate with ecstatic joy. Down on Forbes Avenue, my Pitt students pour into the streets. Peyton leaves the field, and I feel my heart breaking. How can your heart break for a man you don't even know? "Mom," I say into the phone, "how's everybody doing?"

"Well, Scott took off his Peyton Manning jersey, and your dad just kicked a bucket full of spare car parts all over the garage."

After we say good-bye, I pace my apartment, trying to calm down. I log onto the home pages of the *Indianapolis Star* and the *Pittsburgh Post-Gazette* to see the headlines. At a Pittsburgh hospital, the heart-attack man regains consciousness and asks his doctor who won. In Batesville, my father and brother go for a long walk together. They never walk anywhere, not even to the corner store for a gallon of milk, but they just don't know what else to do with themselves. I wish I had someone to commiserate with, but there's no one around except Steelers fans.

It's the day after the Colts lost to Pittsburgh. At a faculty meeting everyone's talking about the game. A colleague notices me sitting quietly and says, "Oh right, you're from Indiana. Too bad."

"It's not too bad," I say brusquely. "It's a freaking tragedy."

He thinks for a second. "Yes, I'd have to agree with you. It's a Greek tragedy. Or perhaps Norse."

Someday he might write a paper comparing the Colts' 2005 season to a play by Sophocles. Me, all I can do is compare it to my stupid love life. But isn't the correlation obvious? Aren't these Colts fans posting on an *Indianapolis Star* message board saying the same things I've said to myself after losing a big game of love?

"Sometimes Peyton can think too much."

"I love the Blue, but how can this organization not be cursed?"

How many times in love's postseason have I asked myself the question "What's wrong with me?" Here's Colts coach Tony Dungy's answer: "That's the hardest thing, because you do kind of get that in your own mind. You hear enough, 'What's wrong? What's wrong?' Really, most of the time there's not a whole lot wrong. It's very, very disappointing, but you do have to resist the idea that something needs to be overhauled, and I think we'll be able to do that."

I sit down to write an encouraging letter to the Colts. I want to tell them, "Guys, I know about heartbreaking losses." I want to tell them, "Don't stop believing!" I start writing, and somewhere along the way, I realize I'm writing a pep talk, not for them but for me.

So that's how this whole thing starts. I tell myself, *Cathy, if the Colts can come back in 2006 and try again, so can you.*

If you build it, he will come.

—*Field of Dreams*

---

# TRAINING MONTAGE

## OR

# Nothing (and Everything) Happens During the Off-Season

---

*Cue "Theme from* Chariots of Fire*" by Vangelis*

It's the week after the Colts lost to Pittsburgh, and I need to get back on the playing field of love. Either that or I need to buy a house. One of the two. I pick buying a house because it scares me less. I log onto a Web site, enter my preferences, and click around to see what's out there. I tell a realtor I'm ready to finally put down some roots, and a week after the Super Bowl, she fixes me up with a two-story brick house in the Polish Hill neighborhood of Pittsburgh. The house is very old but totally refurbished, which is good, because I've had it with those fixer-upper types. I tell myself, *You've been a free agent long enough. Be a franchise player.* So I spend all my money—every cent. I sign the papers. I own property in, of all places, Pittsburgh. I move from my apartment in Shadyside to Polish Hill.

That's when I start getting letters about mortgage life insurance. "If something should happen to you," the letters say, "don't you want your spouse and children to be able to continue living in your house?" Sure—if I had them. But it gets me thinking. What happens if I do die? Who gets stuck with my debt? I call Paul, my insurance guy. He says he can't remember the last time someone bought a house but didn't have a spouse or real or intended children to give the house to. Paul says I should see a lawyer and officially leave the house to my "siblings." He even recommends a lawyer friend of his, also named Paul. Paul the Lawyer. In the back of my mind, I think, *Wouldn't it be funny if making out a will is what leads me to my future partner?* Actually, I have this thought a lot, and my single friends say the same thing. It's so rare to meet a single man, or even a potentially single man, that you can't help but wonder: *Are you the man who will be my husband? Is this the story I'm going to tell about how we met?*

My meeting with Paul the Lawyer looms. I tell myself to collect the info that surely he'll need: bank accounts; my TIAA-CREF accounts. Do I have a life insurance policy? Surely I do. But I can't make myself look for this information. The morning of our meeting, I wake up and think, *You know, I don't need this today. This is really bumming me out.* But what if Paul the Lawyer is my Future Husband? Plus, I have nothing else to do today, so why not make out a will? Who do I want to have power of attorney when I become old and incapacitated? Do I want to be kept alive with a feeding tube? I get out of bed, scour my files for account statements and policy numbers, and run out the door.

Paul the Lawyer walks into the waiting room and sticks out his hand. He's wearing a wedding ring. Oh well. In his small office I explain what brought me: I'm single and I don't know if that's going to change and I just bought a house. Paul chitchats, and then shows me pictures of his kids behind his desk. I get this a lot, actually. I try to be friendly to a man my age, and within thirty seconds he finds a tenuous reason to bring up the word "wife" or "girlfriend" or "kids." For a long time, I worried about this. Was I putting out a vibe like I was after them? I don't think I do, but wasn't I wondering if he was single before I even walked in the door? And aren't I glad these men are doing this? Would I rather that they hit on me only to find out later that they're married?

We discuss setting up the will so that my house will go equally to my younger sister and brother, their spouses, and their current and future progeny. Paul smiles. "But it will easy for us to change this when you *do* get married."

I shrug. Is he being patronizing? It feels like he's just rooting for me.

He smiles. "I'll just write in here something like 'Spouse . . .'"

14

"TBA," I offer.

I'm amazed that this lawyer, a stranger to me, is more positive about my romantic future than I am. Paul gets out a form to take down information about my beneficiaries, and I notice that he's covering part of it with his hand. That's because it's set up in two columns—the left side is for *husband* and the right side is for *wife,* and he's writing all my info down under *wife.*

The feminist, intellectual side of me is infuriated—at Paul, at whoever created this form. But there's another part of me that feels embarrassed and completely, utterly alone on the face of this earth. There's an elephant in this tiny Squirrel Hill office, and the only way I can keep myself from bursting into tears is to smile and point out this elephant. (I wrote a whole book about elephants, after all.)

"Can I ask you something?" Paul looks up from the page. "How many women like me who've bought a house on their own come in here and do this?"

He pauses before answering. "I'd say less than one percent of our clients are women like you, single professional homeowners."

I tell him about the form letters that led me to take this step, the insistent question: *If something should happen to you, don't you want your spouse and children to continue living in your house?* Surely I'm not the only female single professional homeowner in Pittsburgh? "So when those women get this letter in the mail, what do they do?"

Paul's voice gets kind of quiet. "I guess they figure there's always a chance that maybe they'll get married someday."

What I don't say is: *They don't want to come into this office because it's tantamount to saying, "When I die, and yes, I will die someday, I will die alone."* Because who wants to say that?

*Cue "Maniac" by Michael Sembello ( from* Flashdance*)*

It's Valentine's Day, and I think I'm having anxiety attacks. Every time I see the Punter, every time I think I *might* see the Punter, my chest tightens like I've had the wind knocked out of me. I start seeing a shrink. This is a new kind of shrink for me, a cognitive-behavioral therapist who uses a dry erase board, multicolored markers, and workbooks that tell me to stop thinking negatively and start thinking positively. I argue with this shrink, who asks questions like, "Okay, so you think the reason he doesn't want to date you is because you are too intense. What is a more rational explanation?" To which I say, "How do you know that isn't the rational explanation?" What keeps me coming back is that this shrink was born twenty miles from my hometown. We are the same age and went to rival high schools but have just now met in, of all places, Pittsburgh. For some reason, I believe this coincidence means that this shrink can help me figure out why my life makes absolutely no sense to me.

"I can't figure out why I'm not happy," I tell her. "I published a book. I teach at this great school. But why do I feel like I have no life?"

"What about friends?" the shrink asks.

"*He* was my friend."

"Don't you have *women* friends?" She asks this a little accusingly.

"Yes," I say calmly. I tell her about my friend Sofia in Alabama, Jillian in Oregon, my sister, my mom. I tell my shrink I have women friends all over the damn country—from my years in college, graduate school, Minnesota, Baltimore, and New Jersey.

"What about Pittsburgh?"

I sigh. "I'm working on it." Sometimes finding a girlfriend is as hard as finding a boyfriend. "A lot of the women I know are married. A lot of them are busy with kids, or they're trying to have kids." I look down at my hands. "I wonder sometimes. What's the difference between them and me?"

"What do you mean?" the shrink asks.

I pause. "What did they do that I didn't do? What do they know that I don't know?"

My shrink sighs. "I think a woman makes a promise to herself about when she will have kids."

I'm amazed by this. "You mean some women consciously say to themselves, 'By the time I'm twenty-seven, I will be married. By the time I'm thirty I will have a child.' Women actually think like that?"

She nods. "Yes, although sometimes it's more unconscious. Did you make yourself a promise?"

I look up at the dry erase board, at the stoplight drawn next to the long list of my negative thoughts. "I promised myself I'd have written a book by the time I was thirty-five."

The shrink nods. "See, you do understand, you just told yourself something different. Did you keep your promise?"

"Yes," I say, but a very negative thought pops into my head. I don't say it out loud, because then the shrink will jump up and add it to the list on the dry erase board. *Maybe I made myself the wrong promise. Or maybe I should have made two promises: a book and a family.*


My gynecologist gives me the bad news: my chances of finding a good man in Pittsburgh are slim. I've come in for my yearly pap smear, and the doctor conducts her interview in her private office at the Magee Women's Hospital. Outside her window, cars stream up Forbes Avenue. She's a shortish woman in her fifties and she adjusts her glasses as she scans my intake form. I know what she sees. I'm a thirty-seven-year-old unmarried female. "Well, Catherine, what brings you to Pittsburgh?"

"Cathy is fine."

"Cathy." She smiles at me like a supportive aunt.

"I just started teaching at Pitt."

"What department?"

"English."

"You're a professor then?" She looks skeptical.

I nod. I get this a lot. I don't look particularly professorial in my jeans and sweater. I can still pass as a slightly aged graduate student. I give her the short version of my peripatetic academic life: teaching gigs in four states, etc.

She clicks her pen. "Are you on birth control?"

"Not anymore."

She looks up over her glasses. "Are you sexually active?"

"No," I say a little crankily.

The doctor chuckles.

In the exam room, she kneads my breasts and says, "You know, Pittsburgh is a hard place for a single woman, especially a professional."

I keep staring at the ceiling light fixture. "Really? Why is that?"

"Do you do regular breast exams?"

"Oh sure," I lie. Lately, my breasts seem as inessential to me as my gallbladder.

At the end of the exam, she snaps off her gloves and says, "Men in Pittsburgh marry early. The ones who don't fall into two groups: the ones that still live with their mothers, and the ones who leave."

"Where do they go?" I ask, sitting up in my gown.

"Well, the professional ones, the ones with something going for them, the kind you're looking for, go to Philly or New York, where the good jobs are. The ones who stay here and don't get married, well, they lack . . . how to say it?" Her voice goes a little dreamy, and she stares at the specimen bottles in her hands. "Drive," she says finally. "They're not much interested in women like us."

I'm not sure if I feel like bursting into tears or screaming, "What do you mean, like us? I'm not you!" But I know that in many ways I am. I picture her driving home to Squirrel Hill or Shadyside at the end of the day, entering her condo, making herself some dinner with the cat sitting on the counter and settling down for the night in front of the tube, which is exactly what I do every night. Things weren't supposed to work out like this for us, but for reasons we can't quite understand, they did. We sit around and wonder what if we'd done things differently—picked him instead of the other guy, picked this city or that job or this college rather than the ones we did. We're both lonely and bored and pissed off. Or at least I am.

"Thanks," I say to the gyno. It's all I can think of.

"Good luck, Cathy," she says, and I can tell she means it.


For the first time in my life, I've got insomnia. My doctor won't prescribe me anything. Instead, she says, "Are you ready to stop smoking?"

I've been thinking about it a lot, actually. I want to start dating, and I can't imagine getting through that much social distress without Camel Lights. But I know that checking the "I'm a smoker" box will limit my options. What if I miss meeting the man of my dreams because I'm a smoker? But wouldn't the man of my dreams understand? Maybe the man of my dreams is a smoker, and I'll miss meeting him because I've quit? It's thinking and rethinking like this that keeps me up until four in the morning every night.

"You know," I tell the doctor, "I think that if they really want people to stop smoking, they should put us in a coma for about two weeks, feed us intravenously, and let the worst of the withdrawal pass, and then when we come out, all we have to do is beat the habit of it."

My doctor keeps her back to me, looking at my chart. She writes something down. Is she writing a note in my file: "Wants to be put in a coma." But it was a joke!

Not really, but sort of.

The doctor suggests acupuncture instead of a drug-induced coma and hands me a phone number. I ask her, "Is it true that some people get Xanax when they are quitting smoking?"

I am not asking for a prescription for Xanax; I'm just asking if it's ever done.

She gives me a level look. "I wouldn't suggest that." So, in about five minutes, I have asked:

1. for sleeping pills
2. to be put in a coma
3. for Xanax

My doctor must be very impressed.

### Cue "Gonna Fly Now" (Theme from Rocky)

My potential new friend Pam drives us over the Sixteenth Street Bridge, slipping under its tiered yellow arches set against a brilliantly blue June sky. We enter Pittsburgh's historic North Side. In so many of this city's neighborhoods, I can almost see the high-water markers of Pittsburgh's floods and famines. The Victorian brownstones lining the leafy Mexican War streets (named for the battles and generals of said war) mark the economic prosperity of the nineteenth century, and the porn theater and check-cashing stores on North Avenue mark the economic decline of the mid-twentieth. When we park, Pam and I lock our purses in the trunk, stuffing lipsticks and credit cards into our pockets.

We're headed to a fund-raiser at the Mattress Factory, a contemporary art museum housed in a former Stearns & Foster warehouse, hence the name. Inside, Pam points to the hundreds of people standing around with drinks and prods me to start conversations with random people, preferably men. This stresses me out so much that I have to retreat outside to the ornate rock garden to have a cigarette, where I start up a conversation, no problem, with three other smokers, a married couple and their friend, who appears to be single. We chat and smoke. The seemingly single guy owns some sort of landscaping business and plays on a softball team. He tells me that his team stops by Gooski's, a bar in my neighborhood, every week after practice. I take a deep breath and try to seem nonchalant. "Oh, I live near there." The single man says, "Do you have a card or anything?" I say no, and he says he doesn't either. "I'd ask for your number, but you'd probably think I was trying to pick you up." I blush and look at my feet. As Pam and I are leaving, I see him chatting up a girl who looks about twenty-three. Not wanting to interrupt, I give my number to his married friends, who say they will pass it on, but I never hear from him.

On the way back to the car, Pam gives me a pat on the back. "You never know," she says. "Maybe something you learned tonight will make a difference later."

I wake up the next morning realizing that I need to bone up on my dating skills. Not that I've ever had any. See, I can stand in front of a classroom as Cathy the Teacher and riff on point of view or postmodernism. I can stand in front of an audience as Cathy the Writer and read from my book without a single stammer. But I can't seem to figure out how to stand in front of a man as Just Cathy and not fall to pieces. So I tackle this problem the best way I know how: I do research. I buy dating books (anonymously on Amazon.com), including *Dating for Dummies, Turn Your Cablight On,* and *He's Just Not That into You.* I rent the first two seasons of *Sex and the City.* I study up. I take notes.

I'm at the payroll office at Pitt when a lady comes out of the back office and announces that Ben Roethlisberger just crashed his motorcycle at Second Avenue and the Tenth Street Bridge. Later, I'm walking down the street thinking about what I've been learning in my dating research. For one, when I'm walking down the street, I should try to make eye contact with men, which I find extremely hard. I couldn't look anyone in the eye until I was seventeen. Also, I need to start conversations with strangers.

Maybe I should use this news flash as a conversation starter? "Hey," I'll say to some Pittsburgh dude at the bus stop. "Did you hear? Ben Roethlisberger was in a motorcycle accident." But how sick is that, using one man's perhaps fatal accident to talk to another man?

By the next day, however, it's clear that Ben will surely live. I'm on the Cathedral elevator. There's an attractive young man in there with me wearing an earring and an iPod. He's at least fifteen years younger than me, but hey, I need the practice. So I ask, "Have you heard how Ben Roethlisberger is today?"

He looks at me. "I'm so *fucking* sick of people talking about Ben Roethlisberger."

I'm so stunned, all I can say is, "Sorry, sorry."

"I mean people act like the world's gonna come to an end!"

"I know," I say. On the local news, it's all Ben all the time.

The elevator reaches my floor. I get off and run to my office.

**Cue "Lunatic Fringe" by Red Rider (*from the* Visionquest *sound track*)**
My friend Jillian calls from Oregon. "So explain to me what following the Colts has to do with dating."

"Everything!" I say, and I tell her how I'm "in training" for my dating season.

She sighs. "Cathy, you are so hard on yourself."

"No, I'm not," I say. Then I pause. "Okay, so I am, but just look how far being hard on myself has gotten me in life."

Jillian laughs. "Instead of Peyton Manning, you should emulate Brett Favre. At least he knows how to have fun." Her tone turns more serious. "Cathy, maybe what you need to be working on right now is convincing yourself you don't have anything to work on. That you're fine the way you are."

I'm quiet for a long time. "But if I'm so great, why am I still alone?"

She sighs. "Because you didn't settle, and that's to your credit. A lot of people settle because they'd rather do that than be alone. And some are just luckier and found the right person already."

I light a cigarette. "How do people meet other people?" I ask.

Jillian humphs into the phone. "I have no freaking clue, babe." She's been divorced for a few years now.

I tell her that romantic comedies, sappy songs, even the stories people tell about meeting each other, they all make it seem as though it's about serendipity, about *not* trying. *I wasn't going to go to the bar mitzvah, but I did, and then there s/he was.* Movies teach us that all you need to do to fall in love is walk around this earth until one day, boom! the love of your life will literally run into you. "I've been patient, Jill. I've walked around on this earth for thirty-seven years, and I've never run into the love of my life, and he's never run into me."

Jill lights a cigarette. "What you need, girlfriend, is practice. Lots and lots of practice. Go out with any guy who asks, anything that moves. You need to get your confidence back."

"Back? I never had it to begin with."

"You're too nervous. Pretend they aren't dates. Pretend they're like research subjects for some anthropological study you're doing."

Late that night, I sit on my deck alone, chain smoking cigarettes, thinking about love and football. What ultimately determines the outcome of these games? Is it about intangibles like fate and chemistry or is it about tangibles like preparation and control? Or is it both? The lesson the Colts keep learning over and over again is that you can have a great team, a great season, home-field advantage, the best QB in the league, but you still might walk away from the season without a Super Bowl ring. The lesson I keep learning over and over again is that I can have a sense of humor, a good head on my shoulders, a kind heart, a nice smile, a decent rack, but I still might walk off the playing field alone. Why haven't the Colts won the Super Bowl? Why am I alone? Are we victims of bad luck, or is there something we should be doing differently? Is it like people keep saying? *Be patient. It'll happen when it happens.*

It's very late now. I can see the three green copper domes of the Immaculate Heart of Mary Church lit against the downtown skyline. A train clatters through the night. On the other side of the Allegheny River is a mountain of golden stars, the streetlights of Pittsburgh's Troy Hill blinking in the distance. But I'm completely in my own head. I'm thinking about instinct, how athletes can perfect their performance by changing their less-than-ideal instinctual reactions and movements into more powerful swings or better throws. They perform a motion again and again. Muscles memorize and absorb until the new motion becomes a new-and-improved instinct. Perhaps I need to unlearn the way I've always played the game of love. I haven't really been trying—so I'll try. And I always seem to like the wrong kind of guy—so I'll like a different kind of guy. It's like John Cusack's character says in *High Fidelity:* "I've been listening to my gut since I was fourteen years old, and frankly speaking, I've come to the conclusion that my guts have shit for brains."

I stub out my cigarette. I have one left in my pack. The next morning, I smoke that last cigarette and decide that it's my last one ever. *If I can change this instinct,* I think, *I can change anything.*

*Cue "Eye of the Tiger" by Survivor ( from the* Rocky III *sound track)*

Tom and Rachel live across the street from me. They're a cool young couple and seem like they must know other cool young people. One night in July I finally work up the courage to say to them, "Hey, you know, uh, I'm sort of single and everything, so do you guys know any nice fellows?" Magically, they do know someone!

"His name's Nick," Tom says. He's a medic. Is that okay?"

"Why wouldn't it be okay?"

"Well, you know, you're a professor and everything. He's kind of salt of the earth. He didn't go to college."

I roll my eyes. "Dude, I'm salt of the earth!"

I'm supposed to go with them to a Fourth of July party where Nick will be. This will be my first social function without cigarettes, so I bring a lot of suckers.

Nick is forty, a stocky, attractive blond with great teeth and a firm handshake. "Great to meet you, Cathy." Everyone's talking idle party talk—summer movies, landscaping woes, recycling—but I want to cut to the chase and find out who this Nick is. I sit down next to him and ask how he became a medic. Our Q&A (I'm the Q, he's the A) goes on for about forty minutes. Before I leave, I hand him my phone number. I learned my lesson at the Mattress Factory. Just do it. "Oh!" Nick says. "Thanks! I was going to ask, but wasn't sure . . ."

As we drive home, I tell Tom and Rachel that he seemed nice but he did most of the talking. "I don't think he listens very well," I say, "but maybe he was just nervous." He calls me a few days later to ask me to dinner.

I went out to dinner lots of times with the Punter, but those don't count as Real Dates. We both knew he had a girlfriend, and as much as I wanted him to kiss me at the end of the night, I knew he probably wouldn't, which made them Pretend Dates. This date with Nick is my first Real Date in—seriously—years. Nick takes me to Kaya, a Caribbean restaurant in the Strip District. He still does a lot of the talking, but I spend most of my days alone with no one's thoughts to keep me company but my own, so I'm quite glad to listen to another human being for a while. Halfway through dinner, Nick takes my hand across the table and goes on talking. Just a simple, human gesture. But I'm undone, ready to burst into tears. It's been so long since anyone besides family or friends touched me that I can't bear it. A few minutes later, I excuse myself to go to the ladies' room. *Get a grip, Cathy. How can you date if you cry every time somebody wants to hold your hand?*

Later, Nick gives me a kiss good night, and I walk into my house feeling elated and emotionally spent. I want to sit on my deck and have a cigarette, contemplate the evening, but I can't. So I fix myself a drink instead (my first since I stopped smoking), sit on the deck, and replay the evening over in my head. It's a blur. It's like watching a movie with the sound off, a DVD with huge skips in it. The plot, the dialogue, it's all muddled. I can't remember anything Nick said. I can't remember anything I said. All I remember is that touch and what welled up inside me— joy and relief and sadness, all rolled into one.

And yes, a few days later, after our second "date" (which consisted of nothing more than him stopping by), I sleep with Nick. I am amazed I still know how. Afterward, Nick asks with an anxious look on his face, "Do you want to have kids?"

*Finally,* I think. *He's trying to get to know me.* It's a strange question to ask on a second date, but given the speedy way we are progressing through things, perhaps not all that strange. "I don't know," I say. "I think it depends if the man I'm with really wants to be a dad and wants to share parenting." I pause. "What about you? Do you want kids?"

He looks up at the ceiling. "I don't know," he says. That's all.

I had sex more times between the ages of sixteen and twenty-two than I have had in the years since, and that is a sad, sad thing. Back then, I was too young and immature to know what my body wanted, what I wanted. Like a lot of young women who don't yet know themselves, I slept with men because it was something very interesting to do, because it was a way to escape before I had the means or the will to do so. Although I wanted very much to love and be loved, I had absolutely no idea how love worked, what it looked like, or even how to recognize it if and when it decided to show up. In my early twenties, after a period I'll call the Wanton Years, I decided that I would only sleep with someone within the confines of a relationship: if I loved him or thought I did, or if he loved me or thought he did. Of course, I sometimes amended this rule to include the status of "liking a lot." Living by this code saved my soul but has rendered me at times more chronically untouched than I can bear.

There are times when my adult life feels like an impossibly long drive. When I was younger, I didn't mind the highway stretching relentlessly before me as long as I had good music, cigarettes, and a Coke. I loved not knowing how much farther. But these days, I can't handle long stretches of nothingness—on the road or in my life. Being a thirty-something single woman feels like driving down an unfamiliar road at four in the morning: no traffic, nothing's open. I'm hours and hours from where I came from, so I can't turn around and go back, and I'm headed to a place I've never been, so I don't know how much farther. Sometimes, I get scared that *this* is the rest of my life: driving a really nice car all by myself.

For our third date, Nick and I go out for Thai food, then coffee. When we pull up at the Starbucks, he says, "Oh, I have bad memories of this place."

"Why?"

He pauses for a second. "I met a woman here, a woman I met on an Internet dating site. I got here, and I realized she'd . . . uh . . . misrepresented herself."

"How?" I'm fascinated.

"Well, she was a lot heavier than her picture."

"Oh." I think for a second. "Was she nice?"

Nick fiddles with his keys. "I don't know. I was really mad, so I stuck it out for about fifteen minutes, and then I left."

I think about that poor woman working up the courage to meet a stranger in a public place, only to watch him run out the door. It makes me want to cry.

"What if she'd used a current picture and just been straight up?"

Nick is really, really uncomfortable. "I'll admit it. I'm not attracted to big women, so I probably wouldn't have contacted her. I wouldn't have gotten my hopes up. That's what I hate. Getting my hopes up. But you know, if she'd told the truth, she wouldn't have gotten her hopes up either."

We're sitting outside the Starbucks, sipping iced coffees through green straws. "Have you met a lot of women that way?" I ask.

Nick nods. "Yeah, quite a few."

"How many?"

"I'd really rather not say." He smiles, but it's forced. "It's embarrassing."

"Why?"

"I don't know. It just is."

I look at the ground. "Have you met anybody special?"

"No," he says. "I've been on a lot of first dates, but not very many second dates."

"Don't you want to go out with them again?"

"Sometimes I do, sometimes I don't. I'll call and leave a couple messages, but if she's not interested, she stops returning my calls."

I laugh. "That's rude!"

Nick shakes his head. "Oh no, I'd rather they let me know like that. I don't want to have to hear that they don't like me." He takes out his cell phone and flips it open. "I call a girl and leave a message. If I don't hear back, I call again. And if I don't hear back after that, I delete her." He flips his phone closed. "Just like that."

"Wow," I say, shocked. "It can't be fun, being rejected like that."

Nick slips his phone back in the pocket of his cargo shorts. "I move on. If she doesn't like me, fuck her."

26

This is the longest conversation on one topic we have all evening.

As he drives me home, I take stock. *How do I feel?* My instincts are telling me one thing (*I'm not connecting with this guy*), but then, I've decided my instincts have shit for brains, so I sleep with him again. I consider this a hopeful act, a positive step, and as I step out of my clothes once again, I give myself a pep talk. *Maybe things have changed since my twenties,* I think. *I'm a mature, intellectual woman, and I can handle the whole sex without love thing without feeling like a floozy. That's society talking. That's my upbringing talking. I define my sexuality. Me and only me! I can handle this.*

A few hours later, Nick goes home, and I realize I can't handle this. I'm a nice girl. Sex without love just makes me too terribly sad.

### Cue "Na Na Hey Hey Kiss Him Goodbye" by Steam (*ubiquitous sports anthem*)

When I bought my house, the Punter recommended a carpenter to me for some work I needed done. This carpenter had an assistant named Dom, a young, strapping guy who mostly held ladders and fetched tools. The last day of the job, I took a picture of Dom and the carpenter for my scrapbook, waved good-bye, and didn't think much more about him until a few weeks later when, out of the blue, the Punter calls.

"How are you?" he asks.

"Oh, fine! Just fine!" But then I tell the truth. "Actually, I'm having a bad night. Almost a month with no cigarettes and I'm going crazy tonight for some reason."

"Come with me to the grocery store," he says. "It will take your mind off it."

On the way to the Giant Eagle, he tells me he just got back from New York City. "How's your girlfriend?" I ask, cringing inside even as I ask.

He fiddles with his CD player. "We broke up, actually. Or at least I think so."

"I'm sorry," I say, although I'm not sorry at all.

At the grocery store, we wind our way down the deserted aisles. It's about ten on a weeknight, and the only other customers appear to be college boys from the Pitt football team buying large quantities of frozen pizzas. In the soup aisle, the Punter says, "The reason I called you . . ." and

I have to look away, I'm so nervous to hear what will come out of his mouth, ". . . is that I was talking to my friend the other day, you know, the guy who worked on your house."

I reach for a can of Progresso Chickarina. "Uh-huh."

"Dom has a crush on you."

I stand there, palming the heavy can. Then I say, "That's why you called? To tell me that a twenty-five-year-old guy has a crush on me."

Completely oblivious, he smiles. "I think it's cute. You should go out with him."

I want to chuck the can of soup at his head. *You idiot! You just told me you broke up with your girlfriend, the reason you said you wouldn't go out with me.* I look the Punter right in the eye. "Okay, fine. I'll do it." And I wheel my cart away.

A few days later, I e-mail my friend Joe, a writer who lives in Cleveland, that I have a date with a twenty-five-year-old. He e-mails back:

> Wow! Congratulations! Don't mention: Hot Wheels, John Hinkley Jr., *The Greatest American Hero, Remington Steele,* or Rush.

### Cue "That's the Way I Like It" by K.C. and the Sunshine Band (*ubiquitous sports anthem*)

I'll admit it: I like a guy who drives a big truck. When Dom pulls up in his big Ford Whatever, I feel like some younger, wilder, alternate version of myself stepping up to the running board to climb inside. As we fly down Bigelow Boulevard toward the Liberty Bridge with the windows down, I study his flame tattoos. Dom is huge: 6 feet 5 inches and just over 200 pounds, but he's gentle and deferential, asking if I'm comfortable, if I like the radio station. Magically, as he's scanning through the channels, I hear the opening notes of Rush's "The Spirit of Radio," and pretend to drum along with Neil Peart. "You like this song, I guess." He smiles.

"Don't you?"

"Who is it?" he asks.

*Oh God, Joe was right,* I think.

As he winds through the South Hills, I can feel Dom's anxiety, so I try to put him at ease, asking questions about his job, his hobbies.

The restaurant is a family place, and we sit in a booth by a window.

Dom asks the server if a friend of his is working. "Nope, not today," she says as she sets down our drinks. He recognizes two friends sitting at a nearby table and gives them a wave. Did he bring me all the way out here to show me off? I find this incredibly flattering, but why does Dom, who is young and handsome, need to show *me* off?

About halfway through lunch, as an uneasy Dom pushes his food around his plate, it hits me: I feel like I'm sitting across from a nervous undergrad who's come to my office hours, or someone at a book signing, a person who's looking at me like I'm a strange and alien life form—The Author. Sometimes I think I spend half my life putting people at ease. *Hey, I'm just a person here. Calm down.* This unsexy feeling grows stronger when Dom nervously starts talking about his favorite book from when he was a kid, *Where the Red Fern Grows.* I don't remember the plot, and suddenly Dom is completely relaxed as he narrates the story of Billy and his coon dogs, who battle a ferocious mountain lion. His voice breaks up a bit as he relates the Indian legend that a sacred red fern grows over the graves of good dogs. "That's where the title comes from," Dom says proudly.

"Yes," I say, my heart breaking a little. "That's right."

On the way home, I ask Dom, "Hey, be honest. How old are you?"

"I'll be twenty-five in a few months," he says.

"Oh God," I say. "I thought you already were twenty-five. Do you know how old I am?"

He looks at me and smiles. "Is this a trick question?"

"No. I'm thirty-seven."

"I think you look younger. Like thirty."

"That's nice of you to say."

"Seriously, you're pretty cute."

"Dom, I don't think we can go out again."

"Why not? The age difference doesn't bother me."

We're in the Liberty Tunnel, and then, with breathtaking suddenness, we're through and facing downtown Pittsburgh. The vista can change suddenly in Pittsburgh. One minute you're in a claustrophobic street maze, and then you turn right, then left, and suddenly, you're in a different world.

When he drops me off, I kiss Dom on the cheek and give him a hug.

"This did great things for my ego, Dom. But the age thing, it bothers me. I'm sorry."

Dom's hands are enormous and reassuring, but he keeps them to himself. "It's okay, Cathy. You're really nice."

### Cue "Rock and Roll Part II," a.k.a. "The Hey Song" by Gary Glitter (ubiquitous sports anthem)

That night I go to a Gist Street reading. They're held in a local sculptor's third-floor studio in Pittsburgh's Uptown neighborhood. Folding chairs fill his living room and kitchen. An old claw-foot bathtub squats in the center of the room, full of ice and beer. A cat winds his way through chair legs and people legs, and always more than a hundred people show up for these once-a-month gatherings. It's a pleasant summer night, everyone in funky glasses and vintage clothes, bearing wine and beer and food, a bohemian potluck supper. There are a dozen colleges and universities in Pittsburgh, the largest being Pitt, Carnegie Mellon, Chatham, and Duquesne. And where there are colleges, there are writers and lovers of writing. There's nothing quite like the first time you find yourself in the company of like-minded people. One of the reasons I love my life as a writer in academia is that no matter where I teach, there's *someone* around willing to talk about books and writing. Pittsburgh's different though. Most of my teaching jobs have been in out-of-the-way towns or small departments where all the writers were friends or at least knew of each other. I'm a small-town girl, after all. There's no rule that says I need to know all the writers in Pittsburgh, but the fact that I don't makes me feel disconnected. *How long before I walk into one of these readings and I know more than one person?*

I know that walking in now is how I make that future day happen, and maybe it doesn't seem like a big deal that I've come here tonight, but know this: walking into a party where I don't know anyone fills me with more social anxiety than my nicotine-deprived brain can handle. I walk into the room, nod to people I don't recognize, and I see Pam across the room. It wasn't that long ago that we were in the courtyard of the Mattress Factory together. I start to wave, but it's not clear if she sees me, so I lower my hand. For a while we were becoming friends, but now we're not. Making friends, I'm learning, is a process as delicate and fraught with mystery as dating. My brain starts repeating a loop of negative thoughts, and I can't shut it off. My chest tightens, my breath becomes shallow. I want to go home, but I force myself to stay. I give myself a task. *Go to the bathtub. Get a beer.* As I do, Joe taps me on the shoulder. He's driven down from Cleveland. I've never been so happy to see someone in my entire life. "How'd it go with the boy?" He grins.

"He was sweet," I say.

Joe says, "So he was twenty-five, huh?"

"Uh, well, he turned out to be twenty-four." Joe laughs and claps his hands. "I should feel great, right? Some hot twenty-four-year-old guy finds me attractive, and I can't bring myself to take it seriously."

Joe takes a swig of his beer. "Well, speaking as the old married guy, I say you should take advantage of this over and over again."

I blush.

"I'm sorry," Joe says. "That was crude. I'm just jealous I guess."

I'm astounded. "Why would you be jealous of my stupid life?"

He looks at me like I'm dense. "Because you can do what you want."

I look at him like he's dense. "I want what *you've* got."

Joe looks off into the distance. "I remember when Connie and I were trying to figure out whether or not to get married, whether to have kids. I don't know why, but I kept stalling and stalling. Now I don't know why I waited so long, what held me back."

I cock my head and look at him. "Dude, you think the reason I'm single is I fear *commitment?*"

"Well, don't you?"

"No!" I practically yell, and a woman sitting nearby with an "I Read Banned Books" button pinned to her enormous purse looks at me. "I want a partner. A friend. I want a family, even if it's just me and him."

"Well, what's stopping you?" Joe says.

I want to strangle him. "Let me put it to you this way. You and I, we're about the same age, both writers, same kind of job. But the way we got *here*"—I gesture to the room, the crowd surrounding us, the cities of Pittsburgh and Cleveland, "was that we had to move around a lot."

"Yes," he says quietly.

I pause for a second. "Let's say you met *me* in graduate school, not Connie." There's a bit of uncomfortable silence. I don't mean this in the romantic sense—I'm just illustrating a point. "Would you have followed my ass around all these years?"

Joe takes a long swig of beer and stares at the bottle. "No," he says finally. "I wouldn't have."

"That's what I'm saying!" I poke him in the chest with my finger.

"Just because I wouldn't have doesn't mean no man would," he offers.

I laugh a wry, bitter laugh. "Well, if he's out there, I haven't found him yet." The directors of the reading series have approached the microphone, telling everyone to find a seat. I look at Joe. "I always think I've picked the right guy. But it seems like every time I start getting a little bigger, he feels a little smaller."

Joe hands me another beer from the bathtub. "I'm sorry."

Later, after the reading, he says, "I'm your wingman tonight." He circulates through the room and in every group he finds a way to ask, "Hey, do you know anybody for Cathy here?" A few months ago, I would have been mortified. Now, I'm just incredibly grateful, even though in the end his efforts don't produce any results. Maybe finding someone is like that Faberge shampoo commercial. *I told two friends, and then they told two friends, and so on and so on and so on.*


When Alex and I broke up, I had no problem being single. It was sort of a relief, actually. No one to think about but myself. But then months turned into years. What was wrong? When I left Alex, I assumed that there would be another man around the corner, because that's how it had always worked before. But during our seven years together, everyone we knew was getting married, starting families. Of course I noticed this. Buying registry gifts was our biggest expense. When we broke up, I was thirty-two. A year later, I took inventory. How many single men did I know? How many had I met, even casually, over the last year? None. Not a single solitary one. Well, no men my own age, that is. I was surrounded by very young single men every day, all day. The only men my age I knew were my colleagues, and they were all married. I went to their parties and met their friends and neighbors, and again, everyone was coupled. Of course they were. This was suburban New Jersey.

When I started telling my friends that I'd like to start dating again, they said, "Hmmm . . . I can't think of any single men." Not one. Or they said, "Not one who is right for you."

"Who do you think is right for me?" I asked.

"Oh, my boyfriend's got some guy friends, but all they do is fish and talk about sports."

"That's what I like," I said.

"No you don't," my friends insisted. "You need someone more educated, more special."

"At this point, I'd be happy with the fisherman who watches football," I told them. How had it come to this? I'd worked hard and sacrificed so that I could escape Indiana and live a different kind of life, and the only kind of men who were left by the time I got there were the same ones I could have married if I'd never left home at all.

*Cue "Centerfield" by John Fogerty (from the* Bull Durham *sound track)*
A few days later, my phone rings. A man I know, Philip, has season tickets to the Pirates, two seats right behind home plate, and he can't go to tonight's game. I have yet to see a game at spectacular PNC Park. So I start making calls. I call Nick, but he has to work. I don't call Dom. I call Joe, but he's out of town. I call my neighbors Tom and Rachel, but Tom doesn't like baseball ("Boring," he says) and Rachel is busy.

My dad calls from Indiana to check in, and I tell him about the tickets. "I'll go!" he says, and actually, if he got in the car right now, he could drive the five hours and make it on time. But that's ridiculous. Surely I'll be able to find someone to go to this game with me, even if it is last-minute. But there's a part of me that knows right then that I won't be able to find anyone, that I'll call a bunch of people who will take a pass for one reason or another, and that I will have to talk myself out of throwing another pity party. I have to stop myself from thinking negative like this, so all day I make phone calls. I leave Pam a message. I call people I teach with, but everyone's out of town. I call the Punter. No answer. Then I start calling my graduate students. All of them have other plans. Finally, I am forced to call Philip and give up the tickets. "Thanks anyway," I say.

On the eleven o'clock news, I learn that the Pirates didn't win the game. There's also a segment on the Steelers' training camp in Latrobe, Pennsylvania, and the status of Big Ben Roethlisberger's cracked noggin, which makes me wonder how the Colts are doing at their training camp in Terre Haute, Indiana. I wonder how Peyton is feeling.

Actually, what I really want to know is this: What did Peyton do when he woke up on January 16, 2006, the morning after the Pittsburgh playoff game? Did he lie in bed and pout? Did he pray? Did he make a sandwich? Did he replay the game film and study where he went wrong? Did he write angry letters to Terry Bradshaw? What did his wife Ashley say to him? His dad? His mom? His brothers? What did he say to himself so that he could come back and try again? And what is he saying to himself right now, as he lies in bed in Terre Haute? How does he keep himself from thinking too far ahead and focus on each day? Can I pay Peyton Manning to teach me how to think like this?

The next morning, my dad calls to ask how the baseball game went, and I tell him that he should have driven the five hours to Pittsburgh after all. Then I burst into tears. "Dad," I say, "I'm trying so hard . . ."

"I know you are, Cathy."

". . . but I gotta get out of here. I'm coming home."

*Cue "Back Home Again in Indiana" as sung by Jim Nabors before the Indianapolis 500*

I love you guys.

—Gene Hackman in *Hoosiers*

---

# PRESEASON
## OR
# Back Home Again in Indiana

---

The five-hour drive from Pittsburgh is my first without smokes, and the passenger seat of my car is littered with gum wrappers and an empty box of Spree. It's exactly three hundred miles from my house in Pittsburgh to my parents' house in Aurora, Indiana, one of the many towns I consider "home." When they moved to the Greater Cincinnati area in 1986, my parents concentrated their house-hunting efforts on the twin small towns of Lawrenceburg and Aurora. They say it was because at the time all three of their high school–aged kids wanted to attend Indiana public universities (in the end only my brother did), but I've always thought my parents focused on Aurora because it was as close as you could get to Cincinnati and still have an Indiana mailing address and license plates.

That night for dinner, we have hamburgers on the grill. Afterward, my dad goes to light a cigarette, but Mom says, "Honey . . ."

"Oh, right," he says. He gets up from the table and walks off the patio into the backyard.

I call after him, "Thanks, Dad."

"How's it going without the smoking?" Mom asks.

"It's still really hard. Just being around Dad makes me want one."

She touches my hand. "I'm real proud of you, sweetie. It's good to have you home."

"It's good to be home," I say, and I really mean it. Sitting there underneath the umbrella-covered table, I lean back in the chair and feel relief and comfort wash over me. I'm with people who love me, who, when they ask, *How are you?* really want to know the answer, even if takes an hour. This relieved feeling reminds me of when I've traveled to job interviews or for readings, of the emotional and social energy it takes to become and maintain this public version of myself. After the last meeting, the last dinner, the last car ride back to my hotel, the door shuts behind me, and I take off my nice outfit, which seems to have weighed a hundred pounds, but really, it was the intangible weight of having to be "on" for hours and hours on end.

Mom sits forward in her chair. "I know it hasn't been easy for you there lately."

"I don't understand it. I've started over in new places before."

"You're older now. I think it gets harder to start from scratch the older you get. And before, you had Alex."

I look up at the sky. "Sometimes I'll wake up and look out my window and think, *Not one single person in this city really knows me.*" My chest tightens just thinking about those scary moments in the small hours of the night. "I don't know what's the matter with me. I thought I was stronger than this, Mom."

I look up, and I see she's close to crying herself. "I don't know how you do it, honey. I really don't. You're the strongest person I know. I think you can do anything you put your mind to. You always have."

And for a moment, I am the woman my mom thinks I am.

"You've never been patient. Give it time, Cathy. You haven't even lived in Pittsburgh a year yet."

I know she's right. I know it takes time. Right now in Pittsburgh, I imagine my neighbors Fred and Joanne are picking tomatoes and peppers from their backyard garden and handing them over the fence to Larry, the guy across the alley who plays the violin. In Bloomfield, Pittsburgh's Italian neighborhood, old men in undershirts are sitting outside a sandwich shop on Liberty Avenue smoking cigarettes. In Squirrel Hill, the Jewish neighborhood, I picture a couple walking their dog down Murray Avenue; they stop outside the Carnegie Library to chat with another couple pushing a baby stroller. There are times as I'm driving alone to the grocery store or on my daily walk when seeing people greet each other like this makes me madly and irrationally jealous. Even here, in Aurora, I am anonymous except to my family and their neighbors. I didn't go to high school here like my younger sister and brother did.

That's when it hits me: I'm not looking for dates in Pittsburgh. I'm not looking to get laid. I'm really not even looking for a husband. What I want, what I need is a family. This realization surprises the hell out of me, and something completely absurd and incongruous pops into my head: a Jennifer Lopez movie I saw with my mom called *Shall We Dance?* It's a scene in which Susan Sarandon is sitting at a bar—I don't even remember who she was talking to—but what she said made me sit up straight in my theater seat.

> We need a witness to our lives. There's a billion people on the planet. . . . I mean, what does any one life really mean? But in a marriage, you're promising to care about everything. The good things, the bad things, the terrible things, the mundane things, all of it, all of the time, every day. You're saying "Your life will not go unnoticed because I will notice it. Your life will not go unwitnessed because I will be your witness."

I say none of this out loud. I don't have any idea how to articulate this longing. It's all of a piece with the ache in my chest, the smell of grilled hamburgers, the love I see in my mother's eyes when she smiles at me, the cicadas buzzing in the summer trees. Across the street, the neighbor boy sits on his porch, teaching himself to play a Jimi Hendrix song on his guitar. My dad flicks his cigarette into the backyard and walks back to us. "Come on, Cathy," he says, putting his hand on my back. "The Colts are on."

This is the first NFL preseason game I've ever watched. The Colts are in St. Louis playing the Rams. Six months have passed since they lost to Pittsburgh, and I still feel like a complete mess. I hope the Colts are feeling more ready than I am for the season ahead. My parents and I settle down in the living room. The stands in St. Louis are only about half full, and there's no pomp and circumstance on the field, no crazy graphics on the television. It's sort of like watching a high school football game on public access, except that Terry Bradshaw, Howie Long, and Jimmy Johnson are there, sitting in director's chairs on the sidelines. It's all very strange, three big guys in expensive suits, looking sort of rumpled and annoyed. Then I realize I've never seen any of them from the waist down; they're usually sitting behind some big desk. It's only August 10, and the Colts haven't yet kicked off, and already all three of them are saying, *What about January? Can they come through in the playoffs?* If you're a Colts player, if you're a single woman, how do you keep from thinking that far down the road every time you take the field?

My cell phone rings. It's my brother Scott, calling from nearby Batesville. "Hey, Cath. You got here okay?"

"Yeah. Hey, are you watching this? You know, I'm actually really excited about the kickoff!"

"I know. Me, too. I really want to see how this Joseph Addai does."

The Colts' newly acquired kicker Adam Vinatieri makes a surprising (and some might say unnecessarily competitive) move to kick onside.

"I'll be damned," my dad says from his La-Z-Boy. "A gadget play."

"I gotta go," Scott says.

A few minutes later, Peyton throws to tight end Ben Utecht for a touchdown. Seven plays, 59 yards, and boom, the Colts are up by seven. But by the second series, the Colts' first string is on the sidelines, Jim Sorgi is calling the plays, and my excitement wanes. By halftime the Colts are down 19–10. They amass only 13 rushing yards in the entire first half, and the commentators can't stop talking about Edgerrin James, Edgerrin James, did the Colts make a mistake not keeping running back Edgerrin James? In the second half Shaun King gets his shot at QB, and Jim Sorgi, the loneliest backup quarterback in the NFL, takes a rest.

I move down to the living room floor and start labeling VHS tapes for Scott, who has agreed to tape the Colts games for me each week and mail them to me in Pittsburgh, because all I can get there are Steelers games. The game grinds on for three hours. First-string marquee players like Marvin Harrison and Peyton aren't playing. They're kidding around with sideline reporter Andrea Kremer. This is when it hits me: the Colts are *losing!* But it doesn't seem to matter. "This is boring," I say.

Dad says, "Not to the guys who are still trying to make the team."

He's right of course. I point to the television. "That's Ed Hinkel. He went to high school with Bob Sanders. They signed him as a free agent this summer."

My dad does a double take. "How do you know that?"

"One of my grad students at Pitt, he's from Erie, Pennsylvania. They're all three from the same high school. He told me to keep an eye on Hinkel."

Without a lot of drama to narrate, the commentators provide exposition about the secondary characters on a team, whose stories are just as compelling—like linebacker Gary Brackett, who walked onto the Rutgers University football team and was captain by his senior year, when he signed on with the Colts as an undrafted free agent. It was right around this time that the hardworking, never-give-up Brackett lost his mother, father, and brother—all in a sixteen-month span. And then there's John David Washington, son of Denzel Washington, who's trying to make the Rams' 53-man roster. The camera shows the actor, tonight playing "Dad," sitting in the stands staring intently at the field.

The game wears on, and I'm labeling the VHS tapes. Sixteen games, sixteen tapes. But I bought two packs of ten tapes, so I have a total of twenty tapes. Four tapes left. I'm using the Colts schedule to label each tape for my brother, and I see that—best-case scenario—he'll need four extra tapes. I label one "Wild Card," one "Divisional Playoffs," one "AFC/NFC Championships," and one "Super Bowl." By creating these extra tapes, am I jinxing the Colts' chances in the postseason? Or am I doing the opposite of that by performing this optimistic act? I can't decide, so I do it anyway.

The Colts end up losing to the Rams 19–17. Mom and Dad say good night and head off to bed. I go into the study to check my e-mail. Nothing. Then I log onto Chemistry.com. Nothing. Oh, by the way, I've been a member for a month now.

I joined Chemistry the night before I first met Nick. I was nervous about that Fourth of July party the next day, and one of my dating books suggested that the best way to avoid feeling overanxious was to always remind yourself that you have options. At that point, I didn't have any options other than Nick. The Faberge Method hadn't worked. *It's time,* I thought. So I logged on.

Chemistry.com seemed like eHarmony—less of a "meat market" than Match.com. I read about Chemistry in an article published in *The Atlantic,* and what attracted me (well, *attracted* is the wrong word, more like "the reason it seemed like the least of many evils") was that they said their clients tended to be people looking for a serious relationship. I doubted I'd unwittingly run into any of my twenty-something students in this more expensive, more exclusive virtual singles' club. Also, Chemistry would make me take a personality test, and I found this reassuring, since I've always been very good at taking tests. As I signed in, I remembered a story I sometimes taught by Bernard Malamud, "The Magic Barrel," about a rabbinical student who hires a matchmaker:

> He had for six years devoted himself almost entirely to his studies, as a result of which, understandably, he had found himself without time for a social life and the company of young women. Therefore he thought it the better part of trial and error—of embarrassing fumbling—to call in an experienced person to advise him on these matters. He remarked in passing that the function of the marriage broker was ancient and honorable, highly approved in the Jewish community, because it made practical the necessary without hindering joy.

I kept repeating that line from Malamud like a mantra *(it made practical the necessary without hindering joy . . . it made practical the necessary without hindering joy . . .)* as I did the thing I swore I would never do: join an online dating service.

I took their very, very long and exhaustive test, wondering what certain questions had to do with love. What did it matter if my index finger was shorter than my ring finger? I didn't know. I just kept going, afraid I'd lose my nerve. Half an hour later, I was still answering questions on my lifestyle preferences, money, interpersonal skills, hobbies, temperament, tone, even sections titled "Subconscious Personality" and "Archetype Assessment." How did I feel about this picture of a man on his knee, giving roses to a woman who looks like she is a bank executive? Romantic, but a little clichéd. When I pass an open window of a private home, do I look in? No, I don't. How do I respond to this mock dating scenario? I've been seeing a guy for a while, but a few hours before a dinner date, he leaves me a voice mail. (I click on the sound clip provided.) Pretend Date says *Something has come up and I can't make it* in a neutral tone of voice. What is the real meaning of the message? The real question was "Are you the type of person who reads too much into things?" Are you the type of woman who's going to spend the whole night worrying whether or not Pretend Date has lost all interest in you and call him back immediately sounding like a whiny wack job? Or are you a diva, the kind of woman who will hold this cancellation against Pretend Date and not take his calls for a few days? Or are you a normal woman somewhere between the two poles of Princess and Basket Case?

I seriously thought about that one question for about ten minutes and came down somewhere in the middle.

Exhausted, I finally got to the part of the enrollment process where I was required to represent myself, but by that point I was tired and traumatized and wanted a cigarette so badly; I hurriedly typed in my eye-catching "headline" and my short profile.

> Headline: "Take me out to the ball game!"
>
> Profile: In the short term, I'm simply looking for someone to do things with. I moved to Pittsburgh recently and would love to see more of the city. I like baseball games (all sports really, although I'm not much of an athlete myself), movies (artsy-fartsy or schlock), lunch/dinner at new restaurants (and just about every restaurant here is "new" to me). If you're handy, I'd love that—not just because I'm moving into a new place, but also because I like a guy who knows a bit about cars and owns his own tools. In the long term, I'm looking for a smart, mature guy who wants to make me deliriously happy, but I don't want to get ahead of myself. Baseball games and summer movies and drinks will do fine for now, thank you.

Honestly, this was the best I could do.

Two hours after I started, I finally entered my credit-card number and was presented with my five matches. It gave me their first names, ages, distance in miles from my house, and these witty, eye-catching headlines.

41

"I can't believe it's come down to this!!!"
"What am I doing?"
"__"
"REALLY tired of the clubs."


My first reaction was, *Okay, so these guys are as nervous about this as I am.* And then I thought, *Come on! Man up, guys, and show a little enthusiasm.*

I studied these five profiles and decided that I was nominally interested in two of them. My two self-effacing matches would receive an e-mail message from Chemistry letting them know of my interest, and they would check me out, and if they clicked buttons indicating their mutual interest, together we would proceed to the Guided Communications Process. Also, at this very moment, Chemistry was sending my profile to men whose test scores somehow complemented my own. How many men would wake up tomorrow and see my clichéd headline "Take me out to the ball game!" on their screen? All of this made me incredibly nervous—my picture and vital details zooming around in cyberspace. I lay in bed that night wondering if somewhere out there in Pittsburgh, a nice man was up late in his apartment, logging onto Chemistry, devouring my profile, clicking the Yes I'm Interested button.

You might think that I had low expectations regarding my chances on Chemistry. You might think that I lay there in bed thinking, *None of these guys is gonna like me.* Oh no! On the contrary. I felt the opposite—optimism. I was relatively certain that I was a great catch, at least on paper. A nice photo. A decent profile. Who wouldn't want to go out with me? The next morning, I ran to the computer and checked my messages. Nothing. *Well, it's been less than twenty-four hours, and it is the Fourth of July,* I thought. *Maybe they're on vacation.*


The morning after the Colts @ Rams game, I make a cup of coffee and go into my parents' study to "check my e-mail," but really I'm logging onto Chemistry.com. My mom walks in. At first I reduce the screen, but then I change my mind. "Mom, come here, I want to show you something."

She sits down next to me, and I explain how this whole thing works. "This is my profile."

"Oh, that's such a nice picture! Where's that from?"

"Scott took it after that reading I gave in Princeton, after my book came out."

"I'm proud of you for doing this," my mom says, "although I wish you didn't have to."

"You and me both, Mom." I click on a different button and explain that every day they send me five matches. Typically, I sort of like maybe one, sometimes none, but none of the guys I've clicked Yes on have contacted me back. I tell her it's been really depressing. "So I thought maybe you could go through these matches with me, so I can get a different perspective. Maybe there's something I'm missing."

My mom looks a little nervous. "Okay," she says. "I'll do the best I can."

The first one is Bob, who's included a few extra pictures of himself, including one in which he's wearing bathing trunks. "Well, what about him, he's attractive," Mom says.

It's true. He has a very nice chest, but it makes me nervous. "Don't you think it's odd a man would include a bare-chested picture of himself?"

Mom shrugs. "Maybe he didn't have any other pictures?"

"Oh God, Mom, of course he has other pictures! What would you think if I put pictures of myself in a bathing suit on here?"

Her eyes get wide. "You didn't do that, did you?"

"No! But what would you think of a woman who did?"

My mom blushes a bit. "That she was a little, uh, loose."

I don't know why, but I feel like I'm giving my mother a test. "So why would a guy use a picture of himself in a bathing suit to show me he's got a nice physique?"

"Because . . . oh, I see! You think he's full of himself."

I nod. "Yeah, or maybe he's sort of pervy, and he's looking for someone kinda pervy like himself." I explain to her that Chemistry screens the pictures for tastefulness, but from what I've seen, some men definitely push the envelope of what the company will accept. "It's like they're trying to send a secret message," I tell her.

"Oh, I see," Mom says. "Gosh, this is really hard!"

"I know! I'm supposed to be clicking through this quickly, you know, using my gut reaction to guide me."

She takes a sip of her coffee and sets it down. "Well, let's see some others and you tell me your first reaction and I'll tell you mine."

Number 2 is Carl. He's a truck driver, judging from the picture of him sitting in the cab of a truck. He writes:

I'm a divorced white male, 5'7". Dark brown hair, blue eyes. I don't lift weights every day but I'm not fat either. I'd like to meet an attractive, articulate gal. Personality and attitude most important.

"What about him?" Mom says.

"Bland," I say. "And he used the word 'gal.' "

"Maybe he's not a good writer like you. Maybe he doesn't know other words to use."

"But it's all I have to go on, Mom, those words!"

"Honey, I just want you to give these guys a chance . . ."

Number 3 is Robert.

I enjoy gambling and sports, it would be nice if you did too. I live modestly and you must too. I enjoy the finer things in life, which can get me behind the eight ball financially but I have a good job to balance that out. The woman that I envision myself with has to be my best friend.

"He likes sports!" Mom says. "He wants to be friends first. That's good."

"What does that mean, *I enjoy gambling?* Sounds like he's got a gambling problem."

"You don't know that, Cathy."

"Mom, he put it right there in the profile. *Loves gambling.* And he says he *gets behind the eight ball financially.* That doesn't sound very stable to me."

"I think he's just being honest. Give him a chance."

I think about the fact that yes, he did provide me with more specific information, more complete sentences, and more complicated syntax than most of the profiles I read. I look at his picture. He's tall, over six foot. Black hair. He's a little younger than me. "Okay, I'll say I'm interested." I click the button and Chemistry will alert Robert the Gambler that I'm interested.

"Good," Mom says, patting my arm. "This is kinda fun."

I groan and click on number 4, Greg.

I am stable in my career and own my own home. I have a dog and she currently is the executor of my will, an item I'm looking to change as the government might frown upon it—thus the reason I am online. I enjoy dining out but would be just as comfortable making dinner at home together. What I'm looking for is a down-to-earth woman who is employed, and confident with herself.

Mom waits to hear what I'm going to say.

"Eh," is all I can come up with.

"He sounds sincere," she says.

"I don't know. He's forty-seven."

She gives me a hard look. "Now, how would you feel if someone younger than you saw your profile and thought you were too old and didn't give you a chance?"

"I don't know, Mom. I wouldn't like it. But I wouldn't necessarily have to know about it, either." God, this is painful. I feel like crawling underneath the pull-out keyboard tray. "It's not just that he's forty-seven, Mom. I know men who are older than that and I find them attractive. It's just that he looks like . . ." I struggle for the right description. "He looks like Dad, or some guy Dad would have worked with. Some guy he'd drink beer with, you know?"

She crosses her arms. "What's wrong with that?"

"Nothing's wrong with that. For you. Or some other woman. It's just not my type, you know? I don't know how else to explain it." I point to poor Greg's picture. "I just don't look at this picture and get excited, you know?"

My mom is quiet for a minute, thinking. "I just think that your type hasn't worked out very well for you. Maybe it's time to look at a different type."

I know she's right. My gut has shit for brains. I'm supposed to make myself get excited about the Eh's and ignore the Wow's, but doing so is a lot harder than I thought it would be.

I bring up the last match, number 5, Terry.

Mom says, "Oh my God, is he holding a gun?"

"Um, yes, I think so."

"Definitely a no."

"Definitely."

We go out on the porch, where my dad is drinking coffee and smoking. "What were you guys doing in there?"

Mom and I sit next to each other on the porch swing. "Cathy was showing me her matches on Chemistry."

Dad sits up in his chair and looks at me. "You're doing the Internet dating thing? I don't think I like that."

I laugh ruefully. "Well, I don't like it either, Dad, but I've got to do something or I'm going to be alone forever."

He looks at my mom for a second, as if speaking for both of them. "Well, then you can just be our daughter forever."

Once, in graduate school, a woman said to me, "Cathy, you are so refreshingly naïve." She meant this as a compliment. Yes, I have some fairly romantic and unrealistic expectations about love. No, I don't have very good instincts about men. Perhaps now that you've met my parents, you better understand the source of my difficulties.

My parents were high school sweethearts. They met in 1962 in a speech class, during their sophomore year at Peru High School. My dad was on the basketball team. My mom worked at Dairy Queen. Apparently, my dad wanted to go out with a girl my mom knew, but they got to talking so much that they decided, Heck with that other girl, they'd go out.

As my dad tells the story, their first date was a hayride. Afterwards, they sat underneath a tree talking. "She was so easy to talk to," my dad remembered. Even on that first date, they talked about where they thought their lives were going. At the time, they both thought they were going to college, but when I asked my dad why they didn't, he just said, "Life had other plans for us." So there they were, my mom and dad, sitting under a tree in the middle of a field in Indiana, and they kissed. It was for my father his first kiss, and for my mother her third. Afterwards, they went out for a Coke. They broke up briefly in 1965, their senior year, but by 1967, they were married, and eleven months later, I was born.

I'm sure there's more to the story than this. I've always imagined it something like the courtship of George Bailey and Mary Hatch in *It's a Wonderful Life.* It makes you wonder: what would George and Mary Bailey say to their daughter, a still-single and disheartened thirty-seven-year-old ZuZu? "Don't worry, sweetheart! There's a man out there who'll lasso the moon for you. Then you can swallow it, and it'll dissolve, see, and the moonbeams will shoot out of your fingers and your toes and the ends of your hair."

Believe me, my parents know a hell of a lot about holding a marriage together, but about the realities of dating, they know jack.


Early Sunday afternoon, my dad and I drive north from Aurora to Batesville. I've got four tickets to the Colts first home preseason game against Super Bowl runners-up the Seattle Seahawks. Dad and I, Scott and Sara are going. It's cool for August in Indiana, and we keep the windows down in his truck. My dad prefers to drive with the radio off, so there's only the sound of wind and tires on the road. Today, Dad is wearing his Colts sweatshirt, and I'm wearing the Colts T-shirt I just bought at the local Wal-Mart. At some invisible point on U.S. 350 North, in the midst of farm fields and rolling hills and ranch houses with two-acre lawns and Mail Pouch tobacco barns, we leave the Cincinnati TV market and enter the Indianapolis viewing area, which means we pass over from Bengals to Colts country.

When we pull into my brother's driveway, Scott comes out of the garage. "Just got back from church," he says. He looks at his watch. "If we wanna get there in time to see the team stretching and stuff, we should leave in about a half hour, forty-five minutes tops." He holds up his bottle of beer, wrapped in a blue kozy. "Wanna beer?"

Dad and I step into Scott's garage. Half of it is taken up by the 1976 Jeep CJ5 my brother is rebuilding. The other half is taken up by the flotsam of life as a midwestern man: his workbench, sawhorses, rolling Craftsman toolboxes (the ones with the drawers), kerosene heaters, lawn mower, weed whacker, drill, air compressor, impact wrench, fishing poles, trash barrel, and, of course, an old refrigerator full of beer. There's a radio on, tuned into Q95 in Indianapolis, and Bob Seger is still singing about love in the summertime.

You need to know this: everything I learned about drinking, smoking, sports, and shooting the shit I learned by hanging out in the garage with the men in my family, a decidedly masculine space I preferred over the domestic claustrophobia inside.

My dad and brother and I stand in the garage, drinking our beers. My back is hurting, so I sit down on an upside-down five-gallon bucket. "How's the dating stuff going, Cathy?" my brother asks after a while. Back in July, I had called him and asked his advice about what to say in my Chemistry profile. This might seem like a weird thing to ask your brother about, but he's the only man I know (whom I haven't dated and don't want to date) who's used the Internet to find dates. His advice: "The picture's really important, but don't say you're a college professor, or all the normal guys like me will think they're not smart enough."

I tell Scott about going through my matches with Mom, and he laughs. I take a swig of my beer. "I've been trying to figure something out. They say you should just let things happen. That you can't plan for or control it."

"That's true," my dad says.

"But isn't it also true that you can prepare for a positive outcome? I mean, you and Sara met on Match.com. You were making some kind of effort." Scott nods yes. They met during the summer of 2004 and married the summer of 2005. "My friend told me I'm being too hard on myself. But isn't being hard on yourself the way you succeed?"

Scott puts his hand on my shoulder. "It's okay. You're doing good, Cath."

My dad says, "But you know, she's really getting the football side of things down pretty good."

"So, what year did Peyton break Marino's record?" my brother asks.

"I think it was 2004," I say. "He threw forty-nine touchdowns in a single season."

"Yeah, but do you know who caught that forty-ninth pass?" Scott asks smugly.

I smile. "Brandon Stokely."

"Whoa!" My dad and brother clink beer bottles.

Another thing I learned in the garage: if you want to be taken seriously by guys, memorize some sports trivia. It works every time.

Why do we follow one team over another? Why do we marry the people we do? So much depends on the mundane practicalities of our lives: where we grow up, where we go to college, where we work. We inherit our parents' predilections in both love and football as surely as we inherit their DNA and political party. And their predilections are a product of the mundane practicalities of their lives and their parents' lives.

The truth is that I grew up a Bears fan. The reasons are anthropological and geographic; when my dad's dad bought the family's first television in the 1950s, it got one station—out of South Bend. So my father grew up in Peru watching Notre Dame and the Bears, and he taught his children to do the same. Like almost everyone in northern Indiana, my family had followed the Bears for several generations before the Colts defected from Baltimore in 1984. And then, just two years after Indiana got its first NFL team, my family moved to Cincinnati, a Bengals TV market. You couldn't watch the Bears *or* Colts in Aurora, Indiana, unless it was a nationally televised game. I doubt that my family would have ever paid any attention to the Colts had it not been for one thing: when my brother Scott graduated from Ball State University in 1995, he got a job in Indianapolis instead of Cincinnati, although he applied for jobs in both cities. He'd followed the Colts in college in the pre–Manning and Dungy days of coach Ted Marchibroda, running back Marshall Faulk, and quarterback Jim Harbaugh. If my brother had been hired by a Cincinnati company instead, I think that his new, still-wobbly Colts mold might not have set—in which case, this whole story I'm telling might have turned out very differently.

Three years later, in 1998—Peyton Manning's rookie year for the Colts—Scott changed jobs and moved from Indy to Shelbyville, Indiana, a town about an hour and a half from my parents. The Colts went 3–13 that year, and it wasn't such a hot year for my brother either. During the week, Scott went to work, came home, and watched TV or spent time in the garage, rebuilding a 1979 GMC Jimmy. On Saturdays, he watched TV or worked on the Jimmy. But Sundays were all about the Indianapolis Colts. Most weeks, my parents and/or my sister would drive from Aurora to Shelbyville to watch the game with him. They made that drive because they loved him, because they knew he was lonely, and because they knew that these games, these gatherings, were what he looked forward to all week.

In 1999, when I came home for Christmas from Alabama or Minnesota or wherever the hell I was living at that point, I was invited to take part in the Sunday ritual. Understand: this was a Very Big Deal, this invitation. That year—that glorious year—the Colts were on a roll. By the time I showed up in week 16 of the regular season, the Colts were 12–2 and they hadn't lost a game since early October, way back in week 5. Scott was euphoric but worried that my presence might ruin the Colts' chances. Every week, he did the same things, wore the same clothes, drank the same beer, watched the game with the same people—and they'd been winning week after week. When I arrived in Shelbyville with my family, Scott told me, "I love you, Cathy, but if they start losing, would you mind . . . I don't know . . . going for a walk or something?" The Colts defeated the Browns that day. It was a close game, 29–28. I missed a lot of it, banished to the garage or the kitchen every time the Browns surged or the Colts struggled. I thought it was kind of weird, and I huffed and puffed a little every time he ordered me out of the room, but I did it.

Why do we follow one team and not another? Yes, it's about mundane practicalities, about geography and TV markets, but it's also about love. That's how my family and I became Colts fans. My brother loves them. We love my brother. And so we love the Colts.

My brother drives us up I-74 to Indianapolis in the late-afternoon sun. We pass a few cars flying Colts flags from their rear windows, and we honk. Sara is sitting in the backseat with me, and I'm telling her about my last trip to the Hoosier Dome, I mean, the RCA Dome, in 2000. Scott had gotten four tickets to a Christmas Eve home game with the Vikings, and Dad, Mom, Scott, and I went. It was a frigid single-digit day, and we ran through the parking lot, past the parka-wearing tailgaters huddled around their charcoal grills. That was my first NFL football game. I walked out of the gray-and-white Indiana winter, up the concrete walkway, and into Technicolor green warmth. I didn't know much about the Colts then, but the game itself thrilled me. I cheered and shook my fists and stomped. It was like dancing drunk at a wedding, like being wrapped up in sound and light and color and movement.

That season almost everyone had written off the Colts' playoff chances, but if they won their last three games, they had a shot. They'd won the last two, and that day, they won the third—and decidedly: 31–10. Edgerrin James's parents sat two rows behind us, and we took their picture like they were movie stars. The crowd stuck around that day long after the game to celebrate the Colts' ascension to the playoffs. They lost their next game, a wild-card game with the Dolphins, but on *that* day, December 24, 2000, anything was possible.

On our way to the Seahawks preseason game, we walk past the construction site of the new Lucas Oil Stadium, which at the moment is a fenced-in pile of dirt, concrete, and steel but which will be the new home of the Colts in 2008. Outside the RCA Dome, we see the forty-two-foot trailer that's been roaming around small-town Indiana all summer on the "Make It Personal" tour. Embossed with the visages of Colts players, it's a huge fifth-wheel camper that doubles as a traveling museum equipped with interactive videos, a replica of Peyton Manning's locker, a model of the new Lucas Oil Stadium, and a behind-the-scenes look at the Colts. We walk around inside it, and Sara helps me turn the crank on one of those Turn a Penny into a Keepsake machines, transforming Lincoln's face into a horseshoe. Then we get in line to enter the Dome. A woman inspects my purse and points to my two tubes of Spree. "I'm sorry, but you can't bring candy inside," she says.

"I need this candy!" I tell her. "I just quit smoking."

"There's candy you can buy inside," she says.

"Is there Spree? I really need Spree."

She smiles and waves me on.

We walk through the revolving doors of the RCA Dome and buy hot dogs and beers. We've got amazing seats in the twelfth row, right behind the Colts' sideline. My brother walks down the aisle as far as he can to take pictures of the players warming up. I've got that goofy fan feeling: Oh my

God, that's really Peyton Manning stretching out his triceps. There's Dallas Clark and those are his amazing thighs. That's Tony Dungy, and those are really his shoes!

By the time the Colts take the field, the RCA Dome is almost at full capacity, and the crowd goes crazy to welcome them. This is the first time they've run onto this field since they lost to the Steelers here in January, and everyone seems to want to buoy the team with their support. Then it hits me: everyone around me is wearing blue and white. Everyone around me is a Hoosier. Everyone around me loves the Colts. It's the way I felt when I first arrived in Aurora from Pittsburgh, relieved and joyful. I've spent most of my adult life living in self-imposed exile, an Indiana expatriate, but at this moment, I'm home. I feel connected—albeit tenuously—to tens of thousands of people, all occupying the same space. We're wearing the same thing, singing the same songs, screaming the same cheers. I belong to something. I am not alone. It's not a family, it's a tribe, and I never realized until now how much I needed this. Sometimes during the last year in Pittsburgh, I've seen a car go by with an Indiana license plate, or I've seen someone wearing a Purdue University sweatshirt, and I've resisted the urge to walk right up to them and say, "Hi! Are you from Indiana? Me, too!" How is this possible? All I wanted at seventeen was to escape Indiana by any means necessary, and twenty years later, I'm in a very large room with fifty thousand Hoosiers, and I don't ever, ever want to leave.

Like last week against the Rams, the Colts score during their first series. Peyton Manning takes a seat, having completed six of nine passes for 140 yards and a touchdown. Second-string quarterback Jim Sorgi takes the field but is sidelined three plays later with a shoulder injury; this is exactly why the first-stringer doesn't play much during preseason. Sixteen Colts players are missing from the game, including Bob Sanders, Mike Doss, and Montae Reagor, but we do get to see Dwight Freeney sack Seattle quarterback Matt Hasselbeck, and a Freeney tackle is always something worth seeing. With both Manning and Sorgi out, Shaun King mans the helm for the rest of the game and helps the Colts score two more times. But in the end the Colts lose 30–17, their eighth straight preseason loss.

They're closing down the RCA Dome now. Back in the fourth quarter my dad disappeared to go outside and smoke, and we find him wandering around on the concourse. The four of us walk outside, and the inside air pressure that keeps the dome's fiberglass roof aloft rushes at our backs, pushing us out the double doors into the Indiana night, back to our cars, back to wherever we came from.

Back in Batesville, my dad and brother share another beer in the garage while I go inside to use the bathroom. It's late, almost midnight, and Sara is getting ready for bed. I tell her good night and hug her good-bye. *This is my brother's wife,* I think. The feeling is still strange to me, that he's married now, a grown-up man with a wife and nice furniture and a mortgage and a camper and a bass boat.

In 2003, Scott moved thirty-eight miles south from Shelbyville to a rented house on Depot Street in Batesville. He'd been dating a girl from Shelbyville, and when they broke up, everything reminded him of her. It was right around that time that my dad injured his back at work and went on disability. Dad started relying on Scott a lot more for help around the house, and Batesville was halfway between Aurora, where my parents were, and Shelbyville, where he worked. My parents were glad to have him closer, but of course the downside for my brother was that he had no ties in Batesville. That's when I realize that my life in Pittsburgh is just like my brother's former bachelor life. I moved from New Jersey to Pittsburgh (in part) because it was as close as I could get to Aurora without chucking my career, and although it has been nice to be five hours away instead of eleven, my bachelorette life in Pittsburgh feels pretty rootless.

My dad passes me going into the house to take his turn in the bathroom. When I walk into the garage, Scott is standing at his workbench, fiddling with something. I can see that for the first time in his life, my brother is comfortable in his own skin, the awkwardness gone. He is completely himself. I touch his arm. "You know, you seem really happy, you and Sara. I'm really glad."

He looks at me with a strange smile. "I am happy," he says, like he's thinking, *Haven't you been paying attention?*

"I remember when you used to live over on Depot Street." He looks down solemnly. "I think . . . the way you felt when you lived there is how I've been feeling for a while now." I don't even need to describe this. He's my brother, and all I need to do is say "Depot Street," and we both know what we're talking about.

"I know, Cathy," he says. "But I wasn't ever angry about it."

"What makes you think I'm angry?" I ask louder than I intended to, and as soon as I say this, I realize I am angry. I'm mad, but I don't know who or what I'm mad at.

Scott puts up his hands. "I don't know. Maybe you're not angry."

I look out the garage door. "Before you met Sara, did you think about doing all the stuff you guys do together now? Church and softball teams and stuff like that?"

"I tried to sometimes," he says, flipping a bottle cap into the trash barrel, "but I guess it kind of embarrassed me to do those things by myself."

"I know. Me, too."

"Until I met her, I didn't realize how really empty my life was."

I think about this all the way back to Aurora, and a few days later, as I drive back to Pittsburgh.

A reporter sticks a microphone in my face.

**Reporter:** Cathy, what are you feeling right now?

**Me:** Gosh, look how much happier Scott is since he got married . . .

**Reporter:** You don't need to get married to be happy.

**Me:** I know that, dumbass.

**Reporter:** Don't call me dumbass.

**Me:** Look, I did what I was supposed to do. I pursued my dream. I didn't define my happiness in terms of marriage and children. I became a writer. I became a college professor. I teach in the freaking Cathedral of Learning! Yay, rah for me! But don't I deserve a little happiness at the end of the day?

**Reporter:** Be comfortable with yourself. Be proud of what you've accomplished.

**Me:** I *am* proud of what I've done! But haven't I done my time as the strong single woman?

**Reporter:** Why do you call it "doing time"? That's very telling. It implies you see single life as some sort of prison sentence—

**Me:** Oh, shut up and leave me alone, willya?

# The Season

> We always look up to the older sister because they're always ahead of us and they always win.
>
> —Serena Williams

# WEEK 1: COLTS @ GIANTS

## OR

# A Game Called "Who's Better?"

I've watched my share of televised sporting events, but for the past few months I've also become a regular consumer of ESPN and the NFL channel, a reader of *Sports Illustrated* and the online sports sections of several major city newspapers, and I gotta say: man, does following sports take up a lot of freaking time. I'm only paying attention to a single team in a single sport, and still, it's become a huge time sucker. How do men have time for this? There are so many sports channels on 24/7, so many inches of copy and empty Web pages that must be filled with content, so many men (and yes, they are mostly men) whose job it is to fill all those blank spaces with *something*. And so, like men will do, they talk. They tell stories.

In the NFL, for example, the entire season is a novel, and each game is a chapter; each chapter communicates two things: the tangible stuff, like the actual game being played on the field and the statistics like field goal percentages, quarterback ratings, records at home versus on the road and in domes versus not in domes and winning at halftime versus losing at halftime; and the intangible stuff called old-fashioned human drama. Sports writers and commentators know that good stories need characters and conflict, tension and trouble. Obviously, a football game contains external conflict—people actually hitting each other—but inside the hearts and minds of each of those players, there's internal conflict as well: individual conflicts; team conflicts; stories galore. A football game can be as potentially engrossing and surprising as any reality show, and we watch to see how the drama will play itself out, how it's all going to end.

You need to know this: the trick to getting non–sports fans to watch a football game is (oh heresy!) to take the sports out of it, to turn the impersonal game into a compelling story that's not about Xs and Os but about people. Some folks I know in Pittsburgh would rather grade papers than watch a football game, and other people I know in Pittsburgh would rather die than cheer for one of the Steelers' AFC rivals, so this is the e-mail I sent them to convince them to come to my house one Sunday to watch a Colts game with me.

Sunday, September 10 is:

- The first game of the regular season for the Indianapolis Colts.
- The first *real* game they've played since their heartbreaking loss to the Pittsburgh Steelers in the AFC playoffs on January 15.
- The first time in NFL history that two brothers—Peyton Manning of the Colts and Eli Manning of the Giants—have played each other as opposing quarterbacks.
- The day when—finally, at long last—the question of "Who's better? Peyton or Eli?" will be answered. The *New York Times* says, "No season-opening contest in NFL history has generated so much hype. . . . Actual brothers! At quarterback!"
- My thirty-eighth birthday.

It's finally time for the Brother Bowl. Somewhere in the Meadowlands of New Jersey, Peyton and Eli Manning are preparing to take the field. Their parents, Archie and Olivia, and their older brother, Cooper, are putting on their game faces because they know that the television camera will be on them every time Peyton or Eli does something great or something stupid, hoping to catch them showing just a smidge of favoritism.

I am in Pittsburgh, participating in a little sibling rivalry of my own. I've called my sister, Andrea. "How does a Crock-Pot work?" I ask her.

In the background, I can hear her son Clay babbling. "What do you mean, how does it work?" she asks. "You plug it in."

Andrea, who is a good Hoosier woman, has been making stuff in Crock-Pots for twenty years. She knows how to can vegetables. She owns Longaberger baskets. She owns a deli tray and a deviled-egg plate and a casserole carrier. I am a failed Hoosier woman. I have never owned a Crock-Pot—in fact, this Crock-Pot is borrowed from a married friend of mine—and I have no idea how to make deviled eggs.

"Right, you plug it in," I say, "but don't you have to put water around the crock part thing?"

Andrea starts laughing so hard, she's crying. "John, come here," she calls out to her husband. "Listen to this. Cathy wants to know if you're supposed to put water in the bottom of a Crock-Pot!" He chuckles, too.

"What?" I ask.

"How can you not know how a Crock-Pot works?"

"I guess I wasn't paying attention in Home Ec class," I pout.

I love my little sister a lot. She's my best friend, but we still play this game sometimes: Who's Better? We used to play this game constantly. Case in point: I'm twelve, she's eleven. We're on a girl's fast-pitch softball team, the Stealers. It's the championship game, and we're playing the best team in the league, the Tigerettes. I'm the husky girl in center field. Andrea is the skinny girl in right. The Stealers are up three runs in the last inning when the cleanup batter for the Tigerettes steps up to the plate with the bases loaded. She lines the ball to right-center field, and the ball rolls to the fence. My sister gets to it first.

Marilyn, our coach, told all of us outfielders that if the ball goes to right or left, those fielders should flip the ball to me in center. I'm a big girl with a big arm, and I can make the throw to the infield or to the cutoff man. "Gimme the ball," I say. Out of the corner of my eye, I see Tigerettes rounding bases.

Andrea looks at me. "No! I wanna throw it in. You *always* get to throw it in. It's my turn."

"Gimme the ball!" I grab for her mitt.

She's got her mitt tucked under her arm with the ball still inside. Everyone—our team, our coach, the parents in the stands—screams, "THROW THE BALL! THROW IT!"

I can't believe my sister has chosen this particular moment to be the absolute brat I know her to be. "You can't throw it that far! Give it!" I knock the ball out of the mitt, and it rolls to the fence. The two of us roll around by the outfield fence, scrabbling for the ball. I don't remember which of us finally threw it, but by the time we did, it was too late. All the runners scored, and we lost the game.

As I walked from the outfield to the dugout, I figured that everyone would yell at Andrea. Finally my parents and my friends would understand that she was an impossible pain in the ass, that it wasn't my fault, that it was never, ever my fault. But of course, that's not what happened. We both got blamed. Lucky for us, it was a double-elimination tournament. We played the Tigerettes again and beat them. Afterward, we got to ride in the back of our coach's truck, cruising down Broadway screaming the chorus of Queen's "We Are the Champions" at the top of our lungs.

Now, on the rare occasion that we find ourselves playing Who's Better? Andrea always wins in the domestic categories, but I've got her beat in the professional categories. We're both teachers, but I'm a college professor and a writer. She's married with a kid and pregnant with number two. I'm still single. Typically, we don't lord these facts over each other. Typically, my sister does not make fun of me for not knowing how to operate a Crock-Pot, especially on my birthday when I'm already feeling a little blue. "So no water then, right?" I say.

"Right," she says, still laughing. "I can't wait to call Mom and tell her this."

"Whatever."

There's a pause as she gathers her straight face. "So what are you making for your party?"

"Chili and Spanish hot dogs."

Spanish hot dogs are not from Spain, where I'm sure they don't even eat hot dogs. Spanish hot dogs are a delicacy known only to those from my hometown, Peru, Indiana, where one fine day many, many years ago, a man named Bob decided to make a sloppy-joe-like meat sauce and slather it on a hot dog. Meat on meat (brilliant!) topped with cheese (even more brilliant!). Why he decided to call them "Spanish," I have no idea, and I probably don't want to. Bob opened a hot dog stand to sell these delicious torpedoes so that Peruvians could drive up, sit in their cars, and have cute girls hang trays of hot dogs and root beer from their car windows. Then my family moved away from Peru to Cincinnati, a city famous for its chili. An oft-told story in my family concerns the first time we stopped at a Skyline Chili restaurant, where chili dogs are served, and asked if they had Spanish hot dogs. The waitress looked at us quizzically. "Do you mean a chili dog?" and we said yes, but without the beans, and she said, "Well, we don't have anything like that around here. This is Cincinnati, not Spain."

It never, ever occurred to us that Spanish hot dogs were native only to Peru, Indiana. I hope this tells you a lot about growing up in Indiana and growing up in a family like mine.

"Did you chop up the hamburger really good?" my sister asks.

"Yes."

"Don't forget the chili powder."

"I know."

"How many people are coming?"

"I don't know. A lot."

She hears the nervousness in my voice. "How are you feeling today?"

"Pretty good," I say. This is a lie. I don't want to celebrate being one year closer to forty. I don't want the doorbell to ring. I don't want to open the front door of this house—which I bought all by myself and live in all by myself—because then everyone will see the truth: I am alone and I have to throw my own birthday party.


I grew up in the kind of family that celebrated birthdays big-time. It was Your Special Day. You got to pick what the family ate for dinner, what kind of cake or dessert you wanted. Some years the birthday dinner table looked like Thanksgiving, crowded with the five members of my immediate family, plus some grandparents, a best friend, a cousin or two. After dinner we made a production out of opening each card—reading it aloud, laughing if it was funny, oohing if it was sappy. If my Grandpa Day was there, he'd open your gift for you, sliding his pocket knife under the tape to preserve the wrapping paper. "No use letting it go to waste," he'd say, folding it up and taking it home. A year or two later, you might recognize the pink polka-dot paper from your twelfth birthday wrapped around your mom's Mother's Day present.

A birthday is the anticipation leading up to that day and also the experience of the day itself. Like your lucky number or that pair of jeans you always reach for first, a birthday is a bit magical. Here's what I mean: take a wall calendar, any kind—a desk blotter, a freebie from the bank, or a fancy one with puppies. Turn to the month of September. See the square with a "10" in it? To me, that square shines with an enchanted, invisible light. The people who love me can see that light, too, whenever they look at the month of September.

Yes, I'm serious.

I wish I could tell you that I developed more reasonable expectations about birthdays as I got older, but I didn't. My brother-in-law John says that we are the sappiest family he's ever met, that we put way too much emphasis on birthdays. "It's just another day," he says, and we roll our eyes and ignore him. My ex-boyfriend Alex always needed to be reminded that my birthday was coming. "When is it again?" he'd ask. "Wait, don't tell me. The twelfth, right?"

Eventually Alex started remembering my birthday all by himself, albeit a little grudgingly. Once he organized a surprise party for me, but afterward he said, "I felt like you expected me to throw you that party, like you expected me to do something big and elaborate, like your family would do." I lived with this man for seven years, and in all that time, he never understood that I didn't want or expect an elaborate party. All I ever wanted was *for him* to want to make me happy without *my* having to ask to be made happy.

Maybe some people think that's too much to ask for, but I don't. I think it's entirely reasonable to expect a man to love me at least as much as my family loves me. This—I know—is one of the reasons I am still single on September 10, 2006, the first day of the Colts regular season and my thirty-eighth birthday.


It's not even noon yet, and the Spanish hot-dog sauce is bubbling away in my borrowed Crock-Pot. The menu for my party is football food: hot dogs, chili, chips, cookies, beer. Some of my guests will be foodies, more accustomed, I'm sure, to baba ghanoush, Brie, and grilled vegetables. A few months ago, I was invited to a colleague's home for a small dinner party. He lives in Shadyside, a very deciduous and tony neighborhood in Pittsburgh. During the meal the discussion turned to television, and one of the guests (a relative newcomer to the United States) said, "There is this show about the blue-collar humor. A big man who works for the cable company says something again and again."

"Git 'er done!" I growled in an almost perfect imitation of Larry the Cable Guy.

Everyone at the table stopped what they were doing and looked at me.

"My dad loves that guy," I said. Lowering my gaze, I took another bite of salmon.

It happens from time to time—moments like this when my red-state slip peeks out from under my blue-state skirt. I'm still relatively new to Pittsburgh, a city that can't decide if it's more proletarian or more bourgeois. Half of the people who live here, myself included, love that it's both, but the other half very much need to believe that it's a bigger city, like Philadelphia or D.C. I'm aware (probably to an unhealthy degree) that people here are still making up their minds about me, this writer Cathy Day. What will they think when they walk into my house and hear Led Zeppelin on the stereo and see me in a bright-blue Colts T-shirt, stirring a pot of chili?

I can't bear to think about this. I want a cigarette.

Instead, I paint my toenails. I fill the dishwasher. In the bathroom, I set out a few extra rolls of toilet paper. In my study, I straighten my desk and sit down at my laptop. I check the *Indianapolis Star* to see how fired up Colts fans are about the game tonight. Then I check my e-mail. I haven't gotten any actual birthday cards yet, but maybe there will be a few virtual birthday greetings in my in-box. Nope, but there is a message from Chemistry, which says that "Joey" is interested in me.

I click the link, thinking, *Wouldn't it be cool to meet the man of my dreams on my birthday and on the first day of the Colts regular season?* Up pops Joey's profile. He has feathered hair, a gold chain, and a nervous smile. Here's what he has to say for himself:

hi there,sorry i'm no good at this.i am very hard working person.i want someone that won't play games.i want some one that down to earth.and will be true.i am shy at first,but will open up after a while. hope to hear from you soon.

I've only been on Chemistry for a short while, but already I'm sick of profiles like this and of guys like Joey—and it's not because of his hair or the fact that he doesn't use capital letters. It's not because he uses "someone that" when he should say "someone who"—although, okay, sure, that's part of it. And it's not about class. Who am I to say Joey's not good enough for me? I'm from a blue-collar family. My dad drinks Miller Lite and makes his own bullets. My brother only reads the Bible and car magazines. My brother-in-law operates a Bobcat for a living and drag-races in his spare time. I don't say these things to mock them. I'm merely stating the facts. I am proud of and love each of the men in my family dearly, and they would probably love Joey. I'll bet Joey would probably love the men in my family, and Joey would probably love the fact that I listen to Led Zeppelin, watch football, and serve chili and hot dogs at parties. But that isn't all I am, either, and profiles like Joey's do nothing to reassure me that a guy like him will get a girl like me.

I critique writing for a living, so let me tell you what's really wrong with Joey's profile: it is hesitant and vague. Since I started using Chemistry, I have read many, many profiles that begin, "I'm not good at this," or "I don't know what to say," or "How to start?" or the dreaded "I have never done this before." Well, neither have I, buster, but could you try to show a little enthusiasm? I think that anyone over the age of thirty-five feels strange about advertising themselves on the Internet. I know I do. It took me years to work up the courage to do this, and timid, doubtful statements like Joey's just remind me how nervous I am. The other problem with Joey's statement is that it says nothing about the human being who wrote it or about the woman he's looking for. If there's one thing I've learned as a writer and reader, it's that details matter. Show me who you are, don't tell me you're "hard working." That could mean anything. Give me an example. Tell me a story, or at least a revealing anecdote.

I click to look at my own profile, and I read my profile as a stranger might. Is this who I am? A woman who likes sports and movies and will eat anything? Maybe the reason I'm hearing from so many Joeys is because I'm presenting myself as a lover of Joeys, which is true but also not true. In any case, I don't click the button to say I'm mutually interested in Joey, and I close my computer with a sigh. No potential boyfriends today, even if it is my birthday.

I've been thinking about my lame profile for a few weeks, since the day of the Seahawks preseason game. "Come upstairs," I told Andrea. "I need your help."

I saw the look on my sister's face as soon as she walked into my bedroom—the "I'm exhausted and someone else is entertaining Clay and I sure would like a nap" look. She certainly deserved a nap, but instead of letting her take one, I plopped my laptop on her pregnant belly and asked, "Do you ever remember Mom giving us advice about boys? About dating?"

"No," Andrea said tiredly.

"So how'd you figure out what to do?"

She yawned. "I don't think I ever had to 'do' anything," Andrea said. "Not with these." She cupped her breasts with her hands and gave them a little bounce. Even when she's not pregnant, my sister is what you'd call . . . stacked. Andrea gets this from our mother, a trait I was glad not to inherit. My mother's huge bras always scared me when I was a little girl. They weren't lacy and pretty like the bras in catalogs; they seemed vaguely orthopedic, like something you'd have to wear after surgery or an auto accident.

"I think I need to update my profile," I told Andrea. "I'm getting all the wrong guys."

I logged in, and she read my profile. "What's wrong with it?" she asked.

"I don't know, really. Maybe it doesn't say enough about who I am, what I want, my personality. When I read men's profiles, I hate it when they write this vague shit. *I like to hang out with my friends and walk on the beach.* Blah blah blah."

Andrea said, "Well, show me the men you picked."

"Click on 'Active Matches.'"

My sister had never used the Internet for this purpose, to make a connection with a total stranger. Their pictures popped up, and Andrea got this weird, shocked look on her face, like she was being forced to look at porn. I knew exactly how she felt. She read the first profile. "He's got dogs. Why are you picking a guy who has dogs? I'm sure your cat would get along real well with dogs." At least, unlike my mom, she was encouraging me to be a little choosy. She clicked some more. "Oh and this one here says he scuba dives. You can't scuba dive!"

This went on for a while. It was like listening to the scared, fearful voice in my own head. Usually my sister and I take turns encouraging each other. When she's down, I pump her up, and vice versa, but right then she was really bringing me down. I plunked on the edge of the bed. "Look, I'm just trying to be open and willing and not talk myself out of things. What difference does it make if he wants to scuba dive and I don't?"

"What if you marry him and he wants you to go scuba diving? I can't see you doing that."

I wanted to say, *Who says I couldn't scuba dive!? And what do you know about this anyway! You're married and have babies and you don't have to deal with the shit I'm dealing with here!* Instead, I took a deep breath. "I'm trying really hard not to think too far ahead. I have to see it like I'm *just* going on dates."

I realized then that neither one of us had ever Just Gone on Dates. No wonder she couldn't help me.

Andrea clicked around some more. "You have a lot of men on this list." I explained that I'm sent five profiles a day. That's how I've accumulated this list. "So none of these guys have responded to you?"

"No."

"Why not?" She seemed incensed on my behalf.

"I don't know, Andi. They just didn't. I mean, I do it, too—decide I'm not interested."

"But what if you're in a bad mood one day and you click No, but he's really great?"

I threw my hands in the air. "I know! It drives me insane sometimes!"

"What about some of these guys?" She pointed to Charles, a thirty-eight-year-old man who looked like David Duchovny, and Ned, a forty-two-year-old guy who had a motorcycle in every one of his pictures. They'd been in my Active Matches folder for over a month, and I'd never heard anything from them.

"Yeah, I guess I can delete them now. I guess they aren't interested." I point to one, Ralph. "Read this one," I said. Ralph brags that he is a college professor at a Pittsburgh university, that he's "cultured" and doesn't say "warsh" and "tahwn" like most Pittsburghers.

"He sounds like an ass."

"I know! Look at his photos." In one, it looked like he'd taken a picture of himself being interviewed on television. "Can you imagine if I put stuff like that in my profile?!" I put my hands on my hips and spoke in deep bass. "Hey there, baby, let's get to know one another. You know, I've been on NPR. Twice." Andrea laughed so hard, she started crying. I pointed to my chest. "Did I mention I was the solution to the *New York Times Magazine* acrostic?" (All of this is true, by the way.)

"Oh!" My sister wiped her eyes. "Well anyway, I think you should thin down this list. I mean, aren't these people at Chemistry thinking 'Gosh, that Cathy Day sure has a lot of men on her list'?" She was embarrassed for me, bless her heart. And I remembered only too well that it was *exactly* this kind of embarrassment that prevented me from doing anything for years. For me it had come down to a simple choice: I could either bitch about being alone or get over it and reach out to the world. Listening to my sister reminded me that I'd actually come pretty far.

My guests start arriving around six, and soon my house and the deck out back are full of people. There's Tom and Rachel, my neighbors. There's Janet, owner of the Crock-Pot, another colleague who's new to Pitt, and her husband Jerry. He hands me my present, Peyton Manning's Omega card from 2000, which I stick on my fridge. A week ago, Janet asked me to go with her to a Pitt football game at Heinz Field. I jumped at the chance, excited to see the stadium and maybe make a new woman friend. I knew we'd get along when, some time during the first quarter, Janet looked up and around, trying to take it all in—the field, the crowd, the huge sky— and said, "This is *awesome!*" Milling around my house are other colleagues, spouses, their kids, my graduate students. Half of being happy, I'm finding, is making myself go through the motions of it. Throw a party. Invite people. Buy beer. Smile. Take pictures. And eventually you realize you aren't going through the motions anymore; you really are happy.

My cell phone rings. It's Andrea. "How's your birthday party going?" she asks.

"Great!" I say, and I mean it. I feel wonderful.

"Do they like the Spanish hot dogs?"

I lift the lid of the Crock-Pot, which is half empty. "Yep."

"Clay wants to say something to you." In the background, I can hear her saying, *Tell Aunt Cathy happy birthday!* But all that comes out is *buh-buh-buh.*

"Hey, Clay! How's my boy? How's my best boy?"

Andrea gets back on the phone. "He smiled! He always smiles when he hears your voice." This, I remind myself from time to time, is why I moved to Pittsburgh. So my sister's children would recognize my face, my voice, so that I wouldn't be a stranger to them.

Here's the story of my adult life via some birthday snapshots:

**1996:** I'm turning twenty-eight. I'm at the Globe restaurant in Tuscaloosa, Alabama, sitting at a large table surrounded by my friends in the writing program at the University of Alabama. Alex and I spent four years in graduate school, and we're in year two of two-year instructorships that can't be renewed. We're both on the academic job market, and our chances of finding jobs are slim, but I don't want to think about that right now. I want to drink wine and laugh with this table full of smart, interesting people. I'm very, very happy.

**1997:** I'm turning twenty-nine. Alex and I are living in Minnesota. I've just started a tenure-track job at a college there, and he's come along hoping to get a job in the Twin Cities. His job search isn't going well. He's stressed. I'm stressed about my own job and about his stress. All I really remember about this birthday is that I made lasagna.

**1998:** I'm turning thirty. Alex has found his dream job! Unfortunately, that job is not in the Twin Cities, and the week before my birthday, I help him haul all his belongings from Minnesota to Baltimore. Here, my friends, is where my life gets very complicated. I can't bear to spend my thirtieth birthday alone in Minnesota in a half-empty apartment. So I have flown home to Indiana, where my family does its best to re-create the birthdays of my youth, carefully avoiding the subject of why I am there with them in Indiana. Why I'm not in Minnesota with Alex. Or why I'm not in Baltimore with Alex. Or why he isn't in Indiana with me. My family knows me. They know that if they even look like they will ask me one of these questions, I'll burst into tears.

**1999:** I'm turning thirty-one. A Minnesota arts organization has given me a fellowship, and to thank them for this generous gift, I've taken their money, bought myself a leave of absence, and fled the state of Minnesota. Alex and I are living together again outside Baltimore, where he's been working and living alone for the past year. We are not talking about our future.

**2000:** I'm turning thirty-two. I'm living in two places at once: a farmhouse outside Baltimore and a tiny rented room. I've quit my job in Minnesota and was lucky enough (given that I still haven't published my book) to find another tenure-track teaching job within driving distance of Alex—at a small college in suburban New Jersey. Alex and I know many academic couples who aren't this lucky, if you can call it lucky to live two and a half hours apart, to see each other on a rotating weekend schedule. My birthday falls on the weekend that Alex comes to New Jersey, and we take the train up to New York City for the day. That night, we sleep in my rented room—me on the twin bed, him on the floor on an inflatable mattress.

**2001:** I'm turning thirty-three. Alex and I are separated, which really means that we've stopped driving back and forth to see each other. I live in New Jersey. I live in New Jersey? How did this happen? A year ago it was just where I worked, where I lived four days a week, but suddenly, it's my new home. I don't know anyone except for my colleagues in the English Department. I don't really even live in a town, but in a town*ship* where the closest thing to a town center is the 7-Eleven. Everyone in New Jersey, I've discovered, lives in one town and drives forty-five minutes to work in another town. My birthday falls on a Monday. I teach all day, and then a colleague takes me out to eat. I go home that night feeling sorry for myself. Until the next day.

**2002:** I'm turning thirty-four. I'm on the Jersey shore with a girlfriend, drinking beer and looking at the ocean. Back in Baltimore, Alex has a new girlfriend, but I'm still waiting for something to happen. I haven't been on a date in a year. It's been a year since I even met a man my age who wasn't gay or married.

**2003:** I'm turning thirty-five, and I'm still waiting. I have no memory of this birthday.

**2004:** I'm turning thirty-six, and I'm still waiting. I'm back home in Indiana for this birthday. The Colts play their first game of the 2004 season against the Patriots, the team that beat them badly, 20–3, in the AFC playoffs a few months earlier. Trying to redeem themselves and tie the game in the final seconds, the Colts send Mike Vanderjagt to nail a 48-yard field goal. Vanderjagt hasn't missed in forty-two tries and was dead-on perfect in the 2003 season. My family watches in horror as the ball sails wide right. Afterward, we decided to go ahead and celebrate my birthday anyway. We celebrate that Scott is engaged to Sara. We celebrate that my sister Andrea is having her first baby. We celebrate that I've just had my first book. My parents celebrate that I'm home. It's a party like when I was a kid—a big dinner and family and neighbors and beer.

**2005:** I'm turning thirty-seven. I don't live in New Jersey anymore. I've switched jobs (again) to get closer to my family. Pittsburgh is five hours from Cincinnati, which is better than eleven. Now I will be able to drive to family get-togethers, and my family (who refuse to fly) will be able to visit me. Since I don't know anyone in Pittsburgh except for the Punter, I celebrate my birthday in Indiana. My new nephew Clay helps me open my gifts.

**2006:** I'm turning thirty-eight. I'm celebrating my birthday in Pittsburgh by watching the Colts play the New York Giants on television. This is my new life: one foot in Indiana and one foot in the hills of western Pennsylvania.

The Colts' opening drive lasts nearly nine minutes on the clock, an eternity in football game time. Peyton drives 58 yards on seventeen plays, but in the end there's no touchdown, only a 26-yard field goal by Adam Vinatieri, his first regular-season field goal as a Colt instead of a Patriot. He kicks another in the second quarter—Colts up 6–0. Then Peyton throws a 2-yard pass to tight end Dallas Clark, and the Colts are up by a decided margin, 13–0. But then little brother Eli bounces back. With 32 seconds left, Eli throws a beautiful 34-yard pass to Plaxico Burress, followed by a Jay Feely kick, and the Giants have cut the margin to 13–7. The half ends with a powerful 48-yard Vinatieri field goal with no time left on the clock, and Peyton and Eli head to their respective locker rooms with the Giants trailing 16–7.

I'm so nervous that I can't take my eyes off the television. For reasons I don't quite understand, I've convinced myself that my life, my future, is somehow wrapped up in the outcome of this game. I'm convinced that by the end of the season, I will have learned *something* from the Indianapolis Colts—about life and how to live it, about love and how to get it. What does it mean that the Colts are playing this game on my birthday? Their first game since they lost to Pittsburgh. I don't know exactly, but I know it's important. It's magical thinking, but in reverse. I don't believe anything I do will affect whether or not the Colts win or lose. Rather, I believe their winning or losing is a sign, a message from the universe, a 100-yard slip of paper in a fortune cookie. It's like John Madden is speaking right to me when he says, "Let's talk about the Colts. How long is their window going to stay open? How old is Peyton now? He's in his ninth year in the NFL. If they're going to get to the Super Bowl, it better be soon." Why does John Madden keep reminding me that Peyton and I never win the big one, that we don't have that much time left? I know! I'm trying, John! I really am!

Around halftime, I realize that almost everyone has gone home, even Janet and Jerry, and it's just me and my graduate students, who can always be counted on to sit around and drink beer. The Giants have pulled to within two points, and even dour Giants' coach Tom Coughlin flaps his hands, trying to get the crowd into the game. It works. Peyton throws an interception, but when Eli tries to take advantage, he muffs a pass to Tiki Barber and turns the ball over himself. In the fourth quarter, Colts' running back Dominic Rhodes scores a 1-yard touchdown, putting them up 23–14. But the game's not over, sports fans. The Giants score again, which keeps the game close and interesting at 23–21, until in the final minutes, Vinatieri kicks another field goal to seal the Colts win at 26–21.

I'm cleaning up the kitchen when the phone rings. It's my mom. "How was your party?" she asks. I tell her I think it went really well. "And the Colts won! I think it's a sign," my mom says. "This is going to be your year, honey."

Now you know where I get it. Magical thinking is a family tradition.

Nice guys finish last.

—Leo Durocher, Major League Baseball manager

---

# WEEK 2: COLTS VS. TEXANS

## OR

# The Uneven Playing Field

---

Afew days after my birthday, I drive to Shadyside, park on Walnut Street in front of Pottery Barn, and walk to Starbucks to meet a perfect stranger. I don't know this yet, but I will spend a lot of time in coffee shops on Walnut Street over the next few months. This is my Chemistry.com "coffee date in a safe neighborhood." His name is Rick. I'm nervous, but also upset, because I had to spend $99 to meet a perfect stranger named Rick for coffee. Why does it have to be this way? Not just for me, but for Rick, too, and for every other goddamn lonely person forced to resort to these measures?

I give myself a pep talk as I walk past the J.Crew store and the Mexican restaurant. *Stop it, Cathy. That's your fear talking. Relax. Maybe you need to consider this dating thing like a form of self-care, something normal adult women work into their lives, like exercise, manicures, therapy, and buying groceries.*

I'm following all of Chemistry's "First Meeting" suggestions. I have driven to this safe, public venue. My sister knows that I am at this venue and is expecting my call to let her know that I'm still alive once I leave the venue. I will not drink to excess. I will keep my cell phone with me. I will watch for red flags, although Chemistry did not give me a list of red flags, which means I'm supposed to "trust my gut." If my gut says, *This guy is a whack job. Abort! Abort!* I should exit the venue or notify a member of the venue personnel. Maybe the barristas will throw hot coffee at him?

I walk into Starbucks and I see him right away, but he won't meet my gaze, so I walk over. "Are you Rick?" I ask, and he smiles. We make conversation as best we can. I wonder how many First Meetings these young barristas have witnessed. I wonder if this, my first First Meeting, qualifies as the strangest experience of my life thus far. Rick is from Pittsburgh originally and has just moved back. At the moment he's renting an apartment but looking to buy a house. The subject turns to furniture. "I want to get more contemporary-looking furniture," Rick says. "You know, glass and metal."

*Yikes,* I think. "Oh, don't do that!" I say. He looks at me strangely. "I mean you should try to find this Mid-Century Modern stuff. Seems to be all the rage these days." When he asks me what it is, all I can come up with is, "You know, fifties style, stuff from the *Dick Van Dyke Show*." Then, to make him feel better for having lousy taste in furniture, I tell him how a few days earlier, I got three end tables, an Art Deco dresser, a chair, and an outdoor bench from a house down my street. "The owner died and a workman was clearing out the house for the Realtor, and he said I could take whatever I wanted."

"Did you know the owner?" Rick asks.

"No, he died before I moved into the neighborhood. Apparently, the guy who owned the house found out he had cancer, and so he jumped off the Bloomfield Bridge." I look down at my coffee cup. *God, that was morbid, Cathy.*

But Rick doesn't miss a beat. "You know, I work downtown, and this week a man jumped from a twelve-story window right in front of the place where I work."

I think, *Hey, I think I might like this guy!* We've both finished our coffees. "I'm starving," I say, and he concurs, so we walk down the street to a restaurant.

There's one thing you always have in common with anyone you meet online—your experience being online. At dinner, Rick says, "You know, I almost never check my Chemistry account anymore, but the other day I did, and you were one of the five matches."

"Really? You should have gotten an e-mail from Chemistry two months ago saying 'Cathy is interested in you!' You were one of my first five matches when I signed on!" I don't mention that his headline, "I can't believe it's come to this!" was profoundly underwhelming.

Rick says, "No, I never got anything like that."

This makes me incredibly irate. "You know, for the first few weeks I was on there, I had trouble making my profile go active. Every time I logged off, it would change my profile to 'hidden.' So I had them fix it and I asked if all the people I clicked Yes on were notified, and they said yes!"

"I think Chemistry is still in the beta stage," Rick says, gesturing with a french fry.

I give him a blank look.

Rick smiles and explains: he thinks Chemistry launched once they'd eliminated all the major system bugs, but now they're using customers like us to help them work out the minor kinks. "I can't complain, though," he says. "I've never had to pay to renew my membership with them."

"What?" I can't believe this. "Why?"

"It might just be a glitch, but I think it's that they need to keep me on their roster. There are probably far more women members in Pittsburgh than men, so they need as many men as possible to sign up so it looks to the women like they'll be getting their money's worth."

I'm speechless. I take a large gulp of Yuengling.

Rick goes on. "I wouldn't think too many guys in Pittsburgh use Chemistry. It's a pain in the ass—the test you have to take and everything. And you have to wait for *them* to send you just five matches a day. You can't search for yourself and see what's out there. Most guys I know want to control the process." He slips another fry in his mouth. "Are you on Match? You should go on Match if you really want to meet someone."

I explain to Rick that "going online" has been a long process of desensitization. First I joined the Colts fan forum. Then I joined Chemistry. "I thought that using a service that's sort of niche, specialized, was better for me. More private. I don't want my students to see my profile."

"Students?" And so I tell him what I do for a living. Rick smiles. "A lot of women I've met online seem to be looking for a meal ticket. I don't understand how a smart, attractive woman like you doesn't get asked out." I blush and start burrowing through my purse like a squirrel, and as soon as I do, I forget what I'm looking for. "You should change how you describe your body type," Rick says.

"Huh?" I ask, looking up. *Gum. I'm looking for gum.* I return to the purse.

"Yours says 'curvy.' Most guys think that's code for, you know, being overweight."

I look down my shirt. "But the only other choices were 'slender' and 'athletic and toned.' I'm not those."

Now we're both looking at my chest. I'm not a woman who likes to be looked at, so I divert his attention by giving him my theory about why I don't get asked out. I've moved around a lot. I work with men I can't go out with—students and colleagues. Almost all of my male colleagues are married anyway. I don't know anyone outside my department. I don't know that many people in Pittsburgh, period. I don't know many single people, except for my graduate students, whom I can't really hang out with. I could go to bars or clubs, but my girlfriends are married or starting families and aren't interested in that sort of thing anymore. *I'm* not interested in that sort of thing anymore. I shrug my shoulders. "I told a few people I know that I was interested in dating, and I got fixed up a few times, but they weren't right for me."

Then he tells me about his ex-wife, who spent all his money and left him in debt. He tells me about the stripper he dated for a while. Now I understand why his profile said he was looking for a "classy" woman. Rick says, "After my divorce, I moved to D.C. I didn't know a soul. I'd just go to bars by myself."

"I just can't do that," I say.

"I loved being in a place where no one knew me. The slate was clean." Rick touches my hand. "You know, I'm feeling more optimistic than I have in a long time. For a year after my divorce, I just sat around and felt horrible, like I was never going to get married again. During the week, it was okay because I had to work, but the weekends would come . . ."

"Yeah, I know about empty weekends." I pull my hand back, cough politely into it, and rest my chin in the palm.

The waitress takes our plates away and asks if we want another beer. Rick looks at me. I consider the implications of ordering another beer. Am I attracted to him? I'm not feeling anything in the below-the-waist department, but maybe that's a good sign. I'd rather be home watching *Law & Order* than sitting here, but that's my hibernation impulse talking, a tendency I have to fight against. Having another beer implies that I'm enjoying myself. And I am, sort of. Rick is a curious fellow. I say, "Sure, I'll take another Yuengling," and Rick smiles broadly. When the waitress walks away, I say, "I would think that a guy like you—employed, in your late thirties—would be inundated by women looking for a nice guy."

"I wish you wouldn't call me a nice guy. It's like the kiss of death." He tells me about this guy he knows, Lonny, who is not a nice guy. Lonny is married and has a profile on Match.com that he uses to find women to sleep with, many of whom admit they're married, too. He's also sleeping with a fifteen-year-old who he didn't meet online. She is the daughter of a friend of his. The friend has no idea.

Now I really am sick to my stomach. "That's sick," I say. "And illegal. You're friends with this guy?"

Rick shrugs. "We hang out sometimes."

How can Rick be so nonchalant? I feel like a naïve tourist who's glanced into a dark alley. I want to grab a cop and say, "Have you looked down there? Do something!"

Rick peers into his beer. "Why are women more attracted to him than to me? Lonny says I should try being a little bad." Rick gives me this look, hopeful and searching.

"I don't think you want to be like Lonny." I look away, out the window. It's gotten dark, and couples are strolling up and down Walnut Street. "But it's true that some women are attracted to bad boys. Look at movies. Over and over, they show us that all a bad man needs is the love of a good woman."

"What movies?" Rick asks.

"Take *Breakfast Club*. That movie says, 'Don't go for the geek who will probably go to a good college and get a good job after graduation. Go for the cute but tragically misunderstood jock or the poor but tragically misunderstood slacker.' And don't even get me started on *Grease*. I could go on all freaking night about *Dirty Dancing* alone!"

Rick has a bemused smile on his face. "What are you trying to say?"

I take a deep breath. I wish I had a cigarette. "Women love bad boys because movies have warped our sense of reality. They make us believe in long shots. The bad boy is the long shot, the better story. You're the safe bet, but that story's boring."

"Thanks," he says ruefully.

"I say that as a compliment."

Rick gives me a long look. "You sure do think a lot."

I roll my eyes. "Tell me something I don't know."

"You must really like movies," he says.

I think about this. "I don't watch a lot of TV or movies, but I remember things."

Rick cocks his head. "What do you mean?"

"Like I remember where I saw *The Breakfast Club,* who I was with, even though it was over twenty years ago. I see the pictures in my mind." The waitress walks over with our check. "You know how you'll see an actor and you think, 'I know I recognize him from something'? Well, I can tell you what that other movie was. Most of the time."

"Photographic memory," Rick says, reaching for the check. I let him do this. All my research says I must do this. And sure enough, his mood perks up as he lays down his credit card.

"I don't think it's that. It's like everything reminds me of something else. I remember more than I want to." Then I try to recall what our original subject of conversation was. Oh right! Bad boys and nice guys. "Look, you just haven't met a woman who's ready for a real relationship. My friend Sofia says that when we're not truly ready, we gravitate toward people whom we know, deep down, things won't work out with." I finish the last of my beer. "That's what I've always done. I saw your profile and thought, now here's a nice guy I need to pay attention to."

Rick scoffs. "You called me a nice guy again. That implies weakness, and I'm not weak."

I don't know what to say.

Rick offers to walk me to my car. I assent to this. I'm paralyzed by the advice of my friends and by my own contradictory impulses. *Be picky. Be open-minded. Go with your gut. Your gut has shit for brains. Let your emotions be your guide. Don't trust your emotions. Give him the benefit of the doubt. If you're not feeling it, move on.* I can't even answer what seems like the simplest question in the world: *How do I feel?* When we reach my car, we stand there awkwardly for a moment, and then we hug. I feel sort of

Cathy Day

dumb, hugging someone I've known for three hours. He pulls his head back and I realize he wants to do the bold thing that Lonny the Statutory Rapist thinks he should do—kiss me. But Rick is not a bold, manly man. He is a mild man trying to act bold and manly. He has this whipped dog look on his face, and I am full of horrible sadness. I turn my head to let him know, *Okay, you can kiss my cheek,* but he tries to move my head back and kiss me on the lips. Now he's gone too far. His boldness isn't sad anymore. It's creepy.

I take a step back.

Rick looks at me. "Well, do you want to see a movie or something this weekend?"

What does it mean that I feel no chemistry with the first man that Chemistry chose for me? "I'm going out of town this weekend," I say.

He looks down at his feet. "Uh-huh. Okay." Now he's pouting.

For some reason, I feel this need to prove to him that I'm telling the truth. "No, really. I'm going to Louisville for . . ." I've been invited to give a reading at the University of Louisville, but I'm not sure how to explain this to Rick, so I say, ". . . for business. And then I'm going to Indianapolis to see a Colts game with my folks." I volunteer my itinerary, this specific information so quickly that I can tell he believes me.

"Can I call you when you get back then?"

God, I can't stand hurting someone's feelings, and that's most of what dating is—your feelings getting hurt or you hurting someone else's. No wonder I've never really dated. My temperament isn't suited for this. "Sure," I say. "Good night." And I get in my car and drive home. I never hear from Rick again.


The next morning I check my Chemistry account. "No new matches found." No more five a day? My membership isn't even up yet, and they're out of men? And so far, only one of these men has responded to me, and he and I have no chemistry. So I call Customer Service. "Look," I say, "how many men actually subscribe to your service in the Pittsburgh area? Because I've been on this for about three months and I've followed the rules and I check my matches every day and create active matches but no one replies to me." I'm pacing around my study, trying to find the right way to

78

put this. "I mean, well, I'm not ugly or anything, so there must be some reason that nobody responds." I feel like an absolute jerk. "So I was wondering if, you know, maybe I could get extra time on my membership so I can get my money's worth."

The operator says she will talk to her manager, puts me on hold, and comes back with the advice that my criteria are too narrow. "We advise you to expand your search criteria to include a wider geographic area, for example."

"But I don't want to meet a man who lives far away! I've done that whole long-distance-relationship thing already. I'm really trying to put down roots in Pittsburgh." I remind myself that I don't need to tell her all these things.

The operator says she will offer me an extra week on my membership. That's it.

"Well that sucks," I say, thinking about what Rick said about beta whatever and how he doesn't have to pay, and all I get is a lousy extra week. But I don't say any of that. I just think it. "I don't think I'll be renewing."

The operator couldn't care less. She says, "Thank you for calling."

So I log in and change every single search criterion to say "Any." Any race. Any religion. Any body type. Any income level. Any interests and hobbies. Any relationship status except for currently married. Whether they want kids or don't want kids. Basically, any living, breathing dude in Pittsburgh.

The next day, I log in again. "No new matches found."

I was in high school the first time I was aware of being discriminated against as a woman. I've always loved being around sports, and most of my friends were athletes, but I'm not particularly athletic. In junior high and high school I was a manager for the girls' basketball teams, which meant that I generally just hung around and did stuff the coaches didn't want to do. But in my sophomore year I started hanging around the training room with the student trainers, the boys who taped ankles and stuffed tampons up the wrestlers' noses. I was hooked. Between my sophomore and junior year I went to an athletic training camp at Indiana University and learned rudimentary sports medicine—basic anatomy, injury evaluation, when to use heat and when to use ice, how to stretch out a hamstring, that sort of thing. I loved it, and I was good at it. Sports medicine is the only profession I've actually given serious thought to pursuing, other than writing and teaching.

At that time the training room was located inside the boys' locker room; the facilities were designed pre–Title IX. Every day, I had to get myself into the training room before all the male athletes showed up to get changed for practice. If I showed up late and they were already undressing, someone would walk me through the locker room with a T-shirt or a towel over my head. When I started athletic training, I was still so shy that I couldn't look anyone in the eye. But once I hit my stride, once I found something I was good at, a purpose, a place in the miasma that is high school, I looked everyone in the eye. When basketball season rolled around, the head athletic trainer said, "Cathy, you've got the most experience of any of the trainers down here. I'm making you my assistant for the boys' varsity basketball team."

If you're from Indiana, you know this was a big deal. If you're not from Indiana, let me explain: high school basketball matters—intensely. I'd attend all practices. I'd go to all home games and sit with the team, right there for the whole town to see. I'd go to all the away games, on the bus. And I'd be in the basketball team's photo, which might (if we had a good year) hang someday in the hallway of fame with all the other photos of Peru High School teams that had won sectionals and Central Indiana Conference championships. Remember the end of *Hoosiers,* the Hickory team hanging immortally on the gym wall? Even though I wasn't a boy and couldn't play basketball, I wanted a chance to be on that wall, too. I was so excited. And the great thing is that nobody I worked with thought this was weird, that a girl was the student trainer for the boys' team. I was just Cathy. I was the most qualified and I was the best. Sure, sometimes in the training room they'd do dumb boy stuff, like come in limping and ask me to rub out a muscle and then point to their ass or their groin. But it was in this training room that I learned a valuable skill: how to make myself sexually neutral, to turn myself from a female object into something approaching an equal. Sexual tension just distracted us all from our purpose, so I learned how to defuse it, and most of the time, it worked. Eventually, I stopped seeing those boys as boys but as athletes, and they stopped seeing me as a girl but as the trainer who'd tape their ankle fast and solid so they could get back onto the court. At our lockers in the hallways, at dances and parties, it was different, and we were different around each other, but in the gym, that's how it was.

Of course, this blissful unisex utopia could not last. It was 1986. The boys' basketball team practiced and played a mile away from the high school at Tig-Arena, a three-thousand-seat field house built during the Depression. Tig-Arena was located inside the old Peru High School (which was then an elementary school and is now the tribal headquarters of the Miami Indians). My parents went to this old high school. That's where they met, in speech class, and where my dad was a starting forward for the Peru Tigers varsity basketball team. Tig-Arena was a hardwood theater-in-the-round, a gym lifted straight out of *Hoosiers,* and whether it was empty or full of screaming basketball fans, walking inside was like stepping into the past, straight into Indiana basketball history. I knew I'd officially become a small part of that history during the first home game. My mom and dad came, and at one point I looked behind me in the stands and saw them wave at me proudly. That was one of the best moments of my life, and I think of it every time I watch *Hoosiers,* that scene when Gene Hackman takes a deep breath, says "Welcome to Indiana basketball," and strides into the electricity coursing through Hickory High School's tiny gym.

After the game, I went into the bowels of Tig-Arena to take care of my usual aftergame duties. I was in the middle of cutting off some guy's ankle tape when, out of the corner of my eye, I saw a pink blob in a towel enter the training room. "What's she doing here?" the pink blob said, but I kept my head down, my gaze averted. Turned out he was a ref from a neighboring town who hadn't been warned I'd be there. Apparently, he needed to go through the training room to get from his locker room to the showers.

On Monday morning, I was called to the athletic director's office. Gold plaques and pennants adorned the walls, and boxes of uniforms and letter jackets were stacked in the corners of the room. The AD cleared his throat. "I'm sorry, but we can't let you be the trainer for the boys' basketball team."

"Why not? Guys are trainers for girls' teams."

"That doesn't have anything to do with it. We just can't have you down in the training room at Tig-Arena."

I was one of the editors of the school newspaper; I knew how to argue my case. "But the men's team job always goes to the student trainer with most seniority. That's me. It's not my fault that ref walked in. I didn't even see anything. Can't you just warn refs they can't walk through there?"

He cocked his head and stared at me. "No."

I didn't know much about Title IX then, but I knew enough to bring it up.

The AD just rolled his eyes at me. "I've been hearing stories about some of the hijinks going on down in the training room. From now on, you will transport a training kit to the girls' locker room and do whatever you need to do there."

"Why can't we move the training room so that everyone can have access to it?"

He'd just about had it with me. "Maybe someday we'll have the money to do that, but right now, we don't."

I sat there stunned. "This isn't fair," I said, and he hustled me out of his office.

The head trainer appointed Stuart, a nice guy with less experience, to be the trainer for the boys' basketball team. I took over his job training the girls' basketball team. And all was right with the world, I guess. I told myself it was okay. What did I think? They were going to tear down Tig-Arena so I could fulfill my hoop dreams? When the season was over, I quit training forever.

A few days after my $99 date with Rick, I fly to Cincinnati. My parents pick me up, and we drive down I-71 to Louisville. My parents are along for the ride. Maybe this makes me a dork, but when I have to travel as Cathy the Writer, I really like bringing my folks along. It's a good trade; they keep me calm when I'm anxious and they get a little vacation out of it.

On the way to Louisville, I tell my mom that when I get back to Pittsburgh, I have an appointment with someone at Great Expectations, "the nation's premiere destination for meeting and dating quality singles," according to their Web site. "I get to talk to a real person. I hope it works better than this online stuff."

"I sure hope so," Mom says. "Hey, you met a guy from Chemistry? How'd it go?"

"Not so great," I say. "He told me he doesn't even pay for his membership."

"Why not?"

I look out the window at the green trees rushing by. "I think it's because they need to keep enough men on the roster to convince women like me to buy a membership." Then I tell her what the customer-service person said, about expanding my search criteria.

Mom is turned around in the passenger seat. "Well, why don't you look for men in Indianapolis? Or Cincinnati?"

I roll my eyes at her. "Mom, I'm trying to make Pittsburgh my home. I need to date a man who lives there."

"But what if you met a nice man in Indiana or Ohio?"

"What about my teaching job?"

She sighs. "I just wish you could live closer."

This is an old, old discussion in my family. For a long time my parents asked why I couldn't just teach at a college in Indiana or Cincinnati. Gradually, I introduced my parents to the fiction writers who hold tenure-track positions at a number of Midwestern colleges and universities. "See," I pointed out to my parents, "unless one of these people switches jobs or retires, I'm SOL." When that didn't work, I used a different analogy. "See, academics are like NFL football players. We have to go wherever there's a job. Peyton Manning can't say, 'Hey, I'm from New Orleans so I will only play for the Saints.'"

I'm thankful when my dad's cell phone rings, ending (for now) the discussion. It's his lawyer, he mouths to my mom, and they both get very tense. My dad has filed a personal injury suit against the railroad, and after four years of depositions and wrangling, it's finally winding down. Here's what I remember: when my dad moved our family to Aurora in 1986, he never imagined that within a decade the jobs at the railroad yards in Cincinnati would slowly disappear. To avoid being transferred, he had to take any job available. Sometimes he was an inventory clerk. Sometimes he was the janitor. Sometimes he was a forklift operator in the locomotive and car shops. My dad was in his fifties but often doing the work of a twenty-year-old kid. In April 2001, he had to move some brake beams from the forklift to a rack. He performed this duty as he was trained, but he felt his back go *ping!* My dad limped over to his boss and said, "I'm gonna cut out early and go see my chiropractor and see what's the matter." He didn't fill out an injury report. Over the years, he'd seen men file false claims against the railroad, "deadbeats and dirtbags" he called them. But ever since that day, my dad has lived in chronic pain. He's on disability. My mom has health problems of her own, but will have to keep working. My parents put three kids through college and mort-gaged the house over and over because they assumed they'd *both* be work-ing full-time until they retired. My dad's three herniated discs changed all that. A relative of ours suggested my dad file a lawsuit. Dad didn't want to. Dad didn't want to be associated with those "deadbeats," but he couldn't provide for his family anymore. He had to do something. At first, the law-yer said my dad had a really good case, but that missing piece of paper, that injury report, was a big problem.

A few years into the lawsuit, my father went to watch his lawyer depose his old boss and fellow workers. As soon as the railroad's lawyers saw what the line of questioning would be, they hustled the other men scheduled to be deposed out into the hallway. The boss, who remained on the stand, admitted that yes, my dad's explanation was correct, but the other men, who desperately needed to hold down their jobs, all had a different story to tell. *They* knew how to unload those brake beams. If Mr. Day had done it differently and incorrectly, it was *his fault.* My dad came home from that deposition heartsick and angry. He spent most of the evening on our porch drinking beer and chain-smoking. "I just never thought people could be like that to each other. Lying. Talking other people into lying." He shook his head. "I should've done like those other dirtbags done. That's what I get for trying to be a nice guy." He hasn't been the same man since.

My dad finishes the call with his lawyer and clicks his cell phone shut. "They made an offer," he says. He repeats the figure. It's really, really low. Because of this injury, he's missing out on at least seven years of salary.

Mom laughs. "They can't be serious!?"

It's very quiet in our car as we make our way to the Seelbach Hotel in downtown Louisville, the setting of Tom and Daisy Buchanan's fictional wedding in F. Scott Fitzgerald's *The Great Gatsby*. We drop our bags off in the four-star hotel room and go downstairs to the bar. My dad and I order two single-barrel bourbons, and my mom gets a Coke. Over dinner, my dad doesn't say much. Mom touches his hand. "There's no use worrying about it. We're here to have fun and spend time with Cathy. Try not to think about it."

Dad says, "I don't know how to do that." He lights another cigarette and gets up to smoke it outside. My mom's got asthma.

I say to my mom, "So that's where I get it."

"What?" she asks.

"Dwelling."

She shakes her head in dismay. "It's like the needle gets stuck on a record in his brain, and he just can't give it a nudge so he can hear the rest of the song."

I take a sip of my bourbon. "I know what that's like."


I tell the following story about my dad quite often, especially when my students come to me asking various forms of the question, "What should I do with my life?"

One summer when my sister, my brother, my mother, and I were all in college at the same time, my dad pulled double shifts for two weeks straight to make some extra money. Toward the end of the second week, it fell to me to get him up. I entered the bedroom, the afternoon light filtering through the slatted blinds. "Dad! Time to get up!" I said in a cheery voice. He didn't move. I said it again, right into his ear. Still, no movement. I rocked his shoulder. Nothing. There's a reason for the cliché, "It was like waking the dead." Finally he started the climb out of the blackness of sleep. "Dad, maybe you should call in sick."

"Time and a half," he muttered.

He worked all evening, all night long, and the next morning when I got up, I found him sitting at our kitchen table in the usual pose, elbows on his knees, smoking a cigarette. Dad looked up at me and confessed, "I didn't have no business driving yesterday. I didn't really wake up until I hit Colerain Avenue." I made myself a cup of coffee and sat down at the table. Dad said, "Cathy, I just want you to promise me one thing. Make sure you love going to work every day. All my life, I've been beating my dick in the dirt so my kids could have a better life. I don't care what you guys wanna do. If you come to me and say, 'Dad, I love digging ditches and that's what I wanna do,' I'll say, 'Okay by me.' If you kids wind up hating going to work as much as I do, then what was all this shit for?"

After my reading at U of L, we check out of the Seelbach and head up the long stretch of I-65 to Indianapolis. There's a book release party at a Barnes & Noble in Carmel, and a bunch of Indiana writers I know will be there, including my college writing mentor, Gus Walters, whom I haven't seen in a few years. We pull into the parking lot of the bookstore, which anchors a high-end strip mall. As in most Midwestern cities, an interstate highway surrounds Indianapolis, an enormous wreath dotted with multicolored lights: B&N green, Best Buy blue and yellow, Office Depot red. My parents and I walk into the store, past the book-laden tables and calendar displays, and see Gus standing next to the magazine racks. He gives me a hug and shakes the hands of my parents. "Great to see you all again." I once sat in this man's office and said, "Oh, my family doesn't really want me to become a writer." Why would I say such a thing? Here's what I think: in order to be a writer, I needed to leave home, but I didn't have the nerve. I needed to give myself a reason to leave. So I told myself (and others) a story about rebellion, about being tragically misunderstood. To my own shame, I believed this story was true for a long time. I hope that by now Gus has forgotten my fiction or, if he remembers it at all, he's smart enough to realize it was fiction—especially since I'm standing here in Barnes & Noble with my supposedly nonsupportive parents.

I take a seat at the front of the store for the scheduled reading. Gus approaches the mic and begins reading his essay, and I'm transported back to 1990, when Gus gave a reading to a packed auditorium of faculty and students. From where I sat, his life looked like utopia to me. *He's a writer, he has a nice little family, and he gets to stay in school forever!* I thought. *I'll just do what he did.* With equal amounts naïveté and determination, I did exactly that. I went to the same graduate writing program he did. I was even friends with some of his old friends. When I showed up talking about Gus, Gus, Gus, his friends assumed I'd had an illicit romance with him. They told me this, years later, and it made me mad. I didn't sleep with him. I wanted to be him.

After the reading, Gus introduces me to his girlfriend. He and the wife I knew are long divorced. We talk about our jobs. Most days, we love what we do and whom we do it with, but ideally, I'd like to be further west, and ideally, he'd like to be further east. "Geography," he sighs. "It's an academic's huckleberry." It occurs to me that in many ways, I *have* become Gus, except that the happy little life I thought he had was just a story I made up in my own head.

There's a movie theater near our hotel showing Mark Wahlberg's *Invincible,* the true story of Vince Papale. Sort of a *Rudy,* but about the Philadelphia Eagles instead of Notre Dame. My mom and I figure this movie should cheer my dad up, but he wants to stay in and see if Notre Dame can come back and beat Michigan, so Mom and I go see *Invincible* by ourselves. I'm not the only woman in my family who likes a good sports movie. Halfway through, my mom whispers, "This is just like *Cinderella Man.*"

I whisper back, "And *Rocky.*"

"*Remember the Titans.*"

"That one with Dennis Quaid about the pitcher . . ."

"*The Rookie,*" Mom says. "We have that on DVD."

My family typically stays quiet during movies, but in this case, we're not talking over any important dialogue or anything. It's The Training Montage, set to Canned Heat's "Let's Work Together." Plus, it's the middle of the afternoon in Indiana and Notre Dame is playing Michigan, so the theater is almost empty. No one can hear my mom and me playing Dueling Sports Movies. But once Greg Kinnear gives his Dick Vermeil locker-room speech, we grow quiet and listen.

We need to find the soul of this team again. The soul that drove great Eagle players. They weren't just out here playing for themselves, they played for a city. The people of Philadelphia have suffered. You are what they turn to in times like these. You are what gives them hope. Let's win one for them. Let's win one for us.

My mom turns to me and says, "That's what you're doing with this . . . whatever it is you're doing. You're turning to the Colts. They're giving you hope."

It's dangerous to pin your hopes on the outcome of a football game. We walk back into the hotel room. It's dark and cold, the curtains drawn. My dad's sprawled on the bed with a bag of Doritos and what's left of a six-pack of Miller Lite chilling in the sink. He doesn't even look up at us when we walk in. "I thought those Irish would come back and win it for me, but no such luck." Then he looks at my mom. "The lawyer didn't call." A few minutes later, he's asleep.

Is it true that Nice Guys finish last? In real life, the playing field is almost always uneven, and the Dirt Bags usually win, but we don't tell stories and make movies about them. We tell stories about those rare occasions when the Nice Guys win. Like in 1954 when a little high school in Milan, Indiana, won the state basketball championship. Like in 1980 when the American hockey team beat the unbeatable Russians. Like during the Depression, when the smaller horse (Seabiscuit) beat the bigger horse (War Admiral). We need these Nice Guy stories the same way we need to believe in the American Dream and God, because without hope, life is just too damned depressing.

I knew going into the RCA Dome on Sunday, September 17, 2006, that the playing field was uneven. The Houston Texans have never beaten the Colts. Even Texans quarterback David Carr admits, "Coming up here is a chore." Maybe they aren't ready for Indy's fans—their "twelfth man"—and the famous amount of noise generated at the RCA Dome; Carr gets sacked on the first snap and fumbles on the second. The Colts capitalize on this turnover and score when Peyton Manning throws a touchdown to Brandon Stokely, who missed all of the preseason with an injured ankle. Actually, Stokely reinjures his ankle catching that touchdown pass, but says later that it was worth it because it energized the team. As if they needed more energy. Four minutes later, the Colts score again when Joseph Addai slips out of the backfield on a blitz attempt by the Texans and scampers with the ball into the end zone right in front of us—his first NFL touchdown. By the third quarter, the Colts are up 20–3. Then Peyton finds Bryan Fletcher, and the score is 27–3. With 3:17 left in the third, Vinatieri kicks a 38-yarder and extends the lead to an almost embarrassing 30–3. Thank God the score by the end of the game is a less awkward 42–24.

Without the drama of a close game, my mom and dad and I have to find other things to enjoy and appreciate: the taste of the beer and hot dogs, the waves of screaming that pummel our chests, the thrill of watching a perfectly thrown spiral fall into the hands of a swift receiver. The day provides plenty of opportunity for aesthetic appreciation. Peyton Manning completes passes to nine different receivers, finishing with over 400 passing yards, the seventh time he's ever done this. Marvin Harrison has over 100 yards receiving, passing Art Monk into fifth place on the NFL's all-time receptions list. Defensively, the Colts sack David Carr—already the most-sacked quarterback in the NFL—four times.

After the game, we make our way to the car and begin the long drive back to Aurora. We pass a Lees Inn, and I say, "Hey, isn't that where me and Alex met you when we were moving from Alabama to Minnesota?" That was nine years ago. We were in the first of our many Ryder trucks, and we met my parents to swap an air conditioner for a coffee table and say good-bye.

Dad's driving, and he looks at me in the rearview mirror. "I remember that when you guys drove off together, I told your mom it wasn't going to work."

I've never heard this story before. "Why didn't you say something?"

Mom turns around in the passenger seat and looks at me. "Would you have listened?"

I look down at my sandaled feet. "Probably not."

"There was nothing we could say to you right then," she says. "You were just going to have to figure it out for yourself."

I remember Mom crying that day. I thought she was happy that I was driving off into the sunset with the man of my dreams. My God, I'm forever telling myself the wrong story.

> If you're not making mistakes, then you're not doing anything. I'm positive that a doer makes mistakes.
>
> —John Wooden, UCLA basketball coach

## WEEK 3: COLTS VS. JAGUARS

### OR

# Schadenfreude Chili

O n Monday I fly back to Pittsburgh. Driving into the city from the airport means going underground through one of the tunnels that burrow through the South Hills. I still remember my first trip through the Fort Pitt Tunnel. I had flown in for my job interview at Pitt, and the cabdriver drove me past the malls and suburban shopping areas outside the city. But unlike in Indianapolis, these stores were perched on hills above the highway, their tall signs floating in the air like kites. Then the cab started downhill, lanes narrowing, a knot of roads and highways. The cabdriver said, "Now be sure to get a good look when we come out on the other side." And as we emerged from the tunnel, the windshield became an enormous postcard of downtown Pittsburgh, framed by yellow bridge girders. In Indiana, you can see things coming from a long way off: a stoplight, a storm, a city. The hills of western Pennsylvania prevent you from being able to see ahead too much. You turn a corner and boom, you're confronted by an inspiring view, and boom, you turn another corner and the view is gone. Even today, driving into Pittsburgh for perhaps the fiftieth time, the city's beauty catches me by surprise.

That night after my class, I come home and watch *Monday Night Football*. It's the Steelers versus the Jaguars, the latter of which the Colts will be facing this Sunday, so I watch the game to see how tough the Jags are.

Answer: very tough. They hand the Steelers their first loss of the season, snapping the nine-game winning streak that led them to the Super Bowl. It's the lowest-scoring *Monday Night Football* game in history, 9–0. The most exciting thing about it is watching nervously as the Jags tackle Ben Roethlisberger, who's been weakened by an emergency appendectomy and is playing with a high fever. I keep wondering if he's going to pull his stitches and start bleeding all over the place. *What lousy luck this guy's had,* I think. *Crash your bike, smash your face, your appendix blows up.*

Then I remember Carson Palmer. Or rather, the TV reminds me of him in a preview of this Sunday's game between division rivals the Cincinnati Bengals and the Pittsburgh Steelers. Last January, before they beat the Colts in the RCA Dome, the Steelers beat the Bengals in an AFC wild-card game. On the Bengals' second offensive play of the game, Steelers tackle Kimo von Oelhoffen rolled onto Palmer's left knee, tearing his ACL. Palmer's own doctor called it a career-ending injury, but the Heisman winner vowed to be ready in time for the Bengals' season opener on September 10 against Kansas City. And he was. His rebuilt knee proved strong enough, but there's endless speculation about whether Palmer still has the mental toughness to handle 300-pound men running at him, the will to focus solely on throwing the ball and not dance around in the pocket avoiding tackles, a quarterback condition known as "happy feet."

The sports guys are still talking about the upcoming Bengals versus Steelers matchup as "payback time" when I shut off the television. My living-room windows are open, letting in the cool night air. Normally when a Steelers game is on, I can hear people in my neighborhood cheering, but tonight Pittsburgh is quiet. Their team has lost for the first time since December 4, 2005, a loss to the Bengals that energized the all-but-out-of-it 7–5 Steelers and launched the amazing ride that took them to Super Bowl XL. There's nothing for Steelers fans to cheer about tonight, and they head to bed. I head there, too.

Great Expectations is located on Carson Street in a modern office park. I step into a bright office smelling of vanilla candles. The walls are adorned with framed photographs of smiling couples, success stories I'm sure. The girl behind the front desk looks at me and asks, "Cathy?" I nod yes, and she shakes my hand. This is Erica, who called me that day in August when I had two Pirates tickets but couldn't find anyone to go to the game with me. That day she asked, "Do you need help meeting people in Pittsburgh?" and I said, absolutely. Yes.

Today Erica makes a copy of my driver's license and looks at my checkbook. "We check to make sure that there's no one else's name listed on your account. To make sure you're not married," she says with a smile. Then she gives me a form to fill out, and I realize that Journey is playing over the sound system. This seems like a good sign. After I fill out the information form, Erica leads me to an empty office where I watch an introductory video. The sound track is the Beach Boys' "Good Vibrations."

*"You're givin' me Great Expectations!"*

The tape is full of testimonials from real people, although a couple of them look like actors, such as the amazingly blond couple standing in front of waving palm fronds, testifying how glad they are to have found each other. The couples articulate their fears, which are often a lot like my fears (negative thoughts), and a wise-sounding voice-over offers reassurances (positive thoughts).

*I'm a complete loser.*

"You've reached a special point in your life. You're an attractive and intelligent person seeking the same."

*This is freaking embarrassing.*

"You want to be discreet. We offer quality and dignity."

*Everyone in this city is coupled up except for me.*

"When I looked at all the profiles, I realized that I wasn't alone."

*There must be another way.*

"If what you've been doing hasn't worked, do something different."

*Maybe the only way for me to be a significant woman writer is to live like Eudora Welty and Harper Lee and Flannery O'Connor—alone until the end.* (I don't know for sure, but I may be the only GE client to have this particular negative thought.)

"It's never too late to have love in your life. There's nothing like coming home to someone who will love you."

*Love is supposed to come along when you least expect it, by chance, like in the movies. You get your heel stuck in a sewer grate, and just then a huge metal garbage thing starts rolling right for you, and Matthew McConaughey jumps in and saves you!*

"Take chance out of the equation."

I have to admit that the video does its job. Already, I feel less weird about being in this office.

After the video, I go back out to the waiting room and talk to Erica. "You said on the phone in August that you'd been using Chemistry. How's that working?"

I tell her about my recent phone call with them. "I think they don't have enough male members," I say, and Erica looks down at her desk quickly, like she's uncomfortable but trying not to show it.

She changes the subject. "So, you're a professor. At Pitt! Wow."

"Yep," I say.

Just then, Polly enters the office a little breathlessly, wearing a summer dress, high heels, and a shrug. She and Erica exchange a look I can't decipher, and then Polly sticks out her hand to greet me. I'm taken aback for a second by Polly. I mean, I'm from a family of big-breasted women and I've seen some cleavage in my day. But wow. And she has that Playboy centerfold makeup job: lips heavily lined outside the natural lip line, eyes substantially smoky. *Why is she dressed like this?* I wonder. I try not to think about it. We go into her office to talk.

Polly looks at the information form and the first thing she says is, "So, you're a college professor! I'll bet that a lot of men find that intimidating."

"I guess," I say. "I don't know. They don't exactly tell me that to my face."

Then, for a while, we're just two women talking about dating. There are framed pictures behind her of a child. She tells me she's divorced and that she came to GE in order to start dating but ended up working for them. "I didn't meet my fiancé through GE, but coming here and getting back into dating made me ready to meet him," Polly says. I like that she's honest about this. "What made you choose us?" she asks.

I explain. I'm not a big fan of exclusive clubs, but in this case, I like that GE screens its members. Also, if some guy is a crazed lunatic or nothing but a player, he's probably not going to walk into this place and pay money. I'm nervous about using a dating site like Match.com because I don't want students or people who've read my book to see my personal information. "I get weird e-mails from people sometimes," I explain. It's relatively easy to Google me and find out where I teach, find my e-mail address. I tell Polly about the teenager who walked into my office in the Cathedral of Learning last year, closed the door behind him, and handed me a copy of my book. I didn't recognize him, but it was early in the semester. I thought maybe he was one of those kids who skips the first week of classes and then shows up begging to be forgiven. Turned out he wasn't a Pitt student. He was a high school student from Florida visiting a relative in a Pittsburgh hospital and had picked up a local paper to pass the time. There happened to be an interview with me and a photo in that issue. Bored or intrigued or both, he walked to a nearby bookstore to buy my book. The bio said I taught at Pitt, and he realized he was in the Pitt campus bookstore, so he asked where the English Department was, walked across the street to the Cathedral, and boom, showed up at my office, where I happened to be holding office hours. I was both flattered and frightened by the experience.

I also have my own domain name—most writers these days do—so by making it easy for readers and students to find out more about me, I've made it easy for *anyone* to find me. I tell her about the guy who started e-mailing me after he read my book, about how he said he knew me, how I changed his life. Then he showed up at one of my readings (my itinerary is right there on my Web site), which scared me a little. A few months later, someone we knew in common e-mailed me and told me he'd died. It wasn't a suicide, but the details were certainly strange. He was in a convenience store, grabbing microwavable sandwiches out of the cooler, unwrapping them, and stuffing them in his mouth. An employee threw him out, and in the scuffle, he choked on the sandwich. When he tried to motion for help, the convenience store employee thought he was just drunk or high, and he died right there on the sidewalk.

Polly says, "Oh my goodness!"

I tell her that after my book came out, I started getting e-mails from people I hadn't heard from in decades. "My mom sent me this article!"

they said, or "I saw your name in my local paper, and I Googled you!" Sometimes it was really nice to hear from these people. Sometimes it was not. Once upon a time, if you wanted to get in touch with a long-lost love or friend, you had to hire a detective, make a serious effort. Now it's so easy to connect, it's a bit scary. "Look," I said, "I'm not famous, not by any stretch of the imagination, but I'm not anonymous either."

Polly tells me she knows just what I mean. She shows me a framed picture sitting on her desk. "My dad." She tells me about his connection to September 11. That connection, that information is so specific that if I told you now, you could Google and find news stories about him, his obituary, the names of his survivors, and thus find Polly. "You wouldn't believe the e-mails I get sometimes," she says. "People want to share their conspiracy theories with me. Or tell me about *their* family members who died that day."

We get down to business. I tell her about my lousy luck with Chemistry.com and my concern about getting my money's worth at GE. Polly gives an assuring nod. "Let me tell you we have a lot more men as members than women!"

"Really?" I say. I'm surprised.

"A lot of the men who come in here have been on Match.com and they're tired of dating women who're just looking for a sugar daddy."

Maybe she's right. I think about what Rick told me about his ex-wife who spent all his money. I think about some of the "red flag" questions on Chemistry. Once you enter the Guided Communications Process with a potential match, you each choose five to ten questions from a long list of prompts for the other to answer. "How do you feel about sharing money?" You move a cursor along a spectrum from "very strongly" to "not strongly at all." Whenever I got this question, I never knew how to answer. If you feel strongly about sharing money, does that mean you're a gold digger? I don't really care about sharing money—I make my own—so I guess that makes me not a gold digger. Even seemingly benign questions regarding your attitudes toward family, religion, or tidiness could be red flags. I didn't enter the Guided Communications Process with too many men, but more than a few asked me this question: "Do you think it's important to be sexually adventurous in a relationship?" To me that was the player looking for another player question. Which is a shame, because it *is* important to be sexually adventurous. But if a man asks a perfect stranger that kind of question, he's looking for a particular kind of woman. And she's not me.

Polly and I haven't started talking about money yet, but I suspect that Great Expectations is more expensive than Chemistry or Match.com. I calculate the logic. Basically, if I join this service, I will pay to distinguish myself from the divorced mother of three who works as a secretary—as if *that* woman is necessarily "after some guy's money," when maybe she's someone who would be a great partner but also needs money. By joining this place, I'm saying, *I've got enough money and don't need a man's money.* But aren't I also saying I want a man with enough money to come here and find me?

"So your male members are trying to avoid needy women then?" I ask Polly. "How do you weed out normal men from crazy men?"

Polly rolls her eyes. "Let me tell you, I've heard things in this room you wouldn't believe. One man came here wearing his dead wife's clothes. He handed me a book on being transgendered. He was waiting to get the surgery."

"Wow."

"Sometimes men will come in here and say stuff like all women are gold diggers or cheaters, and I tell them they should go get some therapy and come back in a year or two. They're not ready."

"That's good advice," I say, "But you know, that's what's hard. In order to enter into this"—I gesture to the desk, the computer, the office, Carson Street and all its bars and restaurants, the city of Pittsburgh—"you have to be both cautious and open."

Everyone tells me, over and over and over again, *Love will come when you least expect it,* but I've been walking around *least expecting* love for five years, and that tactic isn't working. So I walk into this place. I have great expectations. I'm going to start walking around *expecting* love, but I'm learning that there are three problems with this new tactic:

1. If you expect to win, losing hurts, and if you keep losing, it's hard to keep playing, hoping that maybe this time, this guy, this date will work out.

2. Being proactive smacks of desperation or seediness. I can't shake the feeling that I'm purchasing a male companion.

3. I feel like I'm giving up on real love. That love has become a numbers game about percentages and profiles and criteria. Would Chemistry have worked better for me if I'd cheated on my profile and said I was thirty-four or thirty-five rather than thirty-seven? How many men make thirty-five their cutoff? How many men *didn't* I meet because I told the truth about how old I am? But do I want to meet a man who doesn't want to date a woman over the age of thirty-five? How many men didn't meet me because I said I was "curvy" and they thought I was fat?

Modern dating is hell if you're someone like me who can't stop thinking about the choices I didn't make. What if I'd gone to a different college or graduate school? What if I'd moved from Alabama to Minnesota *without* Alex? What if he hadn't gotten that job in Baltimore? In those alternate realities, a time line of choices I did not make, am I married to Alex or some other dude? Is there a kid? Is there a book? Is it the same book I wrote? Am I happy? God, I would gladly go back in time and make different choices if it meant that I wouldn't have to be sitting here in the Pittsburgh office of Great Expectations with Polly and her porn-star lips. Of course I don't say any of this to Polly, but it's swimming around in my head when she brings me back to reality by showing me laminated sheets of sample profiles. Four guys. None of them strike my fancy. Polly can see this by the expression on my face.

"The great thing about what we do here is that each of our members has photos and a video. You get to hear them talk, see them. It's much easier to get a first impression this way. Plus, we do the photos and videos ourselves. We have our own photographers, so you know the images are current and accurate."

"I've heard some people on Match actually use other people's pictures," I say.

"Yes, but that doesn't happen here."

Polly finally whips out the laminated sheet that describes the different packages: Diamond, Platinum, Standard. The differences depend on how much access I want, how much assistance I desire (if Erica and Polly help me out, it's called "personal shopping"), and for how long. If I meet some-one interesting or just need to stop dating for a while, I can institute an "unlimited freeze," which stops the membership clock. Then Polly turns the sheet over so I can see the prices. I catch my breath. "Oh my God, I just bought a house. I can't afford this!" The numbers are all mid to high four figures. My $99 date with Rick seems cheap in comparison.

Polly says, "Well, I really want you to join us, Cathy, so let me call cor-porate and see if I can work something out." She leaves me in the room with an anxious weight on my chest. A few minutes later, she returns. "Well, I told them you were a friend of mine, and here's what we can do." I can either pay $1,795 with so much down and so much per month or I can pay $1,595 all at once and get an Introductory package that has the same offerings as the Standard package with unlimited freeze and two months of personal shopping.

"Um, I don't know how much money I have right now. Can I have a calculator?" Polly hands me one from her desk drawer and leaves me in her office again. Luckily, I just entered in my recent checks and receipts but haven't subtracted them all from the balance. I feel like I have about $2,000 in my checking, but the month's not over. I'm right. That's about how much money I have. In the world. I peek my head out the door, and Polly comes back in. "Can I think about this?" I ask.

She shakes her head. "No, this is a one-day offer. If you come in next week, I can't promise you the same rates."

I feel like I'm buying a car, and I'm no good at wrangling and barter-ing. I tell myself, *I knew when I walked in I was going to do this no matter what. It's why I walked in the door in the first place. Don't get happy feet, Cathy. Stay in the pocket. Stay strong.* So I decide to put half on my credit card and write a check for the other half.

Erica comes in and explains that I'll come in the following Friday to make my video and have my picture taken. Polly looks up from the pa-perwork in front of her. "Erica, I think Derek would be good for her. Let's call him."

Erica nods.

"Who's Derek?" I ask.

"He's our photographer. He's really good. You'll love him." Polly looks up at Erica. "We need to find her a really good guy. What about John?"

Erica looks a little taken aback, but nods her head.

A thought rises into my brain, working its way out of the knot in my chest. Maybe this moment is scripted. *This is where they act like my girlfriends. They already have someone in mind for me. His name is John.*

When I finally leave the office, I realize that two and a half hours have passed and no one else came in all that time. I feel like I just stepped off the set of a David Mamet movie, and behind that closed door, Erica and Polly are blowing out the scented candles and taking down the pictures of happy couples just before they head to the bank.

*You're just scared,* I tell myself. *Those women were real. They told you things about themselves. When people become real to each other, they don't take advantage of that.*

I walk to a Qdoba and see three attractive men eating lunch together. One of them looks at me and I think *Dude, I wish you would ask me out and save me from this.* But it's too late.

I go home and there's the new Crate and Barrel catalog. I just spent the same amount of money I could have spent on a dining room table, which I actually need. But don't I need love, too? I can't bear to think about this, so I take a nap.


That night I call my sister to tell her about GE, although I don't tell her how much I spent, even when she asks me five times. Andrea asks, "Wait, what happened to Nick?"

I've seen him (but not slept with him) off and on since July. "I don't know," I say. "He still calls me, but sometimes I don't pick up the phone. I can't tell if I'm just scared of relationships in general or if he just isn't the guy."

In the background, I can hear Clay playing with his Limbo Elmo. Andrea says, "I think that if you really liked him, you wouldn't be able to stop yourself from calling him or seeing him."

"I know you're right, but what if my instincts are just all messed up. And what feels 'right' is really what's wrong and what feels wrong is really what's right?"

My sister sighs. "Cathy, you wear me out."

"I know. Thanks for listening to me," I say. "Hey, how do you make Cincinnati-style chili?"

"Why?"

"The Steelers are playing the Bengals Sunday. I'm having some people over."

"I thought you were going to follow the Colts this season."

"Their game isn't nationally televised. I'm stuck with the Steelers again."

"You don't even like the Bengals, Cathy." Andrea watches a lot of Bengals games. Her husband, John, grew up a fan of all Cincinnati teams.

"Sure I like the Bengals," I lie. "Chad Johnson. Carson Palmer. That dude whose name I can't pronounce."

"Hoosh-mand-zaa-deh."

"Right," I say. "Look, the Colts aren't playing the Steelers this season, but the Bengals are. Cincinnati is sort of my other hometown city. This is my only chance for a little payback."

"Aren't most of your friends Steelers fans?"

"Yeah."

"Are you going to tell them it's Cincinnati-style chili?"

"No."

"That's mean." She giggles and gives me the recipe.


"What's the spaghetti for?" My neighbors Tom and Rachel have come over to watch the game with me. I make myself a plate to show them. Crumbled oyster crackers on the bottom, spaghetti noodles, then chili (I've used cinnamon and vinegar to give it the Cincy taste, but skipped the cloves), then mounds of grated cheddar cheese.

"What gave you the idea to make chili like this?" Tom asks.

"Oh, it's just a Midwestern thing," I say.

Cincinnati chili actually comes from Macedonia. In 1922, Tom and John Kiradjieff opened a small Greek restaurant, the Empress, in the Queen City. Hardly anyone in Cincinnati wanted to eat Greek food and the restaurant might have failed had the Kiradjieffs not added chili to the menu—and added Middle Eastern spices to it and served it on spaghetti.

As the game begins, I tell Tom and Rachel about the Achilles tendon that's holding Palmer's knee together. "This woman named Julie Di Rossi was hit by a drunk driver in Houston," I say. "She was an organ donor. Her parts are in like fifty other people. She saved his career."

"How do you know that?" Rachel asks.

"My parents live around Cincinnati. That's all they talk about there. Carson's knee."

"Like Ben's head this summer," Tom says.

"Exactly."

The Bengals struggle in the first quarter but dominate the second. Tom and Rachel notice that I'm cheering for Cincinnati. "We thought you were a Colts fan," they say, mildly annoyed.

"I am," I say. "It's a Midwestern thing, I guess."

In Indianapolis, the Colts defeat the Jags 21–14, but the best I can do is watch the Bengals win 28–20. The Steelers have suffered two losses in a row. I wave good-bye to Tom and Rachel, their bellies unwittingly full of Cincinnati chili.

# WEEK 4: COLTS @ JETS

## OR

# Against the Odds

Y ou need to know this: for the last three months, I have thought about cigarettes every day, every hour, sometimes every minute. I've done a considerable amount of crying. Every impulse felt wrong. Everything overwhelmed me. Emptying the dishwasher overwhelmed me. During these months, there have been terrible moments when I've found myself standing alone in a room in my house, thinking, *Oh my God, I feel so fucking horrible and there's nothing I can do about it. I'm just going to have to stand here and take it.*

It takes a great deal of strength to stand in a room like that, feeling that utterly desperate, and not run straight to the refrigerator or a pack of smokes or a drink or a pill or the arms of a person who loves you (or is at least willing to pretend to). And someday I hope to be strong enough not to run for the comfort of those things. But for now I need all the help I can get. That's why my coach calls every week and gives me a pep talk. His name is Erik. I have no idea what he looks like, but I talk to him more than any other man in Pittsburgh.

When I quit smoking this summer, I went to a group smoking-cessation meeting sponsored by my health plan. I thought, *Wouldn't it be funny to meet the man of my dreams at a smoking-cessation class?* Turned out that all the other attendees were women, but that's not why I stopped going to the meetings—the available times didn't work with my schedule. That's when they told me about "health coaches," trained professionals who would call me every week or so. Erik and I have been talking regularly ever since.

"So, how's it going this week?" he asks.

"It's been three months without a cigarette," I say. For a while I counted days. Then weeks. I'm not keeping track of days and weeks anymore, and for the first time, I feel like I've rounded some kind of corner.

Erik says congratulations.

I asked for a health coach who's a former smoker, which is how I got paired up with Erik. He doesn't sound very old, but he says he smoked for seven years and has been quit for five.

"How's all that social anxiety?" he asks.

I look out my office window at the birds sitting on my cable line. "You know, I think that I've always had that anxiety but I just masked it by smoking a lot. Now that I'm not smoking, I don't quite know what to do with myself." I pop a Gobstopper in my mouth.

He says he's glad that I've accurately identified the reasons why I smoked, and starts talking about methods to deal with stress. "Often you literally have to change the way you think and adopt a more optimistic rather than a pessimistic view about stressful situations. It's easier to view a situation as hopeless, but it doesn't get you anywhere."

I sigh. "Erik, maybe for some people, all it takes to break the pattern is to recognize that the pattern exists, but it doesn't work for me. We've been talking about a lot of the same stuff for two months now, but nothing's clicked, nothing's changed. I know I'm the only one who can flip the switch, but I can't figure out how to do it."

Erik sighs. "But you have flipped it. You've started the journey. You're realizing that as these situations come up, they have to be dealt with in a new way, not avoid them."

Maybe he's right. For most of the summer, I could hardly stand to leave my house. I avoided doing anything that involved actually having to talk to people. Except for dates. After those, I didn't have any emotional or social energy left. But lately I've been able to go to parties again. Instead of taking breaks to go outside and smoke, I excuse myself to go to the bathroom and walk around the house by myself for a few minutes. "I guess I still need to take smoke breaks, just without the smokes."

He laughs. "See, you're figuring it out. People who fail, who go back to smoking, don't recognize that they faced a challenge and failed. They don't even realize it was a test. You're passing the tests, but they are going to keep coming at you."

Briefly I wonder if Erik is sitting at his desk with a list of prompts, a self-help script, but it doesn't seem like it. He sounds authentic. Then he starts talking about repetitive self-talk. I say, "You mean like chatter? Or like the way athletes psych themselves up before a game?"

"Yeah, I guess you could say that."

"Do you know any sports psychologists? Or any books about sports psychology?"

"Why do you ask?"

"I dunno," I say. "All this self-talk stuff reminds me of that Stuart Smalley skit on *Saturday Night Live.*

Erik laughs. "I'm good enough, I'm smart enough . . ."

"And doggone it, people like me!" I finish. "See, athletes talk to themselves all the time, but it's not so Stuart Smalley–ish, you know? And sometimes athletes get in ruts and they can't turn off the negative thoughts. They can't get in the zone no matter how hard they try or how hard they try *not to try.*"

"I'll ask around and see if anyone knows some good books on sports psychology," he says. "Whatever works for you, Cathy."

"Thanks."

How old is Erik? Is he single? Is he a therapist? Or is he just some flunky at my health plan? I'm afraid to ask, and it doesn't really matter anyway, because who else do I have to talk to about the random shit in my head? I'm just lucky he's listening to me. My closest, most meaningful human relationships are with people I only talk to on the phone.

I ask, "How long have we been talking?"

"Oh, about twenty minutes."

"How long are you supposed to talk to people?"

Erik says sometimes five minutes, sometimes a half hour, depending. But not to worry. He's got time today. "You're a lot more analytical about this stuff than most people," he says.

I sigh. "Yeah, I get that a lot."

"If I could leave you with something positive, I'd say give yourself some credit for all the things you're doing to try to change. In many ways, you're becoming a completely different person."

After I hang up, I feel physically spent and on the verge of tears. So instead of sitting around crying, I drive to Pittsburgh's Waterfront, our shopping mecca, and go to Barnes & Noble. I don't go to the self-help section. I wouldn't be caught dead in the self-help section. I go to the sports section and select two books on sports psychology (I can't wait for Erik's recommendations) and biographies of Peyton Manning and Larry Bird. There's an attractive guy my age nearby with his young son who looks about four. For a time, the kid was content to play with the books on the lowest shelf, but the novelty of that has worn off. He wants to go to the children's section. Now! He pulls on his dad's cargo shorts. "Wait a minute, buddy," the man says as he scans the shelves for a few more precious seconds. There's no way I can get this man to look my way. I'm not even a blip on his radar.

The next morning, I get back from a run and my phone is blinking. It's a voice mail from Erica at Great Expectations; she's calling to reschedule my photo shoot. "The photographer is held up out of town, and Polly and I *really* want him to take your pictures, so this will be worth your wait." Erica says she will call me next week to set up a new time. I take a shower and head to Oakland. I've got a coffee-shop date of sorts.

It started a month ago at a university reception. I was accepted into a pilot program called Pitt Partners, a way to connect with faculty from other departments, something that's actually incredibly hard to do at a school this big. At dinner, I noted that the two men in my small group were both married, but of the four women, two of us were single. She and I exchanged e-mail addresses. During cocktails, I chatted with a very nice woman who said she'd been working at Pitt for twenty years. After our second or third chardonnay, she joked, "So what made you apply for this program? A c.v. boost?"

"Nah, I'm just looking for a date." I paused. "I'm kidding." I paused again. "Sort of."

"Oh, I know just who you need to talk to." She wrote an e-mail address down on a cocktail napkin. "She's a good friend of mine, been through this herself. Tell her I sent you."

I do as I'm told. After a brief e-mail exchange and a consultation of our calendars, I have a date to meet Dr. Judy Coombs. I cross Forbes Avenue and head into a coffee shop. She's arrived first (I've seen her picture on her department's Web site) and is sitting at a table by the window sipping tea. She wears her gray hair in a bob, a blue sweater set and khaki pants, but the Birkenstocks and the Whole Foods canvas tote give away that she's an academic. "Judy?" I ask.

She looks up at me and smiles widely. "Cathy! So nice to meet you. Sit, sit."

Her generosity and warmth put me at ease. I set down my coffee and she tells me her story, which starts off a lot like mine. She arrived in Pittsburgh in 1980, single and in her early thirties. She married a local man, raised a family, got tenure. When that marriage ended a few years back, Judy went back on the market. "The odds weren't good for me," she says, but she tells me that she did find a boyfriend. "A lot of my friends think he's not right for me, that I've settled, but I know myself. I don't like to be alone. I'm happy." Judy smiles at me encouragingly. "Tell me your story." And I do.

Dr. Judy Coombs is a researcher, a woman who works with numbers all day long, and she lays it all out for me. "You are at a statistical disadvantage. You're a bit of an anomaly. You're the same age as most associate professors, but because you changed jobs for personal reasons and had to start over, you're still an assistant. Your cohort is about ten years younger than you. Plus, you're working-class, first-generation-college, but a lot of the people you work with are the children of academics or professionals. You're a writer, not a researcher, not a scholar. You don't do the same kinds of things as most of us here. Then there's the fact that you're single while most people your age are coupled up. So you're the odd one out on many fronts. Finding someone like yourself is going to be very, very tough. You might need to just give up on that idea entirely."

I sit there quietly in my tiny café chair. I wish I had a fork so I could stick it in my eye. "Surely I'm not the only single professor in Pittsburgh. I wish local universities could do something to help us find each other."

Judy scoffs. "Oh, you don't want to look for male academics."

"I don't?"

"They're a highly coveted commodity, especially here in Pittsburgh. They're stable, smart, and they have their pick of female graduate students."

"Oh."

I can almost see Judy doing the calculations in her head. "The truth is that educated professional men are not a large demographic in Pittsburgh. If that's what you want, you'll be competing for them in a very large pool. Statistically, you're better off looking elsewhere, at a demographic that's less . . . desired. Your odds would improve."

Judy is talking tactics and strategy, how to make the most of a shitty situation, but I feel like I've just been told there is no Santa Claus. I want my illusions back.

"What about Internet dating?" she asks. "Have you tried that?"

"Sort of," I say and tell her about Great Expectations.

"That sounds like a good idea," she says. "It puts you in a smaller but more appropriate pool. But I'd be curious about how many male members there are here in Pittsburgh. The kind of men who can afford a service like that, a lot of them left Pittsburgh when the economy went south."

I think, *This is exactly what my gynecologist said!*

"How's this Great Expectations working?"

I look down at my lap. "Well, it's not right now. They canceled my photography session today." Then I tell Judy about Chemistry.com.

She tells me something that surprises me a bit—she knows all about Internet dating. "After my divorce, I spent a lot of time searching. I worked at it very, very hard. It became like another job."

"I know what you mean," I say, "and I haven't really tried that hard."

"What age did you put down?"

"Thirty-eight. That's how old I am."

She nods. "That might be part of the problem. A lot of men probably put their cutoff age at thirty-five. Any woman who is older than that they assume is desperate for a child." She squints at me in the afternoon light streaming through the plate-glass window. "You don't look thirty-eight. You should change your age to thirty-two or thirty-three."

I tell her what Rick my $99 date said, how I shouldn't be honest about my "curvy" body. "It's like everyone *expects* these profiles to be inaccurate," I say. "It's like the speed limit. Sixty-five miles per hour means seventy."

She nods. "What did you put down as your profession?" Judy asks.

"Teacher," I say. "There was an option for 'professor,' but I didn't select it." I'm suddenly ashamed of myself, sure that this feminist scholar will chastise me for dumbing myself down in my profile.

Instead she says, "That was probably a good idea." She sits back in her chair and takes a wistful sip of her tea. "My husband worked for one of the steel companies. We'd go to parties at the homes of his colleagues, and when people asked me what I did, you could see them actually take a step back from me."

I shrug my shoulders. "What's a smart girl to do?"

Judy looks up at me. "Why don't you change the variables a bit? If you're not popping up on their radar because of your age, put down a younger one. If they're passing you over because you seem too smart and intimidating, make up another identity. Make up a bunch of different ones and see what happens."

I want to ask, *Is this what you did? Conduct your search for love like a science experiment?* But I don't have the nerve to ask. So I say, "If I met someone who then confessed that he'd lied about who he really was, I'd be upset."

Judy Coombs shrugs. "By the time they meet you and like you, who cares?"

The strategy she's suggesting sounds calculated, but really, is it that different from some of the other choices we make in our lives? I consider my college days. Rather than compete in a losing battle with the perky, pearl-bedecked girls at my own college, I spent most of my weekends at a nearby all-male college. My high school boyfriend had gone there, and even after we broke up and he graduated, I still knew his friends. I didn't think of it this way at the time, but wasn't I increasing the likelihood of being noticed by going to a world bereft of females? I was increasing my odds; what's the difference between doing this consciously or unconsciously?

If I'd met Judy Coombs a year ago, I would have said she was being unnecessarily alarmist. Now, I think she's absolutely brilliant. "I had no idea finding someone in Pittsburgh would be so tough. I figured since it was a college town, a city, it was a lot better than suburban New Jersey."

She sighs. "I'm really sorry, Cathy, but the odds are still against you here."


Before I left my job in New Jersey, I had a mandatory meeting with Dr. Hattie Greggs, a senior faculty member of the college. Officially it was an exit interview, but unofficially it was an attempt to persuade me to stay. I knew Hattie well enough to know something about both her personal and professional life. She'd been hired with much fanfare during my first year at the college, and I'd worked with her on various university committees. Her ex-husband was a renowned scholar at a New York university, and they shared custody of their son. I'd heard through the grapevine that she'd started dating again. There were many times during my last few years in New Jersey that I considered approaching her to ask, "What are you doing? Is it something I could do, too?" But I never did. The ivory tower is full of single professional women, but in my experience, they very rarely talk about the similarity of their situations.

I was feeling mighty down the day of the exit interview. When Hattie asked me why I was leaving the college, I paused for a second and said, "Deep, soul-crushing loneliness."

For a second, I thought we both might start crying. Hattie looked deflated, like I'd knocked the wind out of her with those words. "I know what you mean," she offered. But then she recovered herself. She stood up from her chair, smoothed her blue skirt, and gave me a firm, businesslike handshake. "Good luck, Cathy."


I come home from my date with Judy Coombs and sit down at my laptop. I want data. I want figures. I want statistics. And now that I am finally looking for them, they are easy to find.

I find an article informing me that in 2006, Forbes.com ranked Pittsburgh thirty-second out of forty U.S. cities in terms of "livability" for singles. This is actually an improvement over its ranking from 2002 to 2004, when, for three years in a row, it ranked dead last. This factoid generated a whole lot of bad press for Pittsburgh, which responded in a number of ways, one of which was the creation of the Pittsburgh Singles Volunteer Network. "Hey, that sounds cool!" I say out loud to the walls of my study, but then I read on and discover that they just closed their doors in June. "Great," I mumble. The criteria for this "singles livability" ranking were:

1. nightlife (based on the number of restaurants, bars, and clubs)
2. culture (based on the number of museums, pro sports teams, live theater and concert venues, and university population)
3. cost of living alone (determined by average starting salary and the cost of an apartment, a Pizza Hut pizza, a movie ticket, and a six-pack of Heineken)
4. online dating (determined by number of active Match.com profiles per capita)
5. coolness (based on area's diversity and number of "creative" workers—artists, scientists, teachers, musicians)
6. projected job growth over the next five years (determined by economic stuff I don't understand).

Pittsburgh scored worst in number of online dating profiles per capita, projected job growth, nightlife, and coolness. However, in terms of the cost of living alone, Pittsburgh ranked fifth in the nation. These statistics pretty accurately sum up my existence. I have enough money to go to museums and concerts and ball games, but don't have anyone to do these things with, so I go out and buy an affordable pizza and six-pack of Heineken and drink it by myself in my very affordable house.

I find more statistics. According to the U.S. Census Bureau, from April 1, 2000, to July 1, 2006, Pittsburgh experienced a population loss of approximately 59,000 people (attributed to both death and migration). This number doesn't strike me as out of the ordinary until I realize that New Orleans experienced the biggest population loss in the country—291,000 due to Hurricane Katrina—and Pittsburgh is number two in the net "losers" category. Experts point to the collapse of the steel industry twenty years ago and the mass exodus of Pittsburgh's then–younger generation—people who are now my age—who fled west and south, where the jobs were. Those who stayed in Pittsburgh were close to retirement, and now, twenty years later, the diehards are . . . well . . . dying.

Of course! It's the economy, stupid. Just as the railroad industry sent my family packing to Cincinnati, Ohio, the steel industry (or lack thereof) sent men of my age and demographic packing, too. In my fiction writer's mind, I create Allen, the man I'll never meet because of the collapse of Pittsburgh's industrial economy. He couldn't find a good job after graduating in 1991 from Duquesne with a degree in communications. He migrated to Florida where he found a great job and a woman named Maggie. They had a son. Then they had a divorce. Allen used to come back to Pittsburgh every summer to visit his folks, but since they both died last year, his only connection to his hometown is the occasional Steelers game on TV. He's a Floridian now, a Jaguars fan. He reads the Chucks (Palaniuk and Klosterman) and subscribes to *Sports Illustrated.* His secret wish is to visit Tokyo and he still loves watching *The Simpsons.* Last Christmas, Allen bought his son a vintage Ramones T-shirt, but Maggie made him take it back. He loves to go to his son's ball games, even though it means running into Maggie and her new boyfriend, Roger. Allen thinks maybe he's ready to start dating again, but he wants to find a woman in Florida, not Pittsburgh. Oh, Allen! You are just an amalgam, and I know you don't literally exist, but I wish we could have met.

Wait. There's more.

Researchers at a number of British universities found that a high IQ helps a man's chance at marriage but hampers a woman's. For men, with each 16-point increase in IQ, their chances for marriage increase by 35 percent. For women, with each 16-point increase, their chances for marriage drop by 40 percent.

I am stunned.

I read a review of Sylvia Ann Hewlett's *Creating a Life: Professional Women and the Quest for Children,* which claims that 55 percent of career women over thirty-five are childless.

I am more stunned.

Wait. There's more. Hewlett says, "Nowadays, the rule of thumb seems to be that the more successful the woman, the less likely it is she will find a husband or bear a child. For men, the reverse is true."

I think about the professional men and women I know, the people I've worked with at four different colleges and universities. Using this very unscientific, anecdotal methodology, I realize that many of my female colleagues were single (never married or divorced) and often childless, while almost all of my male colleagues were married, usually with children. In almost every case of my married male colleagues with kids, their wives were the "trailing spouse" and had given up their careers (either temporarily or permanently). I think about what I know about the personal lives of my single female colleagues, stories like my own—the years pursuing a graduate degree, then a tenure-track job, the moving around, the fretful balancing of their careers with their boyfriends' or husbands' careers. I once joked with a friend that it seemed like a marriage (especially one that included kids) could only support one dream, not two. And now, suddenly, I'm realizing which dream almost always wins.

For years I've walked up and down the stairways of the ivory tower, chatted at copier machines, drunk beer with men and women whose relationships were all unique, full of conflicts and pain and joy, but all of a sudden, their stories, like my own, have become evidence of these horribly depressing theorems. I've been looking right at the data for years, living it even, but I never really saw the situation as anything other than "just the way life goes sometimes."

A reporter sticks a microphone in my face.

**Reporter:** Cathy, do you think it's really fair to say that every man who has a career and a family is necessarily happy?

**Me:** No, maybe not. But at least he has the *opportunity* to have both. I have to pick one or the other.

**Reporter:** That's not true.

**Me:** Look at the stats. It's *often* true.

**Reporter:** You already chose.

**Me:** When did I choose? Everyone said I should pursue a career that makes me happy.

**Reporter:** You foolish, foolish woman. Don't you see? Marriage, family, it's all about sacrifice and compromise. You're not willing to do that.

**Me:** Who says I'm not willing to sacrifice and compromise? You know, you're really starting to piss me off! All I'm saying is that things are supposed to be fair.

**Reporter:** Are you for real? Who said life is fair? Life, love—it's all a game, and some people are better at that game than other people.

**Me** (*Pause.*): I'll bet you have a husband and kids, don't you?

**Reporter** (*sticks her chest out proudly.*): Yes, I do.

**Me:** Great! Good for you! Look, I'm not competing with you, okay? I'm not trying to say my life is better than yours. Why are women always trying to one-up each other? This is exactly the kind of shit my sister and I used to pull on each other. All that feminist rhetoric about sisters sticking together is crap!

**Reporter:** Are you done?

**Me:** Yeah. I guess.

With a heavy heart I watch that Sunday's game between the Colts and the Jets. With 2:24 remaining in the game, Peyton Manning completes a 2-yard pass to tight end Bryan Fletcher, ending a 68-yard drive. Colts 24, Jets 21. The Colts offense retreats to the bench, but before they can even sit down, the Jets kick returner Justin Miller runs the kickoff 103 yards to give the Jets a 28–24 lead with 2:20 remaining. Peyton Manning has just picked up the phone to talk to the quarterback coach Jim Caldwell when he looks up and sees Miller run down tiny little Martin Gramatica, the Colts temporary replacement kicker for Adam Vinatieri. Manning hangs up the phone and quickly puts his helmet back on.

Such shifts in such a short time: the Colts win! No . . . now it looks like the Jets will win! The Colts need a scoring drive. They need a touchdown, not just a field goal. They have no time-outs. I need a scoring drive in my life, too. No time-outs. Time's running out on me biologically. The game is rigged, the playing field uneven. I can blame Pittsburgh and the economy. I can blame male privilege. I can blame the crazy academic job market. The odds are too much against me. I should just forfeit the game and accept it: this is my life.

But Peyton Manning doesn't forfeit because the odds are against him! He straps on his helmet and calmly drives his team back down the field—again!—capping it all off with a 1-yard quarterback sneak and, in an uncharacteristic show of emotion, spikes the ball in the end zone. Colts 31, Jets 28.

The crowd in the Meadowlands can't believe the Colts just scored again. After the thrill of that kickoff return, the Jets figured there was no way Indy could come back and score again in two minutes. But they did! Game over.

But no! With just eight seconds left, Jets' quarterback Chad Pennington throws a short pass to Leon Washington, who runs for an 8-yard gain, then laterals the ball to Brad Smith! Another lateral! Then another! If the Jets can keep the ball going, they'll win the game! The crowd goes wild. The wind has filled their hopeful sails once again, and they watch the ball toss this way and that. Again, another lateral! And then two fumbles with re-coveries by the Jets, until center Nick Mangold loses the ball at the Colts 35 and Indy's Jason David falls on the ball to finally—*finally*—finish the game.

It's impossible to watch the end of this game and not think about "The Play." How many people at the Meadowlands or watching the game on TV are thinking about that day in 1982? Doesn't everyone see the Stanford band already on the field celebrating their victory, dodging the Cal Golden Bears, who pass crazy, desperate laterals to each other until announcer Joe Starkey yells, *"And the Bears!! The Bears have won! The Bears have won! Oh, my God! The most amazing, sensational, dramatic, heart-rending . . . exciting, thrilling finish in the history of college football! California has won the Big Game over Stanford! Oh, excuse me for my voice, but I have never, never seen anything like it in the history of . . . I have ever seen any game in my life! The Bears have won it!"*

Even if you weren't watching that game (I wasn't), even if you weren't even born yet in 1982, you have seen "The Play." It makes every list of outrageous, unexpected moments in sports history. Hell, in TV history. We love watching "The Play" because it makes us believe there's always a chance that we can beat the odds. I want to believe in comeback stories, but I can't get Judy Coombs's kind, sympathetic face out of my head. She wants me to face the facts: most of the time, for most people, "The Play" doesn't happen. It's a fluke. A statistical anomaly, but still . . . as I watched the Jets throwing those desperate laterals, a part of me was almost rooting for them. Because I'm a romantic. Because you just never know. Because despite all evidence to the contrary, I can't stop believing in miracles.

There are approximately 150 plays in a football game,
and there are only three or four plays in any game
which make the difference between winning and losing.
No one knows when the big play is coming up.
Therefore, every player must go all out on every play.

—Vince Lombardi

# WEEK 5: COLTS VS. TITANS

## OR

## There's No "I" in "Team" (But There Is a "Me")

On September 24—the day the Colts beat the Jaguars and the Bengals beat the Steelers—a man named Rashad Wayne was driving a Capital City Produce Company truck on a highway outside New Orleans. For reasons that remain unclear, his truck crossed three lanes and fishtailed across Interstate 10, hitting the right retaining wall and sliding along the top of it before landing back on its wheels. When the police responded, they found the thirty-two-year-old driver still behind the wheel with severe head injuries. He was pronounced dead at the scene.

It's unclear if Mr. Wayne's brother, Colts wide receiver Reggie Wayne, got the call about the accident before or after the Colts versus Jaguars game, but it is certain that immediately after the game he flew to New Orleans to be with his grieving family. During that week Wayne spoke on the phone each day with his coach, Tony Dungy, who was only nine months removed from losing his son James. Wayne said, "You are at a situation in your life when you are at the lowest point, and just to hear from somebody that has actually been through it, it helps you out a lot. Coach Dungy is a strong man, a strong soul, so he knows exactly what's going on." Wayne considered sitting out last week's exciting Jets game, but his mother told him that his brother would have wanted him to play. So he did, catching four passes for 74 yards. After the game, Wayne said, "I knew he was watching and I wanted to go out and play for him and get a big win for him. It's been rough. It's my brother, and we were close. I felt he wanted me to come back and play."

If there is one thing I've learned in the last year, it's that people need people. If you want someone to get your back, you need to get theirs. So that's why I'm driving my friend Janet to take her cat Chloe to a vet's office in Greenfield. On Shady Avenue, I tell her, "The first time I came here to look for an apartment, I got lost right around here for like an hour. I got off the Parkway to go to Squirrel Hill and ended up somewhere in Homestead. I ended up driving around in circles in Schenley Park."

Janet turns around in her seat to try to comfort Chloe. "Shhhh. It's okay." Then she turns back around. "Thanks so much. I don't think I could have found this place." Janet and her husband Jerry have lived in Pittsburgh for two months now and know even less about navigating Pittsburgh's street maze than I do.

I turn left into the tree-canopied tunnel of Beechwood Avenue. "I still owe you for taking me to that Pitt football game." I don't tell her that football game saved my life. Or rather, I don't tell her that finding a woman friend who also likes football saved my life.

Eventually we find the vet's office. When the nurse calls Chloe's name, Janet asks, "Do you want to go back there with me?"

I look up from an issue of *Cat Fancy*. "Do you want me to?"

Janet nods. "Last time this happened, it was sort of traumatizing."

I completely understand what she means. I've got a cat. Actually, I used to have two, but one died last year. My mom and dad were taking care of her for me in Aurora while I was on my book tour, but when I got back, Mom said, "It's time." She's a hospice nurse after all. She and Andrea both went with me to the vet. We all cried so much that we made the vet cry, and he euthanizes animals every day. On the drive home I carried her on my lap, wrapped inside a towel nestled in a cardboard box, while my mom drove. About halfway home, my cat's bowels loosened, and the Jeep filled with the smell of shit, which made me start crying again. I got my two cats when I was a graduate student at Alabama, and they patiently followed me—to Minnesota, Baltimore, New Jersey, then Pittsburgh—as I pursued my career. They'd stuck with me longer than some of my best friends, longer than Alex. My mom drove up Hanover Avenue, and we found my dad in the backyard digging a hole in the half-frozen ground.

As I walk back to the examining room with Janet, I try to imagine getting through that day a year ago without my parents, without anyone. Well, I'm a strong person. I *could* have done it, but who the hell wants to go through a day like that alone?

The vet explains to Janet that Chloe's anal glands are impacted. Cats have anal glands? Who knew? "That's what I thought," Janet says. "This happened a year or two ago."

The vet explains that this sort of thing mostly happens to dogs. "Sometimes what comes out is the consistency of peanut butter. Sometimes it's soupier. How would you describe Chloe's feces?" I'm standing against the wall, trying not to gag.

The assistant holds Chloe down on the table while the vet "manually expresses the glands." Janet parks herself right in front of the cat's face to offer reassuring looks. At first, Chloe just looks mildly uncomfortable. But then she starts a low-timbred growl that becomes a definite howl. The vet keeps expressing. Chloe struggles, and then the desperate screaming hits us all hard, right between the eyes. The vet pulls out her finger, the assistant lets go, and Chloe leaps off the table and starts rebounding off the walls, like a furry rubber ball. All four of us stand back, recovering from that horrible sound. I say, "Um, shouldn't you sedate the cat?"

The vet decides that, yes, this is the best course of action. The assistant asks for Janet's phone number, then mine. "Not me," I say with a nod. "It's her cat."

The nurse sort of rolls her eyes at Janet.

Later, we walk out of the office. "I think they thought we were a couple." Janet laughs.

The same thing happened a year ago with the Punter. I needed a minor outpatient procedure, but they told me I wouldn't be allowed to drive myself home afterward. The Punter was the only person I knew in town at the time, so I asked him if he'd be my designated driver. Before my procedure, I asked, "Could you send one of the nurses into the waiting room?" I gave them the Punter's name. "Tell him it's going to be a little longer than I said before, and if that's a problem to let you know." A few minutes later, the nurse brought the Punter into my examining room. I wasn't wearing any pants, and only a sheet covered my legs.

"Oh!" we both said at once, embarrassed.

The nurse looked at us. "What?" she said. "Didn't you want to speak to your boyfriend?"

"He's not my boyfriend . . ." I said.

. . . *but he is my Pretend Boyfriend,* I thought.

In the six years I've been single, I've had a steady succession of Pretend Boyfriends: male companions who play a stand-in role for Real Boyfriends. For a single woman, Pretend Boyfriends fulfill your social and emotional (but not your sexual) needs. You go to the movies together. He takes you to the doctor. You shop for groceries. He calls you when you're sick. You forward him funny e-mails. He's the last person you talk to at the end of a long, draining day and the first person you call when something really great happens. When you're out in public, you don't mind that people must think he's your significant other. I know what you're thinking. You're thinking, *Well, what's wrong with friends?* Absolutely nothing, except that when you're really, really bored and lonely—and I mean the kind of loneliness you feel to the core, inside every cell in your body, and outside your body, too, like a haunting—when all that empty time stretches out in front of you like Kansas, when you're absolutely sick with loneliness, a Pretend Boyfriend is a topical cream when what you really need is something systemic, like intravenous antibiotics. My friend Sofia (who is happily married, by the way) is the one who warned me that Pretend Boyfriends bring both comfort and danger. "It doesn't even matter if you secretly have a crush on them or not. As long as they're there, you're not going to work to find the partner that you really need. Maybe you *need* to get really lonely. Maybe instead of covering up the hole, you need to look inside it. See how much you have to give to someone who is really going to be there."

After we leave the vet, Janet and I have lunch together. She asks me if I want to do something Saturday. That's when I realize that in the last few weeks, she and her husband have become my joint Pretend Boyfriend. We go to the movies together. I took her and her cat to the doctor. Janet calls me when I'm sick, and I forward her funny e-mails. Often she's the last person I talk to at the end of the day (but the last person she talks to at the end of the day is Jerry, of course). I love them both, and since I met them, I haven't been nearly as lonely—but I haven't been on a date, either. Believe me, I would rather spend time with Janet and Jerry than be alone, write checks to Great Expectations, or have depressing cups of coffee with Judy Coombs.

I make up a story about how I have to work on Saturday. Janet says, "Thank you so much for helping me today." I give her a hug, our first hug. And then I drive away. It makes no sense, really—walking away from people who make you happy. But I do it because deep down I know that the moments of joy I experience in the company of friends aren't enough to sustain me anymore.

The next day, my neighbor Tom comes over to help me stain my deck. Actually, I'm *paying him* to stain my deck, but I don't want him to feel like an employee or anything, so I'm out there helping. Deep down, it pisses me off that I have to pay anyone to do this. It's too big a job to do myself. I have no one to give a honey-do (or even a honey-*let's*-do) list to. If they lived closer, my dad or my brother or my brother-in-law would stain my deck for a case of beer and a hug. On Hanover Avenue, work like this is accomplished communally; my dad needs his deck stained, so a buddy helps him, and the next weekend his buddy needs to replace the alternator in his truck, so my dad helps him. It's the same for women, just that the jobs are different; Andrea helps my mom with her quilting because Mom watches Clay twice a week for free. I don't know if it's a small-town thing or a working-class thing or both, but I grew up in a world where people helped each other get by. It's one of the perks I gave up when I moved east, away from my family, away from Indiana, to a world where some people think it's pretty weird when you expect too much of them. Tom would probably stain my deck in exchange for services, but what truly practical skill do I possess? I write sentences. Does Tom need a good sentence? Sure he does. Everybody needs a good sentence. But it's like trading a John Deere tractor for a one-acre plot on a planet that hasn't been discovered yet.

Anyway, it's still great to be outside performing this task. It's a cool, blue morning in early October, sweatshirt weather at last. I dip my brush into the can of stain and spread it across a wooden step. "Do you mind if I tell you something about your friend Nick?"

Tom smiles without taking his eyes off the spindles he's painting. "Sure," he says. "I wasn't sure if you guys were still seeing each other or not."

"We did for a while but not so much lately." I take a breath. "I'm disappointed, I guess. We never seemed to connect. We never really talked to each other."

He says, "Well, you noticed that right away."

"I did?"

"Don't you remember? After you first met him at that Fourth of July party, you said he talked but he didn't really seem to listen."

"Huh," I say. "I guess I wanted it to work so bad, I blocked that out." I think, *Maybe my gut really doesn't have shit for brains. . . .* I move down another step. I'm glad Tom can't see my face now. I feel more comfortable talking to him like this. "I realized after a few weeks that he didn't know really any basic stuff about me, so I tried telling him. I tried asking him questions so that maybe he'd ask me stuff. But he never did."

Tom's got a theory. "Nick's only got brothers. I think guys raised in homes like that, they talk, but they never really *talk,* you know? Never really learn to listen." I hear the boards above me squeaking as Tom shifts positions. "The house I grew up in, it was all women."

Tom and I don't talk often, but when we do, he listens. He truly focuses, and being the subject of his focus is a bit like basking under a warming light. "Yeah, you know how to communicate. Rachel's lucky." I move down another step. "You know how they say women want a guy like their dad? My dad has three sisters, and my brother has two. I guess I expect men to be like my brother or my dad, but they aren't really the norm."

"No, not really." We paint in companionable silence for a while. I can hear a bus roaring by on the busway below us. Then Tom asks, "So how's it going otherwise? Met anyone else?"

"No," I say. "I'm starting to think it's a little hopeless."

I can hear him chuckle. "No it's not."

I grit my teeth. "Tom, I think there's a lot about dating at my age that you don't understand."

"I'm the same age as you, Cathy."

"But you're a man," I say. I like Tom a lot, but for some reason, I'm all of a sudden incredibly pissed off at him. "A man who's married to a woman who's ten years younger than him, I might add."

There's a pause. "I dated my share of women our age," he says a bit stiffly.

"Great," I say. I move down another step, thinking *On behalf of all single women in their thirties and forties, let me just say thank you so much for dating us.*

I actually have to stop myself from saying this out loud. *What is the matter with me?* I think. *Tom is my friend. I like him. I don't have any right to be pissed at him.* That's when I feel it, forming like a cancerous lump on my right trapezoid muscle, a hideous growth called Chip on My Shoulder.

I've got a meeting with my boss. We chat first. He says, "I hear you're a baseball fan."

"I am!" Then I tell him about the game I could have seen that summer. "But I couldn't find one person who wanted to go with me."

My boss wrinkles his brow. "I find that hard to believe. Nobody?"

"I don't know. I'm really trying hard to make Pittsburgh my home, but I can't seem to connect. With people. With the town." I look down at the blank pad of paper in front of me. "I think I need to date."

Lately, I've become fascinated with the different responses I get when I offer this information. Sometimes it's complete nonchalance. Sometimes it's rah-rah enthusiasm. And sometimes it generates uncomfortable silence, as if I've broached an unseemly, private subject, like menstruation or herpes. I worry that people see "dating" as a lowly topic, a girly topic not befitting a grown, professional woman. I certainly saw it that way for a long time. Luckily, my boss just sighs sympathetically. "I don't understand why it's so hard for the junior faculty to meet people. They all say the same thing." I tell him about what Judy Coombs said, but he shakes his head. "Surely it can't be as dire as that for women."

I shrug. "I hear that a lot, but believe me, I've talked to a handful of professional women here, and they say it's pretty dire."

"There are so many doctors and lawyers in this town."

"Sure," I say, "but how do I meet them? Put a sign in my yard? Walk around hospitals?" I fold my hands together. "You've lived here in Pittsburgh for a long time. Do you know any doctors or lawyers who aren't already married? Do you know *any men* my age who aren't married?"

My boss thinks for a second, then shakes his head. "No, I'm sorry, I don't."

*Did I just ask my boss to be my wingman? Yes, I think I just did.*

When I get home, Erica has called, but this time, the caller ID doesn't say "Great Expectations." It says "Mt. Vernon, Pa." I listen to the voice message. "The photographer got held up at one of our other training facilities," Erica says. "So I'm going to call you on October 11 to set up your photo shoot and video. Remember, your membership won't start until those things are completed."

*Sure,* I think, *but I'll bet you've cashed my check! And why do you need a professional photographer? This is the age of digital cameras, digital camcorders. My sister takes better pictures of Clay than she'd get at Olan Mills! Why are we waiting for some dude to show up and click the shutter? And why aren't you calling me from the office?*

And magically, Erica explains. "I brought some work home with me tonight. I remember you saying you'd rather me call your cell phone but I didn't have that number with me here."

Part of me is relieved. Actually, I don't want to make some dumb video or have my picture taken by a stranger for this purpose. But that's what all this is about: perseverance. I have to make myself do my best every single day, even if doing my best means doing something I really don't want to do. My membership on Chemistry runs out on October 13, so I need to get something else going. It's not even working anyway. GE doesn't seem to be working. The Faberge Method (tell two friends and they tell two friends and so on . . .) isn't working. What are my options now? Match .com, I guess. Maybe that's what I'll make myself do on Saturday when I'd rather be hanging out with Janet and Jerry.

That night, Andrea calls. "Clay wants to talk to you! Talk to Aunt Cathy. Tell her about the witch!" I hear him babbling his impassioned baby jabberwocky, and then it sounds like he's licking the phone. Then he drops it on the floor. "Sorry," she says. "He was talking before."

"How was your doctor's appointment?"

"Fine," she says. "I've gained twenty pounds."

"What about all that swelling?" Last week, she couldn't get her shoes on.

"Support hose."

I laugh. "For how long?"

"Until the baby comes." It's the second week in October, and she's not due until the beginning of January.

I tell her what Tom told me about Nick. "I can't believe it," I tell her. "My first instinct about him was exactly right, and I didn't trust it. I'm so confused."

"Who said you shouldn't trust your instincts?"

"You did!"

She sighs. "Well, I didn't mean every single one."


The slot in my front door clangs shut, and my mail hits the foyer floor. I know what's waiting for me downstairs. On Sundays, Scott tapes the Colts game for me in Indiana and drops the cassette in a prestamped bubble mailer. On Mondays, he drops it in a mailbox on his way to work. On Thursday, the game arrives in Pittsburgh. I like getting these packages from my brother. Every week, we are connected in this tiny way. I walk downstairs and, sure enough, I see the padded mailer. This is the Jets game. I pick it up and see that this week, in addition to his return address, my brother has written "Go Colts" on the package, which makes me smile.

Later, I'm standing in my basement, waiting for the spin cycle on my washer to stop so I can put the clothes in the dryer. I look up at the pipes running along the floor joists above my head, and I see the black gas pipe my dad installed back in May when I moved into this house. My parents, my just-pregnant sister, and Clay drove from southeastern Indiana to stay with me for five days to help me get settled in. It's the first time they'd ever done this since I left Indiana for Alabama in 1991. Every other time I'd moved, I was either too far away from them or I had Alex to help.

Standing there in my basement four months later, I remember the day Dad installed the pipe. My asthmatic mom kept an eye on Clay inside my half-empty house while Andrea and I tackled the tiny backyard with a weed whacker. The grass was waist high, and there was some mysterious plant growing back there that was taller than me. Turns out it was Japanese knotweed, a bamboolike infestation which cloaks the hills of Pittsburgh like kudzu. Andrea cut down the stalks and laid them out on an old sheet. I'd fold the sheet like a knotweed taco, sling it across my back, trudge down the hill to a ravine, and dump it over. That morning my dad had measured carefully and gone to Home Depot, clutching a detailed drawing he'd made of all the pipes he'd need to hook up my new gas dryer. He spent the better part of that afternoon doing this plumbing job for me, taking breaks every so often to sit outside on a five-gallon bucket to smoke a cigarette and drink a Miller Lite. Mopping the sweat off his head with a rag, he looked up at Andrea and me working and said, "Boy, it's a jungle out here!"

Suddenly, standing there in my basement, staring at the black pipe, I start crying. It's been a few months since I burst into tears like this. All I can do is wait it out, I guess. When the washer buzzes, I stuff my clothes in the dryer and start another load. I'm still crying as I walk upstairs to get dressed. Shit. I'm late for work. I've been crying for about ten minutes, assuming it would just stop. But it won't stop. Standing in front of the bathroom mirror to blow-dry my hair, I can't bear to look at my own face. I lean against the sink, trying to catch my breath, but now I'm all-out sobbing, close to hyperventilating. Finally, I look up at myself in the mirror. It's like something inside me has cracked wide open, and my face isn't my own. I'm looking at a woman I don't even recognize. "What is the matter with you?!" I yell at the woman in the mirror. "What is your fucking problem?!"

Half an hour later, I finally stop crying. I fix my face, walk to campus, and somehow manage to hold office hours. At six, I walk to a restaurant on Forbes Avenue and take a stool at the bar. I'm meeting someone for dinner, but I'm a little early, so I order a Coke and take a student's story out of my bag to read. Out of the corner of my eye I see him lope by the plate-glass window and recognize immediately the particular slant of his shoulders; he's clutching that familiar brown leather bag stuffed with papers and books. He steps into the restaurant, and I'm mad at myself that even now, all these months later, after all the effort I've put into getting over him, I still can't turn off the electricity that flows through me whenever I see the Punter.

He e-mailed me a week ago and suggested we have dinner to get caught up. After my crying jag today, I definitely should have canceled, but I'm curious why he's asked me here. We sit down in a booth and talk about the classes we're teaching, the music we're listening to. We talk about the actress Sienna Miller, who just called our fair city "Shitsburgh" in *Rolling Stone*. She's in town filming the screen adaptation of *The Mysteries of Pittsburgh*, a novel written by Pitt grad Michael Chabon. Last fall the Punter and I ate at this same restaurant all the time, back during those weeks when we talked and talked and never ran out of things to say. Even now, the conversation still comes easily, like driving a road you know by heart. When our food arrives, he asks, "So, how did things go with Dom? You never told me."

I smile. "We went out once. He was too young for me. End of story."

"Are you still dating?"

Looking down my straw, I take a sip of Diet Coke, then ask, "Why do you want to know?"

The Punter holds up his hands and laughs. "I'm just making conversation. And I care. I want you to be happy."

"I haven't been having a lot of luck," I confess. "It's been hard to find someone I can really talk to."

"I'm sorry," he says.

"What about you?" I ask. I try looking him in the eye, but I can't hold it for more than a second before I have to look at the painting on wall.

He says he and the girlfriend in New York are definitely kaput. "Actually, I've been dating this other woman."

So no, not only is the Punter not dating his ex-girlfriend anymore, he's dating someone else entirely, and it's *still* not me. I grip my hands underneath the table and think, *Don't start crying. Keep it together keep it to-*

*gether keep it together.* I say, "That's nice," and ask what she does, where she lives, if he's happy.

"We mostly just see each other on the weekends," he says. He doesn't seem to want to talk about it anymore, and to be honest, I don't even want to know what I already know. "So, what have you been doing lately?"

"Well, the other day, I went with a friend to have her cat's anal glands drained."

He laughs. "That sounds like a lot of fun."

"Actually, it was the high point of my week. That tells you a lot about my life." He laughs some more. "You know, this reminds me. I think I need to thank you for . . ." I try to come up with the right words. "You kept an eye on me last year. When I didn't know anybody."

"Ah, that's sweet. You're welcome. It's good to know that I made a difference."

I roll my eyes, and he laughs a little. "There was good and bad," I say, "but I should at least thank you for the good." He's blushing now. I wad up my napkin and put it on my plate. "Do you ever feel like you're not connected? Not to anyone. Not to anything."

He looks at me. "Why do you ask?"

I tell him about the pipe.

"A pipe made you cry? That's the saddest thing I've ever heard."

"It wasn't the pipe. It's what it reminded me of."

He shakes his head. "Yeah, I can see your dad sitting there on that five-gallon bucket." The Punter met my parents last fall; they came to visit me, and he volunteered to take us out for dinner. Afterward, my mom said, "I really, really like him," and I sighed and told her, "I know, me, too."

"I miss my family. Isn't that a dumb thing to say? I'm thirty-eight years old." And then I can't help it, but my eyes fill with tears.

A curtain falls over his expression, and he excuses himself to use the bathroom.

Later we're standing at a corner waiting for the light to turn. I can't even look at him. "I'm sorry."

A bus rolls past. He says, "Are you okay?"

"No, not really, but there's nothing you can do about it."

The light's still red. "I don't know what to say," he says.

I laugh out loud at this. It's wry and bitter, a sound I didn't know I was capable of making. "You never do, not when we get to moments like this."

He takes a tiny step backward, and I feel like such an idiot. I turn around and look at him standing there under a streetlight looking at me quizzically. "Look, I'm so sorry. God, I think I'm genetically incapable of small talk."

This makes him chuckle, and I seem to be forgiven, because he leans in to hug me. "Take care of yourself, Cathy." And then the light turns green, and he jogs away from me into the darkness.

I go home and call my sister, who says, "Getting to know him taught you how to recognize what attraction feels like. You need to remember the way you felt with him before, that excitement, and look for it in somebody who feels the same way about you." She's right, but I'm still dejected. As I talk to her, I log into Chemistry and find this:

No New Matches Found

Finding you that special someone with that something special, takes time. We are currently seeking these potential partners for you. Please check back with us soon.

Note: Number of new matches is based on your search criteria and number of matches in your area.

"I can't take it anymore," I tell her.

"You've got to keep trying, Cathy."

"It's too hard."

"No, it's not. Dating is supposed to be fun."

That's when I really lose it. "This is fucking hard work! Two weeks ago I spent all my money on a dating service that probably won't ever call me back. Did you know that!?"

"Well, you didn't go into any details—"

"It's true! I could have bought a dining room table with that money! I need a dining room table, but I made myself spend it on this stupid service that I'm starting to suspect isn't even a legitimate fucking business!"

"How much did you spend?"

I finally tell her.

"Oh my God. Cathy!"

"So don't tell me I'm not trying, 'cause I am! Every day I go to Chemistry and look at these dumb matches, and most of the time, those men suck, but sometimes they are actually interesting and I click the button that says I'm interested in you, and do you know how many of them click that button in return? Very fucking few. Of the hundreds of men I have seen or who have seen me, I've only gone through the whole damn communications process with three of them. Three! And they all say this lame crap about moonlit walks on the beach and the finer things in life. Whatever! I'm spending a lot of time and emotional energy on this, and the last goddamn thing I'd call it is fun!"

Andrea is quiet for a minute. "What are you going to do?"

Look, I'm not trying to say that my week was anything like Reggie Wayne's. So what? I cried for an hour over a stupid pipe. Big friggin' deal. Reggie Wayne buried his brother. And still he shows up on Sunday at the RCA Dome and marches around before kickoff waving a towel, leading cheers in the west end zone, jogging down the sidelines, pumping up the fans, who chant "Reggie! Reggie! Reggie!" Oh, to be down and despondent and hear 57,000 people saying your name, sending out their thoughts and prayers and good wishes. Sometimes, just having *one person* do that for us is enough. We all need to feel like someone's got our back, right?

The Colts are 4–0. The Titans are 0–4. Nobody expects the Titans to win—and yet at halftime they're up 10–0. With just five minutes left in the game, the Colts are still down 13–7 when Peyton throws what will become the winning touchdown to Reggie Wayne. It's his first touchdown of the 2006 season. The Titans' safety hits Wayne hard, knocking him out of bounds. Reggie gathers his wits about him, shakes it off, and returns to the end zone. He kneels on one knee and points his index finger at the sky.

If Reggie Wayne can lose his brother, come back, and do this, then surely I can stop feeling sorry for myself and get back into the game, too. So I do it—the one thing I really didn't want to do. I register for Match.com.

I think about all the things I've learned in the last few months, about the kind of woman I am and the kind of man I'm looking for. I describe all of this with as much specificity as I can muster.

> I care about other people. I'm a little shy until I'm comfortable. I always clean my plate, and I always tell the truth. I'm not a diva or a princess. My best friend says that I'm funny, although she usually says this when I haven't tried to be funny. Actually, I take things too seriously sometimes, so it would be nice to find someone who could make me laugh more. I'm smart, semi-intellectual, but I don't rub it in. I can fend for myself, but I like being taken care of, too. I've always been driven and motivated, and I've accomplished a lot in my life that I'm very proud of, but those accomplishments didn't bring me the happiness I thought I'd find—because I didn't have anyone to share them with. My ideal match is unpretentious and kind and smart and funny. You're comfortable in a variety of social situations—at a cocktail party talking about pop culture or something you just read, or on a barstool arguing about sports or the best band of all time. You like going with me (if you can) when I have to travel or socialize for work, but also like staying home with me to watch the tube or the big old sun go down. Above all, you want to make me deliriously happy, and you want me to return the favor.

And at the end of my profile, I write this, although I'm not sure if it's an appropriate thing to say:

> Your married friends keep insisting, "It'll happen when you least expect it." And then they turn around and say, "You can't just sit around doing nothing." So what does this mean? Are you supposed to try or not? Like me, you decided to split the difference and post your picture and profile and see what happens. You wish you could meet someone the old-fashioned way, whatever the heck that means. You've had some disappointments, and sometimes you're convinced that there's no one left for you, but you don't give up. You keep trying because you believe the right one is out there for you, and you know that you're the right one for a girl like me.

Clear eyes, full hearts, can't lose.

—*Friday Night Lights* (the TV show)

---

## WEEK 6: BYE WEEK

### OR

# Oh, the Movie Never Ends

---

S o I put up a profile on Match.com. Forty-eight hours later, I walk into Starbucks to meet a man named Stan. His was the first e-mail I received, a response to my headline—the opening lyrics of my favorite Journey song: "Just a small-town girl, living in a lonely world." His opening salvo was: "Don't stop believing. Perhaps you're journey will have a happy ending. Let's talk."

Okay, so he spelled "your" wrong, but at least he read what I wrote.

Stan walks into Starbucks breathless and sweaty. I'm sort of touched that he hurried. He's wearing a light-purple dress shirt and gray slacks.

We shake hands. "Did you just get off work?" I ask.

He looks down at his shirt. "No, I've been to the gym and showered." I'm also sort of touched that someone would dress up for a coffee date with me.

Stan tells me some of his Match.com horror stories. "One woman said she was intelligent and educated, and when I used the word *incredulous,* she asked me if I'd made it up. Another woman I was e-mailing with said she enjoyed current events, and then said she wanted to keep her real name secret, so I wrote back and said, 'Yeah, like Valerie Plame,' and she said, 'I think I worked with her once. Isn't it funny we know someone in common!'"

This makes me laugh.

"What about you? Had any bad experiences?" Stan asks.

"You're my first," I say. "I mean, you're the first person I've met."

He looks surprised. "Really? Do you mind if I ask you what kind of response you've been getting?"

I look down into my coffee. "I got like ten e-mails and twenty winks."

You need to know this: a "wink" is a button you click to say "Hi," a virtual equivalent of the real thing.

"The first day?" Stan asks.

"The first couple of hours."

Stan nods. "That's what happens to the new ones. You get inundated. I've got my search criteria set to show me newest profiles first. I'm always checking."

"Why?"

He shrugs. "I've already seen the women who've been on there for a while."

"So I'm fresh meat."

Stan smiles. "Sort of, yes. When a new woman pops up, you've got to act fast." I picture Stan at home in front his computer. He's playing Match.com the way I've seen men play Madden NFL 08 on Xbox—with absolute focus and boyish glee.

He tells me he's been on fifty dates in three months.

"I'm incredulous," I say. "How is that even possible?"

"Well, maybe it's more like thirty . . ."

"Still, that's like ten dates a month. That's a lot. How do you have the time?"

"Mostly it's one date and out," Stan says, then he frowns. "I remember one time I met this woman for coffee and when she got up to use the bathroom, she walked back and grabbed her coffee and said, 'In case you try to poison me.'" Stan's expression says *Isn't that the craziest thing you've ever heard?*

I say, "Are you sure she didn't say 'drug me'? Maybe she thought you were going to slip her a roofie?"

He crosses his arms. "I would never do that!"

"But she doesn't know that." I think, *Actually, that sounds exactly like something I'd do—forget my cup then come back for it and say something stupid to explain why I'm doing something weird.*

Stan is getting very fidgety. He's drumming his fingers on the table, squirming around in his chair. Somehow, the subject of our ethnic backgrounds comes up, and I ask him his last name. Stan folds his hands on the table. "Well, I'd really rather not tell you that."

"Why?"

"I told this woman my full name on our first date, and when we met for the second date, she brought my credit report with her. She paid to run my credit!"

"Oh my goodness!" I say.

"You know, you shouldn't give out so much information about yourself," Stan says. "You already told me you work at Pitt. It wouldn't be that hard for me to find out who you are." Stan takes a breath. "Not that I would do that."

I'm a bit startled. "How can anybody ever get to know somebody else if every time they walk into Starbucks, they expect the absolute worst of each other?" I look him in the eye. "Is your name even Stan?"

He gives me a grin. "Yes, that's my real name."

I look at my watch under the table. It's only been fifteen minutes.

Stan starts talking about himself—his family, his job. I sit there and smile politely, like someone listening to a sales pitch. Finally, there's a pause. He hasn't asked me a single question about myself. *Oh no,* I think. *It's like Nick again.* So I ask him what he'd like to know about me.

There's a long pause. "What kind of guy do you usually like?"

I think on this for a second. "It's something I figure out on a case-by-case basis, I guess." I look out the window and see my bus go by. Oh well. The next one will be here in a half hour. "Some people attract us and some people don't. It's chemical, I think, and visual. Unconscious mostly. It's what feels right and comfortable."

"You're very introspective," he says,

I smile. "What about you? Does your mom like your girlfriends?"

"Oh, I don't take women home."

"Really? Never?"

"When you're dating a twenty-four-year-old girl in a belly shirt, you can't take her home to Mom."

*Did he really just say that?* Suddenly, it hits me: Stan is older than me, and I feel like I'm talking to one of my undergrads. "Um, are you the only one of your siblings who's not married?"

"Yeah, I'm the only one," he says, chewing on his fingernails. I haven't seen a grown-up chew on his fingernails in a long, long time. "So I take care of my mother."

I'm touched by this. "That's nice."

"She lives in a neighborhood that's going to hell. She's scared a lot at night. And she can't see so well anymore. So I spend the night there a lot." He looks at me carefully, and I can tell he's showing me a really big card to see how I'll react.

I can't wipe the incredulous look off my face. "Really? Why couldn't your mom come to your house?"

"She's more comfortable in her house."

"Uh-huh." Without realizing that I'm doing it, I pick up my book bag and set it on my lap. Abruptly, I stand up. "Yes, I know what it's like to worry about your parents. Actually, I'm leaving tomorrow to visit mine and I need to go pack." This is sort of a lie. It's Tuesday night and I'm not leaving until Thursday. "Um, what do we do now? To end the, uh, date."

Stan stands up too and walks his cup over to the trash. "Well, we can shake hands. Sometimes people kiss."

I take a step back. "Oh! But I've only known you for an hour!"

He doesn't even blink. "We could exchange phone numbers. Make another date. End it now. What do you think?"

And even though I knew a half hour ago that this didn't feel right, I can't bring myself to look him in the face and say, "I don't think so. Thank you but no." So I say, "I really hate to have to make a split-second decision. Why don't I e-mail you later?" and he looks down at the ground. We shake hands, and he turns and practically runs out the door.

Later, a girl sitting behind me on the bus says, "Hey, did you know they're filming a movie in Polish Hill today?"

I turn around. "Today? *Mysteries of Pittsburgh*?"

"Yeah, they turned that Emma Kaufmann building into a police station or something and they're filming a bar scene at Sarney's." The woman is wearing a heavy sweater, but it's a warm night and her face is shiny with sweat. "It's that book by Michael . . . how do you say it? Shuh-bon or Shay-bon?"

"I've heard it both ways," I say.

"Anyway, he must really like Pittsburgh! He wrote that book *Wonderboys* that they filmed here, too."

I can tell she's not going to stop talking until I get off the bus. "Yeah, he went to Pitt as an undergrad."

"Somebody told me they filmed *Flashdance* here, too. And that Jean-Claude van Damme movie they filmed at Mellon Arena . . ." She stares at me, waiting. How does she know I know the answer?

"*Sudden Death.*"

"Can you believe what that Sienna Miller said about us? I mean, I think Pittsburgh's pretty great. Sienna Miller is from England. What does she know? Did you know that in England, their bacon is like all fat? In America, at least it's got a little meat on it, but in London it's all fat. Who wants to eat fried fat?"

I don't know how to answer this question. I hate to be rude, but I turn back around in my seat. She just keeps talking. The bus lumbers down Liberty Avenue, past the stained-glass windows of the Church Brew Works—a microbrewery housed in an old house of worship—and turns left up Herron Avenue. Mine is the next stop. I picture Stan driving down the highway heading to his old neighborhood, to his elderly mother's house, to his childhood bed. The woman behind me is still talking about bacon, and I wonder how I ended up here, stranded on the island of misfit toys.

The 54C lets me off in Polish Hill. One of the many things I love about my neighborhood is that it looks like the kind of place where my family would have lived if we'd settled here long ago. It's a working-class neighborhood built into the cliffs above the Strip District. It's a bit old-worldly, with narrow streets winding past tiered row houses. Polish Hill hosts four bars and one enormous, copper-domed church. Instead of heading home, I walk down the street to Sarney's Bar. I've passed it many times, but its façade is nondescript, nestled between two houses, and I always wondered if the door might actually open into someone's living room. Tonight, the door is propped open, and I can see that yes, indeed, it is a bar.

There's a small crowd standing outside, who tell me that I just missed Nick Nolte. Apparently, he's playing the main character's father, a mobster. I follow two fellows down Brereton; they're wearing period cop uniforms, circa 1980. They enter the Emma Kaufmann Clinic, built in 1895 by the Kaufmann family of Fallingwater fame. Today, it serves as an apartment building, but the production crew has stenciled the word POLICE in gold over the front door. I follow Brereton toward the Twenty-eighth Street Bridge and see huge trailers parked all the way down the hill. I stand and watch them humming for a while, but it's clear that the shoot is over, so I turn and walk home.

Sometimes when I'm walking around in Pittsburgh, I feel like I'm in a movie I've already seen. Pittsburgh looks like the place you imagine on its many overcast winter days. You could look over the cliff near my house at the industrial rooftops spreading across the horizon. Smoke curls from the smokestacks of the Pittsburgh Brewing Company. The world is awash in gray and brown punctuated by splashes of red brick, and all you'd need to complete the scene is the sound of a factory whistle. But most of those stopped blowing a long time ago. This is the picture of Pittsburgh the world carries around in its head, and in the winter, Pittsburgh does not often disappoint. But when the sun comes out and the sky is blue, and in the high green of summer, and now, in the golden glow of a warm fall evening, Pittsburgh is an enchanted city, even if pretty little Sienna Miller is too stuck-up to notice.

On Wednesday night, I plop down in my La-Z-Boy with my laptop to check my Match.com account and watch the first two episodes of *Friday Night Lights.* As of this moment, my profile has been viewed over five hundred times. I've received over fifty winks and about twenty-five e-mails. Normally, I'm pretty obsessive about answering e-mail quickly. I have a Pitt e-mail address for school correspondence and a private e-mail address for writing and personal correspondence. Responding to those e-mail accounts alone takes up two or three hours of my day. Now I've added all this Match correspondence, too! What was I thinking?

The first thing I do is e-mail Stan, because that's what I said I would do. "Thanks for driving into the city to meet me. It was nice meeting you.

I don't feel like we are a good match, but I hope you find what you're looking for in a woman and a partner." Stan must be sitting at his computer (I get the sense he's playing Match.com constantly) because he writes back right away and says, "Thanks for your candor."

I start wading through the messages. More than half the messages say things like "We have very similar interests and a lot in common." At first, I think, *Great! Wow! This guy really gets me!* And then I read his profile and it says he likes extreme sports and the last thing he read was the back of a cereal box. Oh, I get it. Some men write greeting-card messages: vague and slightly sappy. It's like when I pick a card for my dad that says, "Father, you taught me so many important things in life," he and I both know we're talking about fishing, batting, and checking my oil, but some other daughter might pick out the same card and know that she and her father are communicating about gardening, skiing, and investments. Maybe these Greeting-Card Guys know they don't really have to be specific, that most women will project onto phrases like "lots in common." Okay, so should I ignore the Greeting-Card Guys? I tell myself God is in the details and move on.

A few messages are from men who actually seem to have read my profile and made note of my interests. One guy tells me that one of the bands I listed as a favorite is playing a show in Pittsburgh in a few weeks. One guy offers to take me to a yoga class. Part of me thinks, *Finally! I've spent a year wondering, "Where are all the single men my age in Pittsburgh?" Here they are!* But the other part of me feels like a voyeur, a stalker. I think, *I shouldn't know what kind of curtains a perfect stranger has in his living room or how much money he makes.* I have no idea what to say back to any of these men, so I log off Match and turn my full attention to a game I understand much better—the football game taking place on the pilot episode of *Friday Night Lights.*


What are the chances that a TV show about love and football would debut just as I'm thinking obsessively about those same two subjects? I've been carrying around a hardcover of H. G. Bissinger's *Friday Night Lights: A Town, a Team, and a Dream* since it was published in 1990. Watching the 2004 movie starring Billy Bob Thornton was like watching my imaginary friends come to life. And then comes *Friday Night Lights* the TV show, part soaplike drama, part sports drama. It's got one foot in a typically female space (the relationship stuff) and one foot in a typically male space (the sports stuff).

What I love about the show is that it knows that most of us live in a world where there is no longer exclusively female space and male space. We're all swimming around lost in the murky middle, trying to negotiate with each other, and it's hard. The coach's wife demands that he pay attention to his family and her career as much as his players. Their daughter hates football but ends up dating the quarterback, but she doesn't care that he's the quarterback. She likes him because, like a good woman, he's the primary caregiver of his grandmother with Alzheimer's. The school slut plots her escape, but on her own terms, unlike her scatterbrained mother, who just wants a man to rescue her. Most of all, I love that these characters are battling with each other, not just on the football field, but in pick-up trucks and bedrooms and car dealerships and hamburger joints and around fires in the middle of Texas, in the middle of nowhere, which is where most of the people in this country live. I wonder sometimes if my life might have turned out differently if I'd been able to watch a show like *Friday Night Lights* when I was growing up.

A few weeks after the premiere, I'm talking to Christine, a fellow writer and an academic. "You should watch this new show, *Friday Night Lights*," I say.

"Oh, I can't watch that," she says, waving her hand. "It's got sports in it. Football, right?"

"Sports aren't just for men," I say.

Christine laughs wryly. "They were when I was growing up. I'm pre–Title IX, dear."

Point taken. I try to explain to her why I loved *Rocky* movies as a kid, why the sports narrative is so important to me. I tell her that when I was growing up in the oh-so-enlightened 1970s, there just weren't a lot of stories (in books, on TV, at the movies) about women doing much of anything interesting, so I identified with the male characters. They were in charge. They solved crimes. They kicked ass. They cracked jokes. They stood in front of classrooms and lecture halls. They banged their fists on tables and offered sage advice over tumblers of golden scotch. They sat in front of typewriters and thought Big Thoughts. While the guys worked late into the night, the women brought them coffee, rubbed their shoulders, and told them, "It's okay, dear. I believe in you."

Christine says that when she was growing up in the 1950s, she didn't see any women around (in real life or on television or the movies) who represented who she wanted to be either. "Marilyn Monroe?" she joked. "Please."

"All I had was *Charlie's Angels*," I say.

"Well, at least they got to do something," she says.

You need to know this: growing up, I thought most of the women I saw on TV were a bunch of bimbos. That might sound harsh, but go back and watch the opening credits of *Charlie's Angels, Buck Rogers,* or *Wonder Woman,* and you'll see what I mean. The unintentionally hilarious lyrics to the *Wonder Woman* theme song are still imprinted in my brain: "Wonder Woman! Wonder Woman! / All the world is waiting for you / and the powers you possess! / In your satin tights / fighting for your rights / and the old Red, White, and Blue!" I know, the intent was to present strong, positive images of women on television, as long as the shows still looked *Baywatchy* if you turned the volume down. I was so grateful when I first saw the *Bionic Woman.* Jamie Sommers was the most real woman I saw on TV, and she had bionic legs.

Here's what I learned about womanhood by watching a lot of TV and movies in the 1970s: even the strong, independent female characters completely fell apart if a good-looking man showed up. Case in point: career girl Lois Lane in my other favorite movie, *Superman.* I lost all faith in her when she got the chance to ask the Man of Steel anything, any question, and she asked him what color underwear she was wearing. And who can forget her blathering voice-over during her first flight over Metropolis?

*Can you read my mind? Do you know what it is that you do to me? I don't know who you are. Just a friend from another star. Here I am, like a kid out of school. Holding hands with a god. I'm a fool. Will you look at me? Quivering. Like a little girl, shivering. You can see right through me. If you need a friend, I am the one to fly to. If you need to be loved, here I am.*

Painful to read, isn't it? It's like the horrible poetry moony eighth-grade girls write. This from a writer for a major metropolitan newspaper (okay, so a fictional newspaper), a woman who had supposedly won awards for her prose. So I ask you: faced with the choice of identifying with Superman or Lois Lane, who would you choose?

As for Adrian Balboa, I like her a lot, and even identify with her a bit. She starts off as a shy, bespectacled pet-store employee, a real doormat, but through Rocky's love and support, she transforms into one tough cookie. In the original *Rocky* she delivers one of the most impassioned lines of the whole movie. Once she starts dating Rocky, Adrian's brother Paulie starts feeling neglected. "You're supposed to be good to me," he says petulantly. And she screams back, "What do I owe you, Paulie?! I treat you good! I cook for you! I clean for you! I pick up your dirty clothes! I take care of ya, Paulie! I don't owe you nothin'! And you made me feel like a loser! I'm not a loser!" Adrian transforms into the well-dressed boxing match attendee we know and love. But that's where her Cinderella story ends; she doesn't literally do much in the movies except help Rocky figure out what he's really fighting for. Watch the training montage in *Rocky III*. She appears a few times supporting Rocky, holding his towel, cheering him on. Everyone needs a support system. Everyone needs someone in their corner. But when I saw this movie as a girl, I didn't identify with Adrian. I didn't see these films and think, *I should marry a guy like Rocky Balboa or Superman.* For whatever reason, I thought, *I want to be like Rocky Balboa or Superman.*

I certainly didn't want to *look* like Rocky or Superman. I wanted to look like Jaclyn Smith or Lynda Carter. And it's not that I didn't want to get married. Believe me, I did. Later (after I'd gone the distance and saved the world) I wanted to marry an interesting man, maybe Rocky or Superman, who thought Big Thoughts and banged on a table. But I wanted to be interesting, think Big Thoughts, and bang on a table, too.

It's Saturday. I'm back home in Indiana for my father's sixtieth birthday party. My brother Scott and I have been assigned to drive to Sears to pick up my dad's birthday gift: a snowblower. "Did you go in on this?" he asks.

"No, I got him a Colts jersey. Number 44." It was always my dad's number when he still played sports.

Scott gives me a weird look. "Why'd you get a Dallas Clark jersey? He's not going to be a franchise player."

"How do you know?" I ask gruffly.

"You should have gotten him a Peyton jersey. He likes Peyton."

I spent a lot of money on this Dallas Clark jersey, and I'm very annoyed. "Everybody has a Peyton jersey," I argue. He and Sara have matching Peyton jerseys. "This is more original."

Scott hmmmphs. "You always have to be different."

I cross my arms and stare out the window.

Scott's cell phone rings. He answers and says, "Okay, but where's it at again? What street?" He clicks his phone shut. "They forgot to pick up the pulled pork. We gotta go out to Wayne's Meats in Milan." It's about twenty minutes away.

"Scott, what should I do with all these messages on Match?"

He takes a sip of Mountain Dew. "What do you mean, do with them? You answer the ones you're interested in."

"But what about the ones I'm not interested in?"

"Nothin'."

"Really? I just don't respond?"

Scott shakes his head. "Cathy, you're too nice. You don't have time to respond to every single one of 'em. Seriously, they don't expect you to."

"How am I supposed to know these things? How did you figure it out?"

"A friend of mine told me."

"Oh."

"Want some advice?"

I turn in my seat. "Of course."

"Don't spend all your time responding to the ones that contact you. A lot of guys are like spammers. They just contact everybody, hoping to get a reaction. Figure out what you want and do your own search. That's how me and Sara met."

"She found you?" *How do I not know this?*

"Yeah, I think my search was limited to twenty-five miles, basically from here to the west side of Cincy. But she lived on the *east side.* I think she set her search radius for fifty miles. So she saw me first and hit the wink button. And there you go," he says. "Hey, what happened with that other thing you tried? Great something?"

That's when I realize they didn't call me on the eleventh like they said they would.

A few minutes later, we drive past Milan's welcome sign, which features a basketball emblazoned with 1954. This, my friends, is the real town of Hickory from *Hoosiers*. We make our way past the grocery store and the Dairy Queen, and head into the town proper, a grid of about six or seven blocks. A car in front of us stops in the middle of the street and four girls clamber out and head into the tanning bed/beauty parlor. In an empty church parking lot, an old woman teaches a little boy to ride a bike. We park on Josephine Street in front of Wayne's Meats. Scott gives them our mom's name, and I look around. There's a deer head mounted on the wall and Styrofoam containers of fishing worms in the Coke cooler. A man walks out of the freezer wearing rubber boots and a Carhartt jacket and gives me a wave. I smile back and wander over to the corkboard by the front door. It's crowded with pictures—they're all of people standing next to animals: 4-H hogs and cows, deer and elk slung over truck beds. We pay for the pulled pork and get back in Scott's truck.

The town of Milan doesn't look much like Hickory, its fictional counterpart; with a population of 1,800, it's actually a bit bigger, and the real landscape rises and rolls much more than the fictional one. That's because they filmed *Hoosiers* in northern Indiana. I know this because two years ago I got to meet the director, David Anspaugh. He'd read my first book and was visiting family in Indiana; he called a mutual acquaintance and asked for a personal tour of my hometown. We spent the day before Election Day 2004 roaming around Peru and ended up at Tig-Arena. We walked past the old classrooms filled with toddlers (the Miami Indians run a day-care center there) and entered the gymnasium. A huge bingo sign hung from the field house rafters, and the room smelled like an ashtray, but as soon as we stepped onto the hardwood floor, Anspaugh said, "Wow! This would have been a great gym for the movie." I told him that his location scouts had visited, but we didn't have enough hotel rooms to house the cast and crew.

Then I confessed that the opening credits of *Hoosiers*—the sound of those wistful horns in Jerry Goldsmith's score, the shots of Gene Hackman's car driving down that highway past the fallow autumn fields, crossing an Indiana morning full of pink sky—always made my heart hurt, and he smiled and said he knew exactly what I meant. I remember watching *Hoosiers* for the first time. I was eighteen, holding hands with a boy. A week earlier, IU had won the 1987 NCAA basketball championship, and the entire state was euphoric (well, except for Purdue fans). Sitting in the dark theater, I got chills when one of the players in *Hoosiers* says, "Let's win this game for all the small schools that never had a chance to get here." The dream of becoming a writer was forming inside me. For some reason, IU's recent victory, coupled with my viewing of *Hoosiers*, made me think I might have a shot. I wanted so much to become somebody, to win the game for all the small-town girls who never had a chance to go to college or write a book or see the world. I didn't want to marry the boy I was holding hands with. I wanted to make something like the movie I'd just seen, something about Indiana and the way it made me feel inside.

After the party, after everyone has gone home, I get on the computer at my parents' house to try out Scott's suggestion. I find a guy who says he likes Hemingway, and another who loves all my favorite indie bands. I wink at them both, a virtual flirtation I would never, ever engage in for real. Then I hear my dad come inside. I can tell just by watching him walk, how he holds his body, that he's a little drunk and that his back hurts. The day before, he made a long drive to his lawyer's office in Louisville to sign the paltry settlement agreement and then he drove straight back. He uses the bathroom and then goes into his bedroom. I hear him call my mom's name. "She's outside," I yell back. So he calls to me.

I walk into the dark room. "Did you have a good birthday today?" I ask a little hopefully.

My father is sitting slumped over on the edge of his bed. "I can't reach down. Can you untie my shoes for me?" While I'm bent down, he touches the top of my head. "Glad you came for the party."

I smile up at him. "That's why I changed jobs, Dad, so I could come to stuff like this." I pull off his tennis shoes.

"That's nice." He sighs. "Wish I could do something for you. Looks like I ain't going to be able to leave you kids nothing. Nothing but my debt." Swinging his legs onto the bed one at a time, he lays back on the pillows with a grunt and grimace.

"Roll over," I tell him. He does, and I rub the small of his back. Seventeen years ago, I sat on the edge of this bed, yelling "Time to get up, Dad!" so he could pull another double shift. My father put every dime he ever made into us kids, and now he's sixty with a house he'll never pay off and a back full of pain. All because of a lousy piece of paper he didn't bother to fill out. How is this fair? Forget snowblowers and Dallas Clark jerseys. If I was a good daughter, I'd rub this man's back every night for the rest of his life.

After a while, I think he's drifted off, so I stand up. But he's not asleep. "I always wanted my kids to live close by," he mumbles into his pillow. "We'd buy houses out in the country, and we'd get golf carts and ride back and forth to each other's houses to borrow milk."

You need to know this: he's absolutely serious, and he'd say this even if he wasn't half drunk and half asleep. We say good night, and for a long, long time, I can't sleep for wondering what it would be like if my father's dream came true. It's how millions of other people on the face of this planet live. Why not me? And then I think about Stan from Starbucks, sleeping now in his mother's house somewhere outside Pittsburgh. Who am I to judge him? I'm sleeping in my parents' house somewhere outside Cincinnati. And that's when it hits me: my family has become my Pretend Boyfriend.

We're close, and close don't mean shit. I'm tired of coming close. I'm pissed off right now. You bet your ass I am. I'm sick of coulda, woulda, shoulda, coming close, if only.

—Jim E. Mora, New Orleans Saints' head coach, 1987

## WEEK 7: COLTS VS. REDSKINS

### OR

## Shake It Off, Johnny, Rub Some Dirt on It

**W**hen you're sitting in your living room watching *Monday Night Football* with one eye and checking out the prospects on Match.com with the other, it's hard not to think that you've ended up in some sort of loser's bracket. Because that is the assumption everyone makes of singles in their thirties and forties: *Why are you still single? What have you all done wrong? What's the matter with you?* The assumption is that we have somehow brought this upon ourselves, and as I troll around on Match.com, I realize how much I've internalized that thinking. It's taken me months to convince myself that there's nothing (or not much) wrong with me, and so it's absolutely not fair for me to look at a man's profile and wonder, *Gee, what's your story, dude? What did you do wrong to end up here?*

My brother Scott's advice—to take an active rather than passive role in my search—has paid off. The guy who likes Hemingway has sent me a message. He's returned to Pittsburgh after working elsewhere for fifteen years. Pittsburgh isn't kind to singles, he writes, especially those in their thirties and forties. I e-mail back, asking him why he thinks that is. He says Pittsburgh started declining in the seventies and early eighties with the end of the steel mills and railroad industry. A lot of native Pittsburgh kids had to make a choice to leave and go where the jobs were or stay.

Those that stuck around generally married their high school sweethearts. He says:

> Pittsburgh is notorious for its reputation as being one of the worst cities in America for singles. I say this is due to its image as a dying city and a crippled economy with virtually little opportunity for young college graduates to achieve the "American dream." It is not very progressive, has little to none grassroots movements, its political system is dominated by cronyism, and the weather sucks. But I love it!
>
> Patrick

Patrick the Hemingway Fan is smart! I'm so damn impressed that I don't even care about the depressing content of his message.

There's a message from Chris the Rocker; he's playing the guitar in his portrait, a picture of concentration. That's why I remember him from my days on Chemistry. He didn't pick a smiling-straight-at-the-camera photograph, like most men, but rather one that captured him doing something he loved, an unusual choice. I remember clicking yes a little hopefully, but I never heard from him via Chemistry. So why is he contacting me now, here on Match? I think about asking him this question as I write back, but it seems a bit rude, so instead I ask about his classes. He says he's in graduate school, but doesn't say at what school.

On *MNF*, it's the Chicago Bears @ Arizona Cardinals. At the beginning of the game there's still some activity on Match.com, but it trickles down as the Bears stage one of the most amazing comebacks in NFL history. All activity on Match.com ceases as the Cardinals leave the field visibly despondent and angry. I realize that a lot of men in Pittsburgh probably do exactly like I'm doing: they check their Match.com account in front of the television.

Who am I competing with on Match.com? I log in to Match as a man looking for a woman in Pittsburgh between the ages of thirty-five and forty-five, and what I find blows my mind. Pretty, smart women, one after the other, with stories very much like my own. They love football stadiums *and* art museums. They travel a lot for work, but work just isn't enough anymore. They want something more. They smile broadly, and their profiles are unfailingly positive. Part of me is thinking, *Shit, I've got some pretty stiff competition here!* But the other part of me is so freaking proud of these women. I think, *God bless us, every one.*

Just as I'm ready to turn off ESPN and head to bed, I see I have a new message. It's from Indie Music Guy, a short-haired blond. I saw his profile at my parents' house after my dad's birthday party, and despite all the distractions, I remember thinking, *Now, here we go!* All he says in his message is thanks for winking, he likes my profile, and I have excellent taste in music. He doesn't tell me his name, and yet, I'm pumping my fist in the air. "Hey! I got a message from a cute boy!" My cat just blinks at me and yawns.

Over the next few days, I e-mail back and forth with Indie Music Guy. Yes, I also correspond with Patrick the Hemingway Fan and Chris the Rocker from Chemistry, but Indie Music Guy is the one I'm excited about. Why do I prefer Indie Music Guy? Can anyone really explain this? I saw his profile and I got excited, even before I saw that according to Match .com, we are 95 percent compatible. There's even a table, me in one column and him in the other, and all of our comparison boxes contain a check. We are the same age, and we are both looking for a partner of the same age. We exercise the same amount. We have similar diets, similar interests. We both read books, magazines, and newspapers. He listens to Guided by Voices and Yo La Tengo, and I've seen both of these bands in concert. We are educationally homogamous; I have a graduate degree and he is a few credits shy of earning his. Politically and socially, we're proudly liberal. We're both in helping professions, although we haven't told each other what we do yet. We both have cats. We've both been in long-term, committed relationships, but neither of us has been married. And we'd both like to marry someone who has never been married, if possible. We both believe in a higher power, and someday we both would like one child.

I know all of this before I know his name.

Our e-mail exchange begins. We share an interest in music, so I start with that. "Tell me about the bands that meant a lot to you growing up." He lists them—by decade. Seventies: Led Zeppelin, the Who, the Stones, T. Rex. Hardly surprising. It's the eighties that tell you a lot about someone, and Indie Music Guy likes what I consider to be the "right" bands: Talking Heads, the Police, the Replacements, and the Pixies.

He asks me where I grew up. Where did I grow up? Where do I start? I have to restrain myself from going on too much about that.

I ask him what he does for a living and what kind of graduate degree he's getting. I volunteer a clue to my identity by signing my name, "Cathy."

Indie Music Guy works somewhere in the South Hills as a social worker. He loves his job and he's finishing his master's. He asks me what I do for a living and for fun. He doesn't sign his name.

I tell him I'm a teacher. I tell him what I like to do for fun: read, watch *Law & Order,* have people over to watch football games with me. This time, I don't sign my name.

Indie Music Guy tells me about his job in more detail. He asks if I moved here for my job. He asks me where I live in the city. And finally, he signs his name: Max. *Max!* I'm so elated to know his name, I don't know what to do with myself.

I tell Max why I moved to Pittsburgh. I tell him I live in Polish Hill. I tell him I'm going to see the band Death Cab for Cutie in a few weeks, and he says he once saw them live and was a little disappointed.

It's my turn. I don't know what else to ask. How about his cat? How about where he grew up? I'm getting anxious. How long are we going to e-mail each other like this?

Max grew up in the South Hills. After high school he moved around to a bunch of unnamed cities for reasons he doesn't disclose, but ended up back in Pittsburgh. He's on his way to Goodwill to look for a Halloween costume. "Have a good weekend," Max says.

What the hell? Stan Who Sleeps at His Mom's House wanted to meet me right away. Isn't that the way this whole Match.com thing is supposed to work? I'm getting impatient, but I force myself to wait twenty-four hours before responding. By now it's Sunday, and I'm parked in my La-Z-Boy watching the Colts take on the Redskins. I write Max back and close by saying, "I'd be up for meeting you, if you're up for it, too. You seem like not a stalker. I hope I seem the same." Smiley face. But I don't hit send. Should I bring up the subject of our meeting first, or should I wait for him to do it? *This is dumb,* I think. *Why do I have to wait for him to ask me?*

*Argh!* I pick up the phone to ask my brother what he thinks I should do, but it goes straight to his voice mail. He and Sara are driving back from her sister's in Nashville, but they must be in a dead zone. I leave Scott a message, but I can't wait to hear back from him. *Oh well,* I think, *here goes nothing.* I hit Send.

A few minutes later, my phone rings, and I hear wind in the background. "Are you watching the game?" Scott asks.

"Yeah," I say. "Duh, it's nationally televised this week."

"Well don't tell me anything, okay? I'm taping it at home, and I wanna be able to watch it and not know what happens."

So I don't tell him that defensive tackle Montae Reagor is in the hospital. His car flipped over on the way to the game. Instead, I tell Scott about Max. "We've been e-mailing all week. I keep waiting for him to suggest we meet."

"Maybe suggest talking on the phone," he says. "Definitely do *not* suggest a meeting."

*Shit.* "Why?"

He tells me that he and Sara e-mailed back and forth for a week and then they spent a week or so talking on the phone. "I didn't want her to think I was moving too fast," Scott says. "I think that going right from e-mails to meeting is sort of weird."

"But that's what the first guy I met did, so I thought that was how it worked. Shit. The guy I like, the one with all the same interests, is being all pokey, and then I get stuff like this." I read him an e-mail I just received from a non-pokey guy:

Hi there! This is the reality of dating in late 30s early 40s: You're 38, I'm 41, we both want kids. Lets get together asap and see if there is any chemistry. . . . No time to waste! lol . . . so . . . how about it?

Scott laughs.

I sigh. "Anyway, it's too late. I already suggested we meet."

Scott says, "What'd you say?"

"I tried to make it casual, you know. I said I'd be up for meeting him. That he seemed like a nice guy, not a stalker."

"Cathy, what'd you say that for?" He actually sounds angry with me.

148

"What? Can't I make a joke?"

"You can't joke about stuff like that with people who don't know you."

I don't say anything. Of course he's right.

"Maybe he just wants to be an e-mail buddy," Scott offers.

*E-mail buddy?* "What's that?" I yell into the phone. "You mean there are men on this thing that don't actually want to date me, they just want to yak at me?"

He explains that Match isn't just about dating. There is an entirely different level of communication. "Sometimes people just talk," he says.

"What is the freaking point of that? I don't have time to keep up with my e-mail correspondence as it is, let alone chat with strange dudes I never intend to meet."

His voice is soft and consoling. "I'm just saying that sometimes guys are shy."

"This is complete crap!"

Thank God this is my brother and he knows I'm not really yelling at him, just yelling. "Cathy, it's okay," he says. And even though I'm upset, I feel strangely good, too. My brother and I are talking—about love and football—more than we have in years. Is my brother an expert on these subjects? No, but like most men, he likes to think he is, and I'm going along with this because I want him to be happy. And isn't this what loving someone is all about?

Just then, Peyton Manning turns into a pretzel right before my eyes. The Redskins' Andre Carter tackles his legs and Phillip Daniels takes his neck, and somehow, Peyton's white helmet pops off like a champagne cork. "Oh my God!" I yell.

"What?!" Scott says.

Peyton does a face-plant into the turf and for a second he doesn't move. In the RCA Dome, all over the state of Indiana, people hold their breath. Then he stands up, albeit with a swollen lip. "It's okay," I say. "Don't worry. It's okay."

"Something important just happened, didn't it?"

"Um . . . yeah."

"I can't stand it," Scott says to both me and Sara. I hear him turn on his satellite radio. A few seconds later, he says, "Holy crap! Is he okay?"

"He's up. He just took a time-out." Neither of us says anything for a minute. "Seriously, that was something, Scott. You gotta see it. He gets all twisty."

Later Peyton will tell reporters, "I did that my rookie year, got the wind knocked out of me in Baltimore, I took a time-out and (former coach Jim) Mora yelled at me and said I wasted a time-out. For me to call a time-out there means I needed another minute to kind of get it together."

Scott says good-bye, and I watch the rest of the game alone. Peyton's on fire in the third quarter, throwing three touchdown passes, and the Colts win 36–22. They're 6–0. It's the ninth time in NFL history that a team has gone 6–0 in back-to-back years. The *Indianapolis Star* sports page has a picture of Peyton rising after that hit, and a headline: "Smacked, Then Smokin'."

So if every Colts game is supposed to tell me something about life and how to live it, what's this week's message from the universe? That's easy: I've received an ugly hit, but I must rise from the turf, shake it off, and fight back.

Here's the ugly hit I'm talking about.

Two days ago, on Friday morning, I finally made the call I'd been dreading for weeks. Erica from Great Expectations said she would call me on October 11. That day had come and gone, so I dialed the number for GE in Pittsburgh. A recorded message said, "We're sorry. That number is no longer in service." For five minutes, I stomped around my house, cursing up a storm. My cat just blinked at me and yawned. Then I remembered that the last time Erica called, she phoned from home in Mt. Vernon. The number was still on my caller ID, and I got her voice mail. "Erica, this is Cathy Day, one of your GE clients. We were supposed to talk on October 11. I tried to call the office but the number is out of service, so I had to call this number. Please call me back as soon as possible."

I went on with my day. I tried not to think about it—which is a pretty hard thing for me to do. I caught the 54C to campus. At Craig and Forbes I got off the bus and walked toward the Cathedral, past the Carnegie Museum of Art. The trees surrounding the Cathedral were starting to turn, and orange leaves speckled the grass. It was a postcard kind of day, and as I walked through that perfect picture, a thought flashed into my head: *Three days ago, I was picking up barbecued pork at Wayne's Meats in Milan, Indiana, and now I'm here. This is really my life. I take a bus to work in an ivory tower across the street from an art museum.*

Inside the Cathedral I took the elevator to the fifth floor. I had a class to teach. When I was a shy little girl, if you told me that one day my job would be to stand in front of people and talk, I would have run screaming from the room. I started teaching for one simple reason: economic necessity. The University of Alabama said, "You want a degree? Teach our freshmen how to write and we'll not charge you for your tuition." So I became a teacher, and something miraculous happened. You know how there are some people who stutter except when they sing? Teaching was like that for me. I became this other person who wasn't shy at all. She walked purposefully into classrooms. She made students laugh as they flunked her quizzes. She turned on bright lightbulbs over (most of) their heads. God, I liked her, so much so that I wanted to be her all the time. I know not everyone believes in such a thing as a "calling." It smacks of religious fervor. It's old-fashioned and quaint. But it's the only way I can describe how I feel about the electric exchange of teaching.

When I got home from class that night, my voice-mail light was blinking. The caller ID said the number was private. "Hi Cathy, this is Bridget Rawlings calling on behalf of Great Expectations corporate office. I understand you've been talking to Erica about when you're able to take your photos and videos. I wanted to have her explain, but I'm happy to talk to you about this. It looks like we will be doing that photo shoot the last week of October or the first week of November. There was an issue with signing over the business papers. Now that's been rectified, and we're waiting to forward the lease, so we're all set. We're buying over the existing center. I'm in Hartford at that center." She gives me the number. "I would be happy to speak with you this weekend, or to perhaps give you a call on Saturday or Sunday. I look forward to speaking with you."

I listened to the message again. *What is this woman talking about? Why can't I call GE in Pittsburgh? Why does GE's corporate number come up on caller ID as private? What does a lease have to do with photography? And why didn't Erica call me? Is this Bridget person going to call me or am I supposed to call her?*

And then I did what I should have done months ago. I Googled "Great Expectations."

I discovered that several offices were being sued by the State of Pennsylvania for violating the state's Unfair Trade Practices and Consumer Protection Law. The attorney general, Tom Corbett, claimed that GE falsely inflated the number of singles available in its network and misrepresented the success rate and costs of its services. "Consumers paid significant sums of money for services and results that were grossly overstated and misrepresented," Corbett said. "The biggest draw for singles joining a dating service is clearly the number of other singles in the dating network. We allege that potential clients were deceived about the defendants' pool of available singles, creating false hopes about the odds of finding a match."

I clicked on "Complaints" and found dozens of testimonials from men and women just like me. Some of them were angry, some were embarrassed and sad. One woman wrote, "I will probably never meet anyone, even if it is just for coffee. I really can't believe I was so stupid. I just guess I was so lonely that I wasn't thinking right." A few former employees had written in to say, "Yes, this is a con."

I clicked on an article from Techdirt.com about two women in New York who successfully sued GE for a full refund. More interesting than the article itself were the comments left by readers.

Somebody has to ask. Were the women in question like big fat ugly sweathogs that nobody in the civilized world would even talk to much less want to date?

The article claims the judge said that they were "intelligent, well-spoken and attractive professional women."

Man, why don't these women just find me and buy me a car. I can be a good little man-whore and they can keep me in a manner I want to become accustomed to.

I was ata party a couple years back and talked with a girl who worked at one of those places. It might have even been GE.

The female profile tended toward professional women who had achieved managerial success to the point where they had priced themselves out of the mkt. i.e. They all wanted to marry guys who were more successful than they were, but the guys who were that driven and successful were picking up their potential trophy wives without 3rd party help.

There were thirty more comments, but I couldn't read anymore.

*No, no, no, no. This isn't happening to me,* I thought. I wanted a cigarette. I deserved a damn cigarette. I tried to remember the smart woman who got off the bus and taught a class, the woman who thinks Big Thoughts that other people write down in notebooks. Where the hell did she go? *That's it,* I thought. *I can't do this anymore. For reasons I cannot fathom, I somehow manage to keep losing at this game. It's illogical. It's unfair. I don't understand why this keeps happening to me.*

You need to know this: I took a time-out. I spent the rest of that night curled up in a ball on my bed. But I got up the next day and checked Match.com, and there was a new message from Max. There was still hope. It's like Vince Lombardi said, "It's not whether you get knocked down, it's whether you get up."

*Show me the money!*

—*Jerry Maguire*

---

# WEEK 8: COLTS @ BRONCOS

## OR

# When the Going Gets Tough

---

Three days later I finally pick up the phone. *Wait,* I think, *hold on. Think about what you're going to say, Cathy. Get a game plan.* I have always had a bit of phone phobia; I really don't like making calls. So I write down a few talking points. Then I dial the number.

A woman's cheerful voice answers. "Hello, Great Expectations."

"May I speak to Bridget Rawlings, please?"

The woman sounds momentarily confused. "Oh! You mean Gidgie! May I ask who is calling, please?"

"This is Cathy Day in Pittsburgh. She called me on Friday."

"One minute, please."

The call is transferred.

"Cathy! So good to hear from you! Did you try to call me this weekend?"

"Uh, no. I didn't think you'd be there over the weekend, so I waited until this week."

Gidgie insists they're there seven days a week, although this information was not clear in her voice-mail message.

So I say, "Well, anyway, I understood your message to say that you were going to call *me* back."

There's a brief pause, and she changes the subject. "Yes, well, I'm so sorry about the delay in getting your pictures and videos taken."

"Yes, what is the problem? I don't understand."

Gidgie launches once again into her explanation about franchises and transitions.

"Look," I say, "I don't understand what any of that has to do with getting my pictures taken or why the phone number at the office has been disconnected. Does this have anything to do with the lawsuit against your Philadelphia office?"

A long pause. "No, not at all! We're just having all kinds of problems with this franchise changeover. It's very complicated. But I understand that you're eager to get started. I'd like to offer you more time on your membership."

The last thing I want right now is more time on my membership. "It seems to me that Polly and Erica *knew* that they wouldn't be able to deliver the services they promised right away. They should have told me to come back when this franchise stuff was all ironed out." Searching for an analogy, I look up and see my television. "It seems to me that if you sell somebody a television when you know beforehand you don't have any televisions in stock, that's unethical. Or if you sell someone a television on good faith, and then realize you don't have any televisions in stock, you should be honest with the customer and say, 'Hey, we're out of televisions.' I should be given the option to wait or get a refund and go to another store and buy it. You know, maybe I really need a television right away." I take a breath. *You're rambling, Cathy. Stop talking about televisions.* "My point is that if you don't have the product or the service to offer, but you sell it anyway, that's wrong."

Gidgie uses her calming voice. "I understand you're upset right now. I really do. I really want to make this right." She repeats her offer to extend my membership.

I try to picture this woman. Is she sitting in a real office, painted mauve and pink? Or is she sitting in her kitchen? Or in an office building on a Connecticut highway with a "For Lease" sign in the window? "Ma'am, at this point, I don't even think you are a legitimate business, and I would like to get my money back."

"Cathy, I understand you're upset right now. I understand how it must seem from your end. But I assure you, this is a great company." She says this so convincingly that I actually believe her.

For the last five minutes, I've been walking in circles through my house—living room, dining room, kitchen, hallway, repeat. I'm wearing my pajamas. In the foyer mirror, I see I have raccoon eyes, and I feel so ugly, so small, so stupid. A voice inside me says, *You are a college professor! You are a writer! You are no dummy, and they are taking advantage of you. You aren't going to let them get away with this, are you?* Briefly, Julia Roberts in *Erin Brockovich* comes to my mind. Then Lesley Stahl on *60 Minutes*. Then Christiane Amanpour on CNN. That's when it hits me: *Pretend you're an investigative journalist, Cathy!* "Ma'am, I should mention that I'm a writer." To prove that I'm really a writer, I give her my Web site address, where, no doubt, she will become deeply afraid when she realizes that I wrote a book about clowns. "Gidgie, I think you should do whatever you can to rectify this situation and save a bit of your reputation."

Long pause. Gidgie's tone has a bite now, and when she says again, "I understand you're upset right now," it's obvious she no longer means it. "I will talk to my boss and call you back before five PM today."

"Yes, please do."

Click.


As soon as I hang up, I call my parents and explain. Immediately, they say, "Call a lawyer."

Amazing. I never thought of this. I kept insisting to Gidgie that the situation was unethical—it never occurred to me that maybe it was illegal. I tell my folks, "I feel so stupid."

"Oh, don't feel stupid," Dad says. "Did Mom ever tell you about the encyclopedias?"

I remember them well, I say. I used to read them in bed at night.

"That salesman came to the house when you were just a baby and asked Mom, 'Don't you want your daughter here to grow up to be smart?' And she said, 'Of course I do!' And he said that the encyclopedias were free and all we'd have to do is buy one yearbook each year, but the yearbooks were like five hundred dollars each, and she'd signed the contract saying she'd buy them." In the background, I can hear one of them emptying the dishwasher. Dad goes on. "The salesman saw your mom sitting there, a young mother with a brand-new baby, and knew exactly what to say, just what she'd want to hear. That's what they did to you, too."

"I feel sick."

Dad has put me on speakerphone, and Mom pipes up. "You feel violated!"

I can hear Clay yelling. They're babysitting today. "What's he doing?" I ask.

"He's jumping, or trying to jump," Mom says. "Basically he just throws up his hands and stands there."

"Clay!" I say into the phone. "Mr. Man! How's my best boy?"

"He's smiling," Dad says.

God, I'd give anything to be standing in my parents' kitchen right now. I start singing (badly) an old Cole Porter tune, "Ev'ry Time We Say Good-bye." I've been singing it to Clay in person and over the phone since he was born. It's certainly not a lullaby, but for some reason, he loves it. It's pretty weird to sing a torch song to your nephew, even weirder when you consider it was written by a man pining away for another man. But who cares? Clay always smiles and calms down when he hears it.

My mom pipes up. "How can they get away with this?"

Curled up in a ball on my bed, I think about his question. "Shame," I say. "Their customers feel shame, and they take advantage of that. It's like if you bought some illegal porn and didn't get what you ordered, what are you gonna do, call the Better Business Bureau?"

Dad says, "Call your lawyer and your credit-card company."

"Okay, I will."

Click.

The customer-service guy at American Express listens to my so-called fraudulent charge story. In an unruffled voice, he says I need to contact Great Expectations and find out for sure if they intend to refund my money.

So I call my lawyer, Paul. As I tell him the story, he does a Google search for Great Expectations and finds the same consumer-affairs Web site that I did. Paul says he used to work at the Pennsylvania attorney general's office, and he reads the press release out loud on the phone while I pace around the room. My life has been full of excruciatingly embarrassing moments, but listening to my lawyer read sentences like this is more than I can bear: "In some instances, Great Expectations compared its singles services to 'being a kid in a candy store.'"

"Oh, God!" I moan.

Paul continues. "Consumers typically paid between one thousand and three thousand four hundred dollars for their memberships." He pauses and asks, "How much did you give them?" he asks.

"Um . . . uh . . . almost sixteen hundred dollars."

"Oh! That's a lot. I was thinking you were going to say a few hundred dollars. But you know, Cathy, it's still not enough money to warrant hiring a lawyer." He's quiet for a moment, reading to himself. "Okay, here's the number for the Bureau of Consumer Protection." Paul reads the number out to me.

I write down the number. "Do you think I should call them back today? They said they'd call me back by five PM."

Paul sighs. "You can try, but they probably won't take your call, and that will just frustrate you. Write a letter. Tell them you've spoken to an attorney and that they have ten days to refund your money for failure to render services or you'll file a small-claims case. Put them officially on notice."

I write all this down, too. "I feel so stupid, Paul."

"Don't be!" he says. "I mean, if I hadn't found my wife in graduate school, this could be me. I can completely understand why you'd feel like this was a better option for you than the Internet. I've heard a lot of stories from professional women going through this same thing, trying to figure out a discreet way to meet people."

"Really?" This makes me feel so much better, and for a second I wonder if, somewhere in Pittsburgh, there's another woman just like me who finally worked up the nerve to walk into Great Expectations but was too ashamed to try and get her money back.

"Yes, really," Paul says. "You know, I remember when you first came in here, I couldn't figure out why it would be hard for a woman like yourself to meet someone. You work at a university. But I guess that as a professor, you work with people who have already found their partners. There aren't that many opportunities for you to mingle with other single people, unless they're students." He tells me there's a social organization in Pittsburgh of Jewish singles under forty, organized through local synagogues.

I sigh. "I know, but I'm not Jewish. There's this book I've been reading called *Bowling Alone,* about how nobody belongs to anything anymore. The workplace has become our biggest means of social interaction."

It's sort of odd to be talking to my lawyer about this, but he seems genuinely interested in my plight. He says, "You know, I was born here in Pittsburgh, and every day I run into people I know. If I was single, it would be relatively easy to tell people that I was interested in dating. I probably wouldn't even have to say anything." He laughs. "It's got to be harder for you, coming to a place where you don't know anyone."

"Yeah, it is," I say. "Most of the people I've met in Pittsburgh so far are colleagues or people like you, my lawyer, my doctor, people I have a professional relationship with. You stick out your hand and say . . . what do you say? *Hi, I'm Cathy Day, nice meeting you. Are you married? Oh, well, do you know anyone who isn't?*" I laugh at this.

"I'm sure it's a bit awkward." There's a pause. "Well, I really do wish you luck, Cathy."

I sigh. "I'll keep you posted."

Click.


I call the Bureau of Consumer Protection. A woman answers the phone, and when I try to explain why I'm calling, she cuts me off. "If you tell me your name and address, I'll send you a form and it will be turned over to an agent."

"Okay," I say. I give her the information.

Click.


Then I call my parents back. It's three o'clock, and I've been on the phone all day. Mom says, "This is just a lesson you're learning about listening to your gut. Your gut told you it was a scam, but you didn't listen to your gut."

"I thought it was my *fear* talking to me. How am I supposed to know when it's my gut and when it's my fear?" I look at myself in the bathroom mirror. I'm still in my pajamas. I still have raccoon eyes. "For so long, when I thought about dating, all I *felt* was fear. So now I'm trying to stay positive and quiet the judgmental voice in my head." I've wandered downstairs to my kitchen, although I have no idea why. "Mom, I feel like I've spent my whole life making the wrong choices. You say 'Listen to your gut,' but why the hell should I?"

"What do you mean?"

I go through a list of men I've dated in my lifetime. "Every single time, I followed my gut."

"Well, then if you're choosing wrong, you need to start picking the kind of men you don't normally pay attention to."

"So now you're telling me *not* to follow my gut. Make up your mind. Which is it?" My mom hates it when you raise your voice to her, so I take a deep breath. "I've tried that anyway, Mom. I knew within a half hour of meeting that guy Nick that he wasn't right for me, but I thought, well my gut is telling me *no,* and my gut is always wrong, so I'll do the opposite of what my gut tells me and date this guy. And three months later, I came to the same conclusion I made in that first half hour. But I wasted my time and his and probably got his hopes up about me. But I tried anyway, just to see if my gut was wrong."

"What you need is to learn discernment. You need some guidelines to discern between your gut and your fear."

"Tell me please, where are those guidelines!"

Mom sighs. "Don't be smart."

"I'm sorry. I just really want to know. Everything I feel, every thought in my head, I don't trust any of it anymore. I can't stand it." My voice shakes, and I feel the tears rising up inside me. "What am I supposed to do?"

In the background, I can hear Clay crying. "Hold on," she says, then comes back to the phone. "He wanted me to blow his nose. He needs some Little Noses." She sighs. "You're on the verge of a big breakthrough, honey. I just know it."

"What breakthrough?" I ask, my voice quivering. "From what to what?"

"I don't know exactly, but you'll know it when it happens."

"I want a cigarette," I say. "I'm going to take a nap."

"Go take a nap, honey."

Click.


I wake up around seven and wash my face. Then I sit down at my computer and write the letter my lawyer told me to. That's when I realize I don't know Polly's last name. She scrawled it on my contract, but I can't make it out. Then I remember the story she told me about her father's death on September 11. It makes me sick to my stomach, but I enter those details into Google's search engine, along with the name "Polly," and boom, I've got her last name—from a comment she once left on a discussion board for family members of 9/11 victims.

The first two paragraphs of the letter calmly recount the history of my experience with Great Expectations. But I can't maintain that neutral tone:

> It is my suspicion that the popularity of online dating sites has resulted in a decline in your memberships and the company is struggling financially. It is my suspicion that your employees were well aware of this when they sold me my membership and that they knew they would not be able to render the services I purchased. Taking advantage of lonely people is a truly despicable thing. I got to know Polly and Erica during my time in the office, and I think that my disappointment in them personally almost outweighs my anger at your company.

I tell them I've contacted a lawyer and the Bureau of Consumer Protection, and that I want a refund in ten days. I close by reminding them again that I am a published writer, and that for the sake of their reputation, they should refund my money. I hit Print. An hour later, I call it a day and go to bed. I'm still wearing my pajamas.


You need to know this: I don't give up. I keep trying.

I go to lunch with a very nice woman I met when I visited a local book group. She says, "Surely it can't be that hard to find a nice man in Pittsburgh!" I point out that she's been married for over twenty years. She asks, "Do you mind if I tell some of the women in the group you're looking?" Do I mind? I would give anything to meet a nice man via one of those wonderful women rather than pay $1,595! "Wait!" she says. "I know just the guy! He's a carpenter, but really, he's more of a philosopher." She gives him my vital data, but I never hear from him.

I keep checking my Match account. Max the Indie Music Guy finally responds to my suggestion that we meet and asks me out for coffee—in ten days. I tell my friend Janet, "I'm a busy girl, too, but what? In a week and a half, he doesn't have a half hour for coffee?" Janet says, "Maybe he wants to lose ten pounds before he meets you."

I e-mail Chris the Rocker, the guy whose picture I remember from Chemistry. "So you play guitar?" I ask. "Not anymore," he confesses. His profile said he was in graduate school, so I ask him where. "Pitt," he says. Uh-oh. Then he confesses that he isn't a grad student quite yet, he's *applying* to graduate school and currently finishing his second undergraduate degree. He mentions a class assignment on autoethnography that's giving him fits. Personally, I've never understood the difference between autoethnography (a popular term amongst my colleagues) and plain old memoir, so I ask Chris the Rocker if he knows the difference. He says that autoethnography is a personal account of one's experiences as an outsider in a culture, a more difficult form than "plain old memoir."

He names the book his class is reading. I know this book. The Punter carried it with him frequently. No . . . it's not possible. I e-mail Chris the Rocker and ask, "Who's your professor?"

Yep. You got it.

The same day (I'm serious, the same day), I get an e-mail from the dean's office. The subject line reads: "Faculty Awareness of University Policies on Sexual Harassment and Faculty-Student Relationships." It's a mass e-mail sent to all faculty members. Instead of visiting Human Resources to watch a video or attend a seminar, the university wants me to take an online course to make sure I understand the rules of (non)engagement. So I take the course. There's no policy (yet) on what a faculty member should do when she unwittingly encounters students on Internet dating sites. And there's definitely not a policy about what she should do when she discovers this student is currently enrolled in a class with her former Pretend Boyfriend. Instead, I am offered pearls such as: "The best policy is always to avoid touching someone else unless you are absolutely sure it is welcome," and "This fact is critically important. The statement, 'I didn't mean anything by it,' is not a valid defense of harassing behavior." So I pass the test with flying colors and print out a signed certificate of completion. Then I send an e-mail to Chris the Rocker via Match.com telling him I can't communicate with him anymore.


Maybe it's time to leave these virtual spaces and try a *real* meeting place: a Pittsburgh sports bar on a Sunday afternoon during a Steelers game. My friend Phillip (the guy who offered me the Pirates tickets I couldn't use) asks me to meet him and his friends Quincy (the lawyer) and Marcus (the doctor) at Buffalo Blues on Highland Avenue in Shadyside. All of these men are happily married and my father's age. They're parked at the bar, waiting for the game to start. Marcus is eating a hamburger, and Quincy is reading that day's *New York Times*. I point to the magazine inside, which features a Michael Lewis interview with Dallas Cowboys' coach Bill Parcells. "Did you read that?" I ask, pointing to Bill's face.

"Not yet," Quincy says.

"It's really interesting," I say. In the interview, Parcells discusses his interest in the psychology of his players, namely what he calls "game quitters." To illustrate his point, Parcells tells a story about a thirty-year-old boxing match between the middleweights Vito Antuofermo and Cyclone Hart. In this story, Antuofermo wins the fight by a knockout and afterward, in the locker room, he tells his cornerman, "Every time [Hart] hit me with that left hook to the body, I was sure I was going to quit. After the second round, I thought if he hit me there again, I'd quit. I thought the same thing after the fourth round. Then he didn't hit me no more." Cyclone Hart overhears this admission and begins to weep, realizing that they'd both felt the same physical pain and exhaustion. The only difference between them was this one intangible thing, call it what you like. The will to win. The heart of a champion. The eye of the tiger. The indomitable spirit of man. Nerves of steel. If you could bottle this ineffable substance, you could probably save the whole world. I ask Quincy, "Do you think that's what it is? What determines who will win this game?" I gesture to the large-screen television above our head, where the Steelers and the Oakland Raiders are preparing to take the field.

Quincy takes a sip of his beer. "I think it's a bunch of different things all at once."

I order my second beer. "I've been thinking a lot about this lately and about how it's like love. How much are these things within a person's ability to control? Or is it all just random dumb luck, you know?"

Quincy smiles. "Phil said you were a writer."

I wave my hand. "Yeah, sorry. I'm not so good with small talk."

He ponders the football players on the screen. Then he says, "It's like a car crash. Think about it," he says. "A bunch of tiny things have to go wrong in order to cause a car crash. How many times have you caught yourself falling asleep or accidentally going through a red light, and you think, *Boy, it's a good thing no one else was around.*" Quincy points to the TV. "The players think they're working hard, but sometimes there's something missing, a small slip they can't even feel or see, and when you get enough players doing that, the whole game can turn."

I'm nodding. "Winning, it's like a miracle. A bunch of people all being 'on' at the same time."

Quincy turns on his barstool and stares over my shoulder through the window. "I think about how I met my wife. I could have turned this way instead of that way. I could have gone to a different college and not met her. Or I could have met her when I wasn't really ready to meet her, you know? You can't control it. You can't force it. And if you spend too much time thinking about how to 'make it happen,' you'll drive yourself crazy."

"I know," I say. "Believe me, I know."

Quincy smiles at me again. His eyes are full of mirth and sympathy.

I notice that they're showing the Colts game at Mile High Stadium in Denver on one of the smaller screens, but it's at the other end of the bar. There's one barstool open in front of that TV. I say good-bye to Phil and Quincy and Marcus and sit down with my beer between two very young men. The chain-smoker on my right is rooting for Indianapolis, too, but not because he's from there. "I got a lot of money on this game, and I need my man Tony to pull this one out, ain't that right?" He bumps knuckles with his buddy sitting next to him. They've also got a big bet down on the Raiders.

"You're gonna root for the Raiders? *In here?*" I say.

The three of us scan the room. They're the only black men in a bar full of white guys in Steelers jerseys.

He shrugs. "Don't bother me."

The guy on my left is wearing a Broncos jersey and tells me he was born in Denver.

I smile. "I was born in Indiana."

"Whatever," he says, shrugging his shoulders. "Denver's won thirteen home games in a row. They ain't gonna lose today."

I shrug my shoulders, too. "Whatever." And that's the last thing he and I have to say to each other for the next three hours.

The Steelers are 2–4. The Raiders are 1–5. What a shame that the majority of screens at Buffalo Blues are tuned to this mediocre game that the Steelers lose anyway. The real excitement, the real nail-biter, unfolds on one little screen in the corner of the bar, a game being watched by four people. At halftime the Colts are down 14–6, but the second half—oh, that second half—is magical. Peyton connects with wide receiver Reggie Wayne for three touchdowns. The bettors and I exchange high fives, and I show them that underneath my baggy sweater, I'm wearing a Colts T-shirt. One points at my head and proclaims loudly, "This girl here's my good-luck charm!"

The Broncos guy on my left drinks his beer glumly until the end of the fourth quarter, when Denver's Jason Elam kicks a 49-yard field goal to tie the game at 31–31. "Yes!" he screams, raising his arms. He's the only one in the whole bar cheering for the Broncos, and the bettors and I are the only ones cheering for the Colts.

There's only 1:49 remaining. The Colts need to get in field-goal range. The Broncos have one of the best defenses in the NFL. There are 75,000 Denver fans rocking the house; reporters say they can feel the press box shaking. And the completely unruffled Peyton Manning marches the Colts downfield, no problem. Eight plays, 62 yards. Bingo. With two seconds left, Adam Vinatieri comes onto the field to attempt a 37-yard field goal.

"Miss it!" the Broncos guy yells.

"Make it!" the bettors yell.

The remaining patrons, all Steelers fans, turn their weary heads to our screen. Phillip and Quincy and Marcus have given up on watching the Steelers game and stand behind my barstool.

Vinatieri kicks. Right through the uprights! Colts win! They are the second team in NFL history to go 7–0 in two consecutive seasons! The Broncos fan throws a couple of singles on the bar and walks away. The bettors start making calls on their cell phones.

I order another Yuengling. God, this is the best I've felt all week. Three hours have gone by, during which time I was completely absorbed by the game. I didn't think once about Gidgie or Polly or Max the Indie Music Guy or Chris the Rocker. I didn't worry about the difference between my gut and my fear. Even if Vinatieri had missed that kick, even if the Colts had lost, I would still be thankful for the pure joy of those three hours.

Phillip puts his hand on my shoulder. "Great way to meet a fellow, watching the wrong game," he says.

"I don't care. I had fun," I say. I raise my glass to Quincy. "If you spend all your time trying to 'make it happen,' you drive yourself crazy."

> Sometimes, getting up in the morning and brushing your teeth is the hardest part of the day—it all just hurts.
>
> —Tom Brady

## WEEK 9: COLTS @ PATRIOTS

OR

# A Good Old-Fashioned Locker-Room Speech

Every move Peyton Manning makes (or fails to make) on the gridiron is scrutinized—by the coaching staff, by football fans, by the massive sports media complex. Millions of words have been spoken, written, and broadcast to assess the performance and psychology of this single human being. But I'll bet that Peyton Manning is harder on himself than any Monday-morning quarterback. We all love to criticize a player's performance after the fact. Case in point: it's Monday morning; the Colts won against the Broncos last night, and, depending on how you look at it, I sort of won (because I enjoyed myself immensely) but I also sort of lost (because I didn't meet any potential suitors in a bar full of male sports fans). Monday morning, I get a new message on Match.

Ok, as crazy as this sounds . . . you didn't happen to be out watching the Steelers game last night, did u? I was in Pittsburgh and saw someone that looked incredibly like you and I was like "no way" lol. Anyway, I was staring and this poor woman (unless it was you) had to be thinking "he's nuts" lol. anyway, have a great day!

I write the Sports Bar Staring Guy back, and say yes, that was me if he was at Buffalo Blues. He replies.

lol . . . how strange is that, lol???? have to say that u look even better in person (wink). anyway, it was great to see you.


My mom calls me, and I tell her this story.

"Maybe you shouldn't have watched the Colts game. Maybe you should have watched the Steelers game like everyone else, and then you would have noticed that guy looking at you. Maybe then he would have come up and talked to you."

"Mom, you told me to listen to my gut, and my gut told me to watch that Colts game and not worry so much."

"It just seems like such a missed opportunity." She sighs.

I'm so frustrated, I can't stand it. "Look, Mom, I did my part. I hauled my ass out to a public place crawling with men. It's not my fault that dude didn't have the nerve to come up and talk to me."

"Don't get smart with me . . ." Mom says.

My sister calls, and I tell her the story.

"Why didn't you sound more excited when he wrote to you? He says he thinks you're cute."

"Andi, I've seen this guy's profile. He's not my type."

"Why not?"

I sigh. "He doesn't live in Pittsburgh. He's conservative and he said he doesn't read. And he's not even technically divorced yet."

"Well, it would have been a great story to tell about how you met."

"I know," I tell her, "I love a good story as much as the next girl, but that's not reason enough to date someone."

My brother Scott calls, and I tell him this story.

"Did you see Peyton in the last two minutes of that game?" he says. "He's so amazing. But their run defense still sucks."

God, I love my brother.

You need to know this: I'm playing this game called love to the best of my ability, and you can do your Monday-morning quarterback thing on me, scrutinize my performance and my psychology all you want, but it doesn't equal the pressure I put on myself every minute of every day. For example, everyone says love happens when you're not expecting it—the Don't Try strategy. I used that approach for years without any results, so I decide to do the exact opposite: the Try Everything strategy. Do you know how logistically difficult and emotionally exhausting it is to literally try everything? Actually, it's sort of impossible. So one night, my instincts tell me "Stop trying everything," so I follow my instincts and stop trying for three lousy hours, and what happens? Of course, a man notices me, but I'm not paying attention because I'm not trying. Okay, so he wasn't my dream partner, but the point is, I think the universe is trying to tell me something. It's saying, *Pay attention, Cathy. Don't stop trying.*

But I'm absolutely sick of trying.

What I need is a good old-fashioned locker-room speech, and I know just the one.

In order to enact the Try Everything strategy, I need to take advantage of every possibility. It's like the "Inches" philosophy Al Pacino advocates in *Any Given Sunday.* In his final locker-room speech, he says to his team:

Life's this game of inches, so is football. Because in either game—life or football—the margin for error is so small. I mean, one half a step too late or too early, and you don't quite make it. One half second too slow, too fast, and you don't quite catch it. The inches we need are everywhere around us. . . . That's what living is, the six inches in front of your face.

You need to know this: sometimes when I'm feeling low, I'll look up a bunch of locker-room speeches on YouTube to get myself going again. Or I'll break out a DVD and skip right to the locker-room speech, like a guy fast-forwarding to his favorite scene in his favorite porn. My money shot? A passionate pep talk delivered to a bunch of sweaty men, carefully crafted to incite emotion in the hearts of the viewing audience. The rhetorical strategy follows a tried-and-true formula, with slight variations. First, the soft strands of orchestrated music stirring in the background. Then the bowed heads of the assembled players. They are tired. They are nervous. They need guidance. They need a metaphor. The camera focuses on the coach, who begins with a general status overview and then moves into "the plan," conveyed allegorically in phrases that turn slowly into a refrain.

Sometimes the coach's plan is delivered quietly, like before the last game in *Hoosiers,* when Gene Hackman says, "Well, we're way past big-speech time," and allows the players to speak instead, followed by a reading from the Bible, a short passage about David and Goliath. Sometimes the plan is delivered in a quiet voice that builds into a roaring fire, like Pacino's "Inches" speech or Kurt Russell's "Our Time" speech in the hockey film *Miracle*:

> Tonight, *we* are the greatest hockey team in the world. You were born to be hockey players. Every one of you. And you were meant to be here tonight. This is your time! Their time is done. It's over. I'm sick and tired of hearing about what a great hockey team the Soviets have. Screw 'em. This is your time. Now go out there and take it!

Sometimes the plan is delivered with easy-to-remember simplicity, like Keanu Reeves's words to his team in *The Replacements*: "Pain heals. Chicks dig scars. Glory lasts forever."

As with everything else in life, real locker-room speeches rarely live up to their cinematic counterparts. Former Indiana University basketball coach Bobby Knight is famous for browbeating his players in the locker room. In John Feinstein's classic book *Season on the Brink*, Knight delivers this little motivational speech to former IU player Daryl Thomas:

> Daryl, look at that. You don't even run back down the floor hard. That's all I need to know about you, Daryl. . . . You know what you are, Daryl? You are the worst f—— pussy I've ever seen play basketball at this school . . . that's my assessment of you after three years.

Notre Dame's Knute Rockne gave locker-room speeches that seem ridiculously cornball in this day and age: "We're going inside 'em, we're going outside 'em. Inside 'em outside 'em. . . . They can't lick us 'cause we're going to get in there and fight, fight, fight, fight, fight. What do you say, men?" Steelers' coach Bill Cowher began referencing, strangely enough, Christopher Columbus during the 2005 season. It became clear that in order to make it to the Super Bowl, the Steelers would need to make an improbable journey into uncharted waters: win every single upcoming game, almost all on the road. "Everyone thought Columbus was crazy," Cowher said to his assembled team, "but he sailed anyway and discovered America." And magically, the Steelers kept winning. So Cowher stuck with Columbus, although the metaphor started to break down as he ran out of grammar-school-gleaned information. One week Cowher said it was time to get out the periscope, and the players laughed and asked, "Coach, are we on a submarine or a ship?" But it worked. The Steelers' rallying cry in the weeks leading up to the Super Bowl became "Let's do it for Chris, man! Win one for Chris!"

Locker-room speeches are stirring and sentimental, and if you're the cynical sort, you probably hate them. But if you're a person willing to embrace your inner sap, then I'll bet you love locker-room speeches, too. We all have some kind of fire in our belly, but we can't always light it all by ourselves. We need inspiration. We need just the right metaphor, just the right words, and bingo! The flames roar. I call this inspiration "a locker-room speech," but it can take many forms. It can be an impassioned closing argument or a Senate filibuster speech, real or fictional. It can be an address to thousands of troops preparing for war or to a memorial gathering in a small Pennsylvania town after a battle. It can inspire a whole nation or a single person. It can be a particular song, a powerful image, the smell of napalm in the morning, a Nobel Prize acceptance speech, a Bible verse, or a story your grandmother once told you. A locker-room speech is anything that moves and inspires you.

The written word is nothing more than squiggles on a page, and yet those squiggles have the power to produce physiological responses in the human body. I learned this lesson early and I've never, ever forgotten it. Once I approached my eighth-grade English teacher and told her I wanted to read some serious books, the kind of books that would prepare me for college. But I didn't know what those books might be. She smiled and handed me the Bantam Classics catalog. "Pick out anything you want, and I'll order them for you." I had no idea what to choose, so I picked the ones with the prettiest covers. That's how I came to be reading George Eliot's *Silas Marner*. I was lying on my bed when I came across this passage:

In old days there were angels who came and took men by the hand and led them away from the city of destruction. We see no white-winged angels now. But yet men are led away from threatening destruction: a hand is put into theirs, which leads them forth gently towards a calm and bright land, so that they look no more backward; and the hand may be a little child's.

For a moment, I felt like I was floating an inch off my bed. I decided then and there that *that* was what I wanted to do—write words and sentences that would make other people feel something. I guess you could say that in a way, all I ever wanted to do was write locker-room speeches.

I have a new friend. Her name is Laura, and she's my new hero. She's an Eagles fan, but not because her husband, Ben, is. She's an Eagles fan because *she* is. By day she's an academic, like me, but she also knows a heck of a lot about love and football. Perhaps because she played college sports, Laura talks to me like she's the bossy, benevolent coach and I'm the quarterback who can't quite get her head in the game. Over dinner at Lulu's Noodles on Craig Street, Laura asks me to update her on my season so far. I opt not to tell her about my troubles with Great Expectations. I'm afraid she'll think I'm an idiot. Instead I tell her about Nick the Medic, Dom the Carpenter, Rick the $99 Date, Stan Who Sleeps at His Mom's House, Chris the Rocker, and Sports Bar Staring Guy. I tell her about a new guy on Match I e-mailed with the night before, the Baby Guy, an attractive dark-haired professional. Most of his pictures were of him with an infant, and in his profile he said his son was part of the package.

"His wife must have just died," Laura says matter-of-factly. "That's horrible, but he's probably looking for someone to help relieve him of single parenthood. Smart guy. I'll bet women on Match just gobbled him up."

*Of course!* "I e-mailed him pretty quickly," I tell her, "but he said he'd already met someone. I was kind of disappointed."

"Don't be," Laura says, shaking her head. "Who are you interested in now?" I'm both relieved to talk about this with another woman my age (who is not my relative) and horribly uncomfortable to talk about this with another woman my age (who is a colleague). But Laura seems genuinely interested, so I tell her everything I know about Max the Indie Music Guy. "You're really into him, huh? That's good. Anybody else?" I tell her about Patrick the Hemingway Fan, who e-mails me frequently and wants to meet soon.

"But I've been putting him off," I say. "I want to meet Max first."

"Why?" she asks.

I shrug. "I dunno. I'm more interested in Max than Patrick."

Unlike my sister and my mom, Laura doesn't ask me to think about *why* I like Max better than Patrick. She doesn't ask me to tell her what my gut's telling me and then suggest I do the exact opposite of that. Laura's philosophy seems to be that your gut's your gut and there's not a hell of a lot you can do about it. But she does have advice for me. "So of course the guy you're intrigued by doesn't want to see you for ten days and the guy you're sort of iffy about is the one who wants to see you right away. Of course! But let me tell you something." Laura pauses and leans over toward me. "I know you want to, but don't wait around for this Max guy. You gotta go with what's in front of you. And who wants to go out with you right now? Patrick, that's who." Laura forks up some pad thai and gestures with it. "Aren't you just sick and tired of liking guys who can't decide if they like you or not?"

"Yeah!" I say too loudly. Some students sitting at the next table look over.

"They never send the right signals."

"I know!"

"But you keep watching soooo hard, waiting. And after a while, *everything* starts looking like a signal."

"Right!"

She finishes her bite and continues. "Let me tell you the most important thing I've learned about relationships." Laura pauses for effect, and I'm literally holding my breath. "You have to wait for the man who is going to be invested in you and the relationship at least as much as you." She holds her two hands palm upward to represent a balanced scale. "If the woman's the one who's the most invested, he just . . ." One hand sinks below the table.

"Wow." I take a big pull on my bubble tea. "How do you know all this stuff?"

She smiles. "I learned the hard way, just like everybody else."

Sometimes I have to remind myself that married people haven't always been married, that once they went through this same crap, too.

"Tell you what," Laura says. "Contact both these guys and try to set something up with each one this week. See what happens."

Of course, I e-mail Max the Indie Music Guy first, but he says he has to work all week, and he's getting over a cold. "How about Sunday at eight PM?" he suggests. The Colts are playing the Patriots at that time. I have a DVR, yes, but why do we have to meet so late on a Sunday night? So I write him back and say, "How about six PM?" and I give him my phone number. I don't hear anything in response. The week before, we were e-mailing every day or so about bands and books, and now that I actually want to talk to him, he's disappeared.

Of course, Patrick the Hemingway Fan is happy to meet me, so I do— on Friday at a coffee shop on the South Side. Patrick's nice, he's smart. He just got out of the armed services, but surprisingly, he's not a rah-rah-America-love-it-or-leave-it conservative. He just got a job at a local non-profit, and he's originally from Pittsburgh. He's not weird or squirrelly. He asks me good questions and actually listens to my answers. At the end of our meeting, Patrick says, "You know, I think you're the first woman I've met *on the Internet* . . ." He whispers those three words and looks around, as if we're doing something illegal. ". . . that I think I might actually have something in common with. Can I see you again?"

As I walk down Carson Street toward my car, I call Laura to let her know I haven't been raped or kidnapped.

"How'd it go?"

"Fine. Okay," I say.

"Does he want to see you again?"

"Yep."

"Do you want to see him again?"

I pause. "Yes and no."

"Well, if it wasn't a terrible time, which it doesn't sound like it was, I think you should see him again, just to be sure. He might grow on you."

"Yeah, maybe." I unlock my car and get inside. "Man, I wish I liked him. Why don't I like him? Why don't I ever like the ones who like me?"

174

"I don't know, Cathy. It's the great mystery of life."

"This always happens to me!"

Laura goes into coach mode. "You don't know what's going to happen. You're going to see Max Sunday, right?"

"I don't know. He never wrote me back."

"So do you have a date or not?"

"I don't know!"

"God, that's rude. Weren't you thinking about having people over to your house Sunday to watch the Patriots game?"

"Yeah!" I'm still sitting in my car.

"How are you supposed to know if you can have a party until this dork lets you know if he's gonna buy you a cup of coffee or not?"

"Yeah! I know!"

"Schmoo head. I don't like him anymore. Can you call him?"

"He never gave me his number."

"You go home right now and e-mail him!"

"I will!"

And I do. I drive straight home to e-mail Max. But before I can, I find another message in my inbox. It's an official letter from Great Expectations, dismissing my "accusations and suspicions," and explaining that the franchise has been going through some kind of transfer, which, along with "extemporaneous legal and operational delays" sent the business into limbo. The guy insists that GE is financially stable and able to provide me the promised services, but I'm past the point of believing anymore. He says that, contrary to my theory, the proliferation of online dating services has increased GE's business, "as people realize the virtual dating world is full of fakers, frauds, married individuals, and predators." Well, maybe he's right on that one. He shrugs off the Philadelphia lawsuit as an isolated incident being exacerbated by attorneys hoping for a big class-action payday, and then he offers me access to members in other, non-Pittsburgh locations, in case I want "someone available for dinner, conversation, or a night on the town" to "ease the stress" when I am on the road traveling. Of course! What am I thinking, taking my parents on the road with me to readings? What I really need is a hired gigolo.

I'm informed that, by asking for a refund, I'd be taking money directly from Polly's pocket, and she's left the company for "personal reasons, for which she was heartbroken."

Oh boy. There's no friggin' way I'm getting my money back.

I sit at my desk for a few minutes. I read the letter again. And again. I consider calling Laura or Janet, but I can't. I'm too embarrassed to tell them this has happened to me. I can't bear to talk to Paul, my lawyer, about it anymore. So I forward it to Jillian in Oregon. I think, *Jill's ex-husband is a lawyer,* which makes her both a good friend and my next-best legal authority. Then I call her. "What are you doing right now?" I ask.

"It's Friday night, what do you think I'm doing?" she says. "Having the time of my freaking life."

"Get on the Internet. No, first let me tell you what happened, and then get on the Internet." So I bring her up to speed on the Great Expectations saga. I hear her turn on her computer and listen to her mumble the letter to herself.

Jillian reaches the end. "What the hell? Well, one thing to remember is that the tone is designed to control you. Don't let it. They aren't neeeeeearly as apologetic as they should be. You paid all this money how long ago?"

"Almost two months ago!"

She reads a few sentences out loud again. "I mean, fuck them, a business they describe as 'in limbo' has your fucking cash. They're in no position to scold you."

"Yeah!" I'm sitting in front of my computer, too. "Hey, I'm going to Google his name."

"Okay, I will, too."

Pause.

Jill says, "There are all these letters to the editor he's written."

"Check it out," I say, clicking around some more. "Every single time he writes a letter, he's affiliated with another company." I start writing all the different names down, although I don't know why.

"Why didn't you research this guy earlier?"

"I didn't know who the head of the company was when I signed up!" I remember the analogy I used with Gidgie. "If I bought a television, I wouldn't Google 'Sony' and research the president!"

"No," Jill says, "but maybe you'd do a little research and comparison shop before you bought the television. Did you do that?"

I lay my head down on my desk. "No."

"Why not?"

"I *never* comparison shop, Jill. Alex always did that. My grandparents do that. It drives me crazy. Driving out of your way to save a couple bucks."

"Uh-huh . . ." Jill says softly.

"Okay, so I was afraid to look into things too much."

"Uh-huh."

"Because I thought I'd get nervous and not do this. And then everyone would tell me I was being paranoid and coming up with lame reasons for not getting off my ass and trying."

"*Who* would say that?"

"I dunno. You. Sofia. Everyone who's been on my case about not dating."

"Well, I didn't say you should let yourself get taken advantage of."

"I can't stand it," I say. "This is impossible! In order to show someone who you are, you have to allow yourself to be vulnerable. You have to be open. You have to put information about yourself on the Internet. You have to look at shit you really don't want to see. And then when people take advantage of you or lie to you, you have to turn right back around and try again. I don't want to try everything anymore. Sometimes I just want to go back to the way things were before."

"No you don't, Cathy."

There's a moment of silence. "Jill, which do you think it is? Am I single because of my career, or do I have my career because I'm single?"

"I don't know." She sighs. "What brought this up?"

"What does it mean that most of the women who go to places like GE are professional women? Why are so many professional women alone?"

"I dunno. Because we made different choices."

"I don't know about you, but I was never presented with anything like a choice. Alex didn't say, 'Stay with me in Baltimore. Marry me. Give up your career.' "

Jill's voice is kind but level. "That's why you left. He never asked you to choose."

I feel like the wind's been knocked out of me.

"Did you ask him to choose?" She already knows the answer, but she wants me to say it out loud.

"Yeah," I say quietly. "But he said he didn't want to give up his job in Baltimore. He didn't want to live in New Jersey."

"Well, there you go."

My cat jumps into my lap, and I stroke his head. "This is what I'm saying, Jill. It's not the women who are picking career over marriage and family. It's that men aren't picking women who want marriage and family and also a career. How many men move up the ladder because they're willing to move wherever, work whatever hours, do whatever it takes." I'm getting really worked up now. "Think about it. How many men do you know who've followed their wives through multiple job changes? I only know a couple, and every damn one of them's depressed."

More silence on the line.

"What? It's a coincidence America is full of single professional women in their thirties and forties?" Then I say something I've felt all my life but never quite knew how to articulate—until this moment. "Maybe the real problem is that there aren't enough men around who are *man enough* to help a woman achieve *her* goddamn dream."

Even though we are talking on the phone, Jill and I take a step back from each other, contemplating that sentence. "So, you're saying it's men," she says.

Outside my window, rain falls in the glow of the streetlight. "It's the way they're raised, maybe. They're only comfortable if they feel just a tad bigger. I don't even think it's conscious. It's just what feels 'right' to them."

"I don't understand," Jill says. "What are you saying?"

"I'm saying it's society's fault I'm still single."

"Oh! Society!"

"Look, I think this is a big improvement. At least I'm not blaming myself anymore."

Jill laughs. "That's true."

"Everyone blames single women for being single, even single women themselves. The assumption is you must be fat or ugly or nutty or undesirable somehow."

"Well, people might think that. They don't say it."

"Oh yes they do!" I tell Jill how to find the message board about the two New York women who sued GE, and the ensuing discussion about the plaintiffs. She reads aloud the first posting:

Were the women in question like big fat ugly sweathogs that nobody in the civilized world would even talk to much less want to date?

Jill catches her breath and reads on.

I'd have serviced these ladies, and GE would've kept a tidy, secure profit.

Then the response.

Women don't have to pay to get "serviced." They were hoping to avoid meeting slobs like you.

She skims through about thirty postings from people detailing their visits to GE's offices, the sums they paid, the lack of results.

Listen to you people. No wonder you are single. You're all so bitter. Okay so the service didn't work for you. Maybe b/c you are such a joy to be around and you're all so positive (that's definitely sarcasm). . . . Do you get mad and bitch like this at your gym because in the three years that you had a membership there you didn't get any less fat. No! . . . You people frustrate the hell out of me and I hope that all of you stay single or hook up with one another. . . . This site isn't bringing you any luck finding a date and that is why you are all bitching right? Because you didn't find a date?

"Jesus," Jill says finally. "This is why I'm happy being alone."

"Why can't this process be civilized and humane? This is like, I dunno, voluntarily exposing your psyche to the worst of the human race because maybe, just maybe, you'll find the best. That's why I joined GE. Because they said they could protect my precious little psyche."

"But how could they?"

"They said they wanted to! They said they'd been doing it for thirty years." I sigh. "I mean, sure, it's a business, but when I go to the doctor, I expect her to at least try to help me."

"What are you going to do now?"

"I don't know. I don't want to think about it anymore. I'm sick of thinking about it."

I came to my study hours ago to e-mail Max, but I completely forgot about dating once I got this letter from the dating service that has my $1,595. It's late. The sun has long since set, and I'm sitting in the dark. The computer screen glows.

Jill asks, "Are you still going to try and get your money back?"

"I guess."

"You have to."

"I'd rather go to bed."

"Funny."

"I'm serious. I would rather go to bed than write this mean man and probably get a mean letter back."

"C'mon," Jillian says quietly. "Don't give up, Cathy."


It's 4:00 PM on Sunday, November 5, 2006. Do I have a date with Max in two hours, which is the time I suggested, or a date in four hours, which is the time he suggested? Or do I have a date at all? Should I take a shower and get dressed? I have no idea what to do.

As if she's reading my mind, Laura calls. She says, "I think he should have gotten back in touch with you if he wanted to meet. Tell me again how you guys left it?"

I tell the story once more *("And then he said . . . and so I said . . .")*. I feel like I'm in junior high again.

It's 4:30 PM. I take a shower, but while I'm washing my hair, I decide I am not washing my hair for the sake of Max but rather because it's dirty and because I'm going to invite people over to watch the Patriots game, even if it is last-minute. After the shower, I go into my study and send this e-mail. I had it all written up but didn't send because I was waiting for this stupid man to call me.

Dear Friends,

If you know football, you know why this Sunday's game between the Colts and the Patriots is a big deal. If you don't know football, here's the back story:

2003–2004 season: In the AFC Championship game, the Colts were decisively defeated 24–14 by the eventual Super Bowl champions, the New England Patriots, with quarterback Peyton Manning throwing four interceptions.

2004–2005 season: After a memorable regular season in which the Colts *averaged* 32.6 points per game and quarterback Peyton Manning threw a record 49 touchdowns, breaking Dan Marino's NFL record, a season in which Manning is named the MVP of the entire National Football League, the Indianapolis Colts seemed to be on their way to the Super Bowl at last. But a familiar obstacle stood in their way—the New England Patriots. The Colts could only manage a single field goal. Patriots won 20–3 and went on to win the Super Bowl. Again. It was a heartbreaker, folks.

2005–2006 season: On November 7th, 2005, almost exactly a year ago, the Colts returned to the scene of so much heartbreak— Foxboro, Mass. The Colts hadn't beaten the Patriots in Foxboro since 1996! *Sports Illustrated* put Peyton Manning and pretty-boy Tom Brady on the cover. The Colts entered the game at 7–0 and home-field advantage in the playoffs on the line. And what happened? The Colts trounced the Patriots 40–21 live on Monday Night Football and the curse was broken. With this monkey off their backs, naysayers who claimed Peyton couldn't win the big games started changing their tune . . . that is until Jan. 15th, when the Colts lost to the Steelers in the playoffs, but that's another story . . .

2006–2007 season: Once again, the Colts are 7–0. Once again, Manning and Brady are dueling for top QB honors. Will it snow Sunday night in Mass? Can the Colts make it to 8–0? Are you tired of watching Peyton Manning pitch products rather than pigskin? Are you tired of watching the Steelers lose? Well then, come to my house this Sunday night at 8:15 PM. I can't promise the Colts will win (although, gee, I sure hope they do!), but I can promise an exciting game. Even if you can't come over, you can watch the game on NBC's Sunday Night Football. Yea! This week, the Colts are nationally televised! I'll make some chili and have some beer. If you want to bring something, feel free!

I put on my Colts shirt and make some chili. I go out on my deck and see Heinz Field lit up on the horizon. Who are the Steelers playing today? I don't even know. I live in Pittsburgh—I can literally hear the game— and all I care about is a game that's going to happen in Massachusetts in a few hours. I make a mental note of this fact, then go inside, turn on the TV, and discover that the Steelers are playing the Broncos and Pittsburgh is losing again, 21–10.

It's 5:15 PM. I go upstairs and start putting away my summer clothes and getting out my winter ones. I check my e-mail every five minutes, telling myself I'm checking the Steelers score, but even I know that's not what I'm really doing.

At 5:30 PM, Laura calls. "Did you hear anything?"

"Nothing."

"Doesn't he have your phone number?"

"I gave it to him in an e-mail this week."

"Do you think maybe he doesn't have e-mail at home? Maybe he just has it at work?"

"Maybe." I resume folding a sweater. "I don't care. I wouldn't go right now even if he did call. Tom and Rachel are coming over to watch the Patriots game with me. You and Ben can come, too."

"Thanks, but there's no way I can stay up late enough to watch the whole game."

"That's okay."

"I mean, I'm sitting here trying to think of some freaking reason why this guy would suggest meeting you and then you say, sure, how about this time or this time, and then he doesn't answer? He's just a derelict."

"I have a date with Patrick tomorrow anyway."

"Right!" Laura says. "Heck with Max!"

My phone beeps. It's a local number I don't recognize. "Oh! This might be him calling!"

"Oh my God!" she says. "Call me back!"

Click.

"Hello?"

"Is this Cathy?"

"Yes." I say this one word as nonchalantly as I can.

"This is Max." His voice is boyish, not as deep as I thought it would be.

He tells me he's really sorry. He's had a very busy weekend and apologizes for not trying harder to get in touch.

I want to ask him, *Hey, what's the deal? Are you in a bad place in your life right now? Because if you are, or you're just not that into me, I can move on. I've spent half my life stuck on guys just like you. And I get it. Finally! I'm not going to fight for your attention anymore. You need to fight for mine, dude.* But of course I don't say this. Even I know that would be a little crazy.

I should be cool to Max on the phone, but I can only manage a state of A Bit Pissed Off. I hear myself say, "It's okay."

"How about tomorrow night?" Max suggests cheerfully.

Uh-oh. I have a date with Patrick tomorrow. A horrible notion (*You could meet Patrick another day . . .*) appears over my head, like a cartoon thought bubble, but I let it float up to the ceiling. "I'm sorry, but I have plans tomorrow," I say. "How about Tuesday?"

"Tuesday's good."

We decide on the place and time and say good-bye.

I call Laura immediately.

"Was that him?"

"Yes." I tell her his excuse was kind of lame but seemed sincere.

"Give him one more chance. No more. I went out with a guy like this in high school. Chris Bender. I spent way too much time on Chris Bender."

"I've been dating Chris Benders my whole damn life." I walk into the kitchen to stir the chili and get myself a beer.

"I'm glad he called. That was exciting!" Laura laughs. "That's the most exciting thing that's happened to me all day. All week."

I laugh, too. "Well, I'm happy you enjoy living vicariously through my stupid love life."

My neighbor Tom shows up alone to watch the game. "Rachel's tired. She said 'Go Colts!'" He makes himself a bowl of chili and grabs a beer and watches the first half with me. By the time the Colts have beaten the Patriots 27–20, I'm sitting alone. The Colts are 8–0. Somewhere in the bowels of Gillette Stadium, Tony Dungy delivers this fiery locker-room speech

(I'll see it Wednesday on *Inside the NFL*): "Whatever it takes, we seem to be able to do it. And that's the mark of a good team. A lot of people are gonna say a lot of things about you guys, well deserved! Just don't believe any of it." Their season is half over and they are undefeated. My dating season is half over, and I'm 0–8. This dumb project of mine isn't working very well.

After the game, Andrea Kremer asks about the Colts-Patriots rivalry, and Peyton says, "What's happened in years past is really kind of irrelevant. It's what's going on right now during this season." So true, Peyton! The past is irrelevant. Next week, it's a whole new ball game. I have *two* dates. Also, Pitt will be showing the movie *Friday Night Lights* on campus, followed by a talk by Buzz Bissinger himself. Here's my game plan: I will go out with Patrick on Monday and Max on Tuesday, and on Friday I will take one of these two men to that screening! I will fight for every inch. I will go inside 'em and outside 'em. I will be perfect, because pain heals but glory lasts forever. This is my time! Now, what do you say, men?

A school without football is in danger of deteriorating into a medieval study hall.

—Vince Lombardi

# WEEK 10: COLTS VS. BILLS
## OR
# Who Will Be Mr. Friday Night?

Whether they acknowledge it or not, educational institutions perform a vital but implicit function: they put us in proximity to our future partners. Now, I spent a lot of time in school—twenty years total, in fact—but, for reasons I'm just now beginning to understand, I didn't meet The One. Let me explain why I think this happened.

I did not meet my future husband in grade school. When the other girls said, "Let's go talk to those boys over by the monkey bars," I'd get a nervous stomachache and excuse myself to use the bathroom. Unlike my mother, I did not meet my future husband in high school. I didn't think about marriage because—I can't believe I'm saying this—I didn't want to end up like her: married with three babies by the age of twenty-five. I spent a lot of my childhood watching my parents grow up, and sometimes it wasn't pretty. Plus, we were always broke. Sometimes the hundred-dollar bill in the freezer was all that stood between us and the poorhouse. I had it all figured out: my parents should have waited to settle down. I vowed I wouldn't make the same mistake, even though, yes, I was the product of that so-called mistake. My plans regarding marriage and children were vaguely somedayish. My biggest fear in high school was that I'd get pregnant and boom, my story would be over, just like in "The River" by Bruce Springsteen: "Then I got Mary pregnant, and man, that was all she wrote." I admit this with great chagrin: I thought marriage was a shiny, alluring trap and babies were precious little dream zappers. I definitely needed to get some things out of my system before settling down. So in the fall of 1987, my parents drove me to college. They were both thirty-eight years old, the same age I am as I write this. They didn't even have gray hair yet. As we carried my stuff into my dorm room, I looked at the other kids and wondered why their grandparents drove them to college.

Many people meet their spouse at a university, and I attended a college that assumed this de facto responsibility with great gusto. After my parents dropped me off, I went to my first floor meeting. The resident assistant had taped pieces of paper and pencil stubs in the bathroom stalls, but brought one sheet with her to demonstrate. Cheerfully, she said, "These are called Mash Lists. It's a tradition for freshman girls to keep track of the fraternity boys they make out with, or 'mash' with. I've listed all the fraternities on campus." Her face grew a bit stern. "Just in case you decide to mash with one of the independents, I've included a space for Gamma Delta Iota, also known as God-Damned Independents."

We tittered. Our RA had used a bad word.

She continued. "Also there's a space for the HTH or Home-Town Honey. Now, just make a tally mark by the letters of the house each time you mash with a boy. At the end of the semester, we'll see which fraternity was this floor's favorite. Doesn't that sound like fun?!"

I found this whole enterprise fairly traumatizing. Every Saturday and Sunday morning, I'd sit there, hung over on the toilet, and marvel at the exponential growth of the Mash List tallies. After my freshman year I lived in a sorority house, where we were subtly encouraged to move from "mashing" to actual dating, circa 1958. Gone were the Mash Lists, replaced by candlelight ceremonies. Occasionally, after dinner, we formed a circle in the living room next to the grand piano. The house president lit a candle, and we sang a special song created just for this purpose, something about being a dream girl. If you blew out the candle the first time it reached you, that meant you were lavaliered (which meant a fraternity boy had given you his Greek letters on a necklace). If you blew out the candle the second time around, that meant you were pinned (which meant you wore his pin and yours, connected by a thin gold chain). If the candle started going around the third time, this meant somebody was actually engaged (which I know I don't need to explain). No matter how many times the candle circulated, after the girl blew it out, we'd all sit in a circle on the floor and listen to The Story—how that particular article of jewelry was transferred from man to woman, the circumstances surrounding that transfer, et cetera. Then the boy and his fraternity brothers rang the doorbell and serenaded the girl. The ceremony concluded with the fraternity boy being tossed into a campus pond.

I hope these anecdotes explain why I emerged from college with no practical knowledge about dating. I also hope they explain why a girl like me (who had spent four years in a place like that) would go to graduate school, see a group of young men standing underneath a magnolia tree, and immediately pick the one most likely to break her heart: the moody, dark-haired one smoking a hand-rolled cigarette, wearing a T-shirt that said, quite simply, "Fuck."

That was Alex. To be fair, he always swore he wasn't wearing his Fuck T-shirt that day, but that's how I remember it. We didn't start dating until three long, tortuous years later, during which time I learned some very important things.

- Don't sleep with a man just because he tells you that you're a good writer. Find out if he really means it first.
- Don't bother a male writer while he's writing, but don't expect *him* not to bother *you* when you are writing.
- The time you spend together must not conflict with his schedule, and my God, when he's on a roll or feeling blocked, you must be flexible; but when he's done and wants to spend time with you, be ready.
- Deep down, a lot of male writers don't really think women can write serious literature, although they keep this opinion to themselves so that you will sleep with them.
- A woman writer is emotionally capable of dating a male writer who is better, more talented, and/or more successful than she is, but it rarely works the other way around.

Ah, graduate school. What an education!
At all of these schools a game was being played—the Invisible Game

of Musical Chairs—and some women knew it, consciously or unconsciously. They knew the boys were the chairs, and that when the music stopped, they needed to grab a seat fast. Me? I didn't even know a game was taking place. I saw all these girls walking around in a circle, giggling and whispering to each other, and then all of a sudden, they'd make a fast break for these chair-shaped objects and fall all over themselves in the process, like they were fighting over the bridal bouquet. It seemed ridiculous. So I stood off to the side for a long time, watching.

Then I decided to assume a chair shape. If I was going to be stuck in this room and forced to participate in this stupid ritual, whatever it was, I wanted to maintain a little dignity. Now, my particular response to the Invisible Game of Musical Chairs would be perfect if a girl sitting in my lap did anything for me in the ya-ya department, but alas, it does not. I wanted one of the chairs to get up and sit in my lap, but unfortunately, this almost never happens. Chairs feel weirdly exposed when they have to assume the position of the sitter. It makes them feel very unchairlike. Now, I would have been willing to get up myself and go sit in a chair, but I'd grown to like the dignified, chairlike position, too. All I really, really wanted was for one chair to stop being a lazy chair, stand up, come over to where I was sitting and say, "This game is dumb. I don't want silly girls squirming around in my lap. I want to sit next to you, and I want you to sit next to me. Forever."

That's all I wanted. I didn't think it was a lot to ask, but maybe it was.

On Monday morning, I get up and make a cup of coffee. I sit down at my computer and reread the letter from GE. I no longer feel ashamed. Embarrassment (disguised as a need for privacy and discretion) is what made me walk into their office in the first place, and they are counting on that shame in order to make a profit. Therefore, if I refuse to feel ashamed, they have no power over me. So I write this kick-ass letter, and as it's printing, I shadowbox with my computer screen:

6 November 2006

Regarding your recent letter, I would like answers to these questions:

- How many GE members are there within a 20-mile radius of Pittsburgh? I am not interested in dating outside of the city, and Polly and Erica were well aware of this.

- What is an "extemporaneous legal and operational delay"?

- Isn't it customary to inform a client when delays such as this occur? Why stall me with false claims about photographer no-shows? Why did I have to make repeated phone calls before being informed about the *real reason* I wasn't receiving the promised services?

- Is there anyone currently employed in the Pittsburgh office?

- You admit that the franchise is "in limbo." If there was going to be a delay, why not put my money in an escrow account until services could be rendered?

- Who has the $1,595 I paid to Great Expectations?

- The situation in Philadelphia is a civil lawsuit backed by Pennsylvania's Attorney General, Tom Corbett. He is not an ambulance chaser.

- If it is indeed true that GE is able to provide the services I paid for, why wasn't I contacted to schedule the photography session before now?

Thank you for offering to give me access to members in other cities, but that's not what I'm interested in. Actually, the way you phrased the offer makes it seem as though I am in need of an escort service.

In addition to answers to these questions, I would also like a full refund—whether that money comes from you or from Polly is not my concern. I will also be forwarding our correspondence on to the Bureau of Consumer Protection and to my lawyer.

Sincerely,

Cathy Day

An hour later, I'm driving to the Southside to meet Patrick for lunch. I've discovered a great route through the Hill District, and as I come down the hill on Kirkpatrick, Pittsburgh is spread out before me like an enormous toy train set. Crossing the Birmingham Bridge, I see Downtown sparkling on my right, the houses built into the Southside Slopes in front of me, the Hot Metal Bridge to my left. Everywhere the trees seem to have already turned and dropped their leaves. Did I miss autumn? I'm afraid that I have. That's when I realize that this is the first time I've driven in Pittsburgh on autopilot, without consulting a map. In my head, I know the streets, the route. I know where to park. For the first time since I moved here, I don't feel like I'm in a foreign land.

I know this feeling. It means Pittsburgh is becoming my new home. I remember this particular day from every place I've ever lived outside the state of Indiana. When it happened in Tuscaloosa, Alabama, I was twenty-five, sitting at a Laundromat called the Cleansing Tide. A disheveled woman walked in the door and said to the attendant, "Girl! I feel like the pookie bears done played ball in my head! And that ain't good!" I knew exactly what she meant. A similar moment arrived a few years later, after I'd moved to Minnesota. I was twenty-nine years old, coming out of a liquor store after buying some Leinenkugel beer, looking across the street at the Hy-Vee grocery store. The enormous overcast sky was spitting down snow, and I thought, *This is where I live now.* It happened when I lived with Alex outside Baltimore. I was thirty-one, sitting on the porch, looking out at the blossoming apple orchards, thinking, *This is where I was meant to be.* Then I moved to New Jersey, and sometimes even that place felt "right." And now that feeling is back, that sense that I've become part of a place. I'm thirty-eight years old, crossing the Monongahela River in Pittsburgh, Pennsylvania, on my way to meet a man for lunch. But I can't bring myself to celebrate the long-awaited arrival of this moment, perhaps because I know too well how fleeting it is.

There's a post office on Carson Street. I need to mail the letter to GE, so I call Patrick's cell to see if he'll meet me there. People walk in the door to my left, and each time I turn my head to see if it's Patrick. A man. Not him. A woman. What does he look like? I sort of forget. As I'm paying at the counter, I turn my head and there's a man standing inside the door. He's wearing khakis and a sweater and a backpack, staring at me intently. I think, *Oh! That's him!* I smile as if to say, "I know you're here," and turn back to the postman making change; I realize that I'm ten seconds into this date and there's only one word in my head: "No." But I press on. I'm going to give this nice fellow a chance.

We walk down the street. Patrick points to stores and tells me that this is a good place for live music or that place has great snacks. We eat lunch at a Middle Eastern restaurant. He talks about his new job, and I talk about my job. He talks about being a Steelers fan, and I talk about being a Colts fan. He asks me what I think about the loss of running back Edgerrin James, and he seems to like my answer. After lunch, we walk down Carson Street, killing time. I find myself looking around at buildings, making comments like "Boy, I just never come over here enough."

Patrick points down a side street. "I live just a couple blocks that way." There's a pause. "Would you like to go there?"

I'm sort of shocked. "To your apartment?"

He looks down. "Yeah."

"Um . . . no. I don't think so. I'm fine just walking."

A few minutes later, Patrick stops in front of a coffee shop. "Well, I need to get some work done," he says. "So, I'm going to leave you here."

I give him a hug. "Talk to you later!" Then we wave and walk in opposite directions.

Driving back to Polish Hill, I wonder: Is home a place or a person? Is it a feeling or a fact? If I stay in this city long enough, if I find someone to share my life with here, will I feel the same way about Pittsburgh as I do about Indiana, like my heart is breaking a little? How long before I can come through the Fort Pitt Tunnel and see Downtown through the bridge's yellow girders and feel, not appreciation and awe, but love—genuine love? Something you don't even have to think about. Something that just feels right, something that just is.

It's Tuesday night. As I approach the restaurant where I'm supposed to meet Max, I see him through the plate-glass window, sitting at a two-top. Giving a small wave, I walk inside and find him standing by the door, waiting to greet me. He's wearing jeans, a faded Smiths concert T-shirt, and a jacket. Max smiles shyly and sticks out his hand. A word pops into my head. *Zing!* And I'm so damn grateful for that tiny, weird word. It reassures me that I'm still a woman capable of experiencing pleasure.

We order beers and food and try to tell each other who we are. It turns out Max's job as a social worker is a fairly recent thing. He's actually an artist, a painter. After high school, he went to New York, then Seattle, then Minneapolis, then Philly. Somewhere along the way, he got an MFA.

"Really? Me, too!"

Max cocks his head and smiles. "You said you were a teacher."

The food arrives. Max has a veggie wrap, and I dig into my Pittsburgh salad: a heart attack nestled on a bed of greens. Seriously. I'm not kidding. A salad topped with french fries, sautéed onions and mushrooms, grilled chicken, and melted cheddar. God, I love Pittsburgh.

"I am a teacher," I tell Max in between bites. "At Pitt. But I'm a writer, too."

"Oh, what do you write?"

"Fiction mostly. Short stories. Sometimes essays."

"No, I mean what do you write about?"

I think about this for a second. "I don't know. The circus? Indiana? Whatever interests me, I guess. What do you paint?"

Max smiles. "It's hard to describe."

I laugh. "I know. Tell me about it."

But he doesn't. He asks me a question instead. "Why do you write about the circus?"

So I tell him about my hometown, how it was the winter home of traveling circuses at the turn of the century. "I wrote a book about it."

Should I have kept this a secret? He seems startled for a second. "A book? You've published a book?"

I shrug. "Yeah."

"Oh, I didn't realize. That's really great."

"What about you? What's up with your painting? What are you working on?"

He wipes his mouth. "Right now, I'm pretty focused on the social work."

I get the sense that he doesn't want to talk about his painting. "So . . . how long have you been doing this?"

"Doing what?"

"Match."

He looks around briefly, as if to see if anyone heard me. "About a year."

"I just started. What's your experience been like?"

Max sighs. "Pretty unreal, actually." He tells me that when he first started meeting women through Match, he spent hours and hours studying the details revealed in women's profiles. Using those points of reference, he painted pictures in his mind of each woman, and every time, she turned out to be someone else entirely.

I sit there nodding my head, like I completely commiserate, but the truth is, it's just now hitting me that I've spent the last two weeks painting the same kind of picture of Max. Or rather—wrong medium—making up a story about Max.

"So now I don't allow myself to get worked up about it all."

"What do you mean?" I fork some more Pittsburgh salad into my mouth, trying to get some eating done while he's talking.

"I only check Match once a day, if that. I don't actually go out with too many women from there anymore. I guess I stopped allowing myself to expect much."

The waiter comes and we order another round.

I want to say, *The problem with that strategy is that you come off as rude and uninterested.* But I don't. I say, "It's hard to stay hopeful."

And then, for a long time, we tell stories about all the different places we've lived and the cheap meals we ate when we were really, really broke. We have a third round and open up an imaginary map of America and stick in our pins. There are a lot of pins. We talk about the bands we loved and the people we thought we were when we lived in those places. I ask him if he followed the Steelers in all those cities, and he thinks for a minute and says, "Yeah, sort of."

"Are you glad to be home again?" I ask.

Max looks down into his beer. "Yeah, it's good to be around my family, my old friends. I never thought I'd end up back here. This place, I don't know . . ." He looks out the window and the cars driving by. "It stays with you, you know?"

I roll my eyes. "Oh, I know! That's how I feel about Indiana." Maybe it's because I've had three beers and the date has lasted almost three hours that I say what I say next. "That's what I'm looking for, actually. I think I've finally figured it out. What meeting the right person feels like. It feels like home."

Quickly, I look away, afraid I've said too much, but when I turn my eyes back to Max, he's grinning. "Yeah," he says. "That's a good way to put it."

It's after eleven, too late to call my sister or my friends about how the date went. So I e-mail them.

> And then he walked me to my car and he said maybe we could do something on Thursday! I think it went really well. We closed down the restaurant.

Then I see I have another e-mail from Great Expectations.

> Polly collected your membership fee, and she is no longer in the area. We are under no obligation to return such funds. Since your stance is confrontational, threatening, and accusatory, and you have no desire to work with us, I see no purpose in further addressing your questions. Return of your membership fee will be discussed internally, and you will receive a response within 72 hours regarding same.

I shut my laptop with a sigh. There's no way I'm getting my money back, but tonight I don't really give a shit, because for the first time in a long time I'm happy.

On Wednesday night, I send Max an e-mail to thank him for a nice dinner. I don't ask, "Hey, so are we doing something Thursday?" but I do say "I hope to hear from you soon." My computer dings, alerting me I have a new message from Great Expectations. I don't even open it. I make myself some dinner instead. And then, finally, I do read the message, which, incredibly, says that I'm getting my full refund. I just need to go by their office to sign for it.

I'm speechless. I can't believe it. They're actually giving me my money back. Whoo-hoo! I call my sister. Andrea asks, "Are you going to go by yourself?" No one in Pittsburgh (other than my lawyer) knows about this. However, I don't want to go through this by myself. And then I remember my resolution: Embarrassment is what made me walk into their office in the first place, and if I refuse to feel ashamed, they have no power over me.

I pick up the phone. "Janet, what are you doing on Friday? I need a favor."

On Thursday I wait—again—for Max. In the afternoon I check my e-mail for the twenty-fifth time and see I have a message from Chemistry. Chemistry? Back in September, I told their customer-service person I wouldn't be renewing my membership. Maybe they decided to give me the extra time I asked for? Maybe it's a glitch in the system? The message says that "Robert" is interested. Robert? The name rings a bell. Oh well. You never know, so I log back into Chemistry and check the message. It's Robert the Gambler, the one my mom liked. All I really want to do is ask him, "Were you serious about the whole 'I love to gamble and you must too' thing?" But in order to ask him this question, I must proceed through Chemistry's Guided Communications Process. This summer, I liked the safety of this social buffer, but now that I've been on Match for a while, it's just annoying. In order to e-mail Robert and ask, "Do you have a gambling problem?" I have to pick two preset questions from Chemistry's pull-down menu. So how about:

1. What's the most important lesson you've learned from a previous relationship?
2. [a three-part question that counts as one] Looking back at your life, what has been the most significant "fork in the road"? Do you feel you made the right choice at the time? Would you choose differently now?

Robert's answers are cogent and sound—don't go to bed mad, don't look back, et cetera He also picks two preset questions for me from the pull-down menu. He asks me the "What you learned in a previous relationship" question. I write:

I learned that, gulp, I have to learn to be more selfish. I worried more about what my partner needed than what I needed. I was so worried about whether or not he was happy that I didn't often ask myself, "Am I happy? Am I getting what I really need?" I didn't really know what I needed, let alone how to ask for it. This condition is the curse of Nice People, and it's not easy to get rid of it. "Selfish" might sound like an extreme word, but it can mean something good, too: taking care of yourself so that you can be a good partner for someone else.

Robert's other question for me is, "What I'm generally looking for in a guy." I write:

One of the things I've found myself really paying attention to lately is whether the guy listens and asks questions, whether he seems genuinely interested in who I am on the inside. I also look for and pay attention to whether or not I feel attracted to the guy, whether there's a little "zing!" Attraction is a funny thing—you can't predict it or manufacture it, but I've realized that whatever the heck it is, it's necessary.

Robert must be at the computer, because a few minutes later, I get an e-mail from him. So I ask the question I've been dying to ask since July:

When you say you love gambling and that you want your partner to also, what does that mean? Gambling in the metaphorical or literal sense? Do you mean she should be a risk-taker, or she should have her own bookie? :-)

Robert says that he could really use another bookie. Laugh Out Loud. Then he makes the contradictory statement that I "would have to be willing" to go to casinos "if I wanted." Oh well. Now I know that Robert the Gambler is really a gambler, and I need to walk away—or run.

It's late in the day. The sun's gone down, and I haven't heard from Max. I haven't heard from Patrick either, not since Monday when we said goodbye outside that Southside coffee shop. I picture the sad, knowing look on his face as I turned to walk away, like he knew that was the end of our story. I remember the same look on Rick's face, then Stan's. And none of them contacted me again after showing me that face. Did they lose interest in me? It's more likely that they realized I wasn't interested in them.

And how sad is that? Near-perfect strangers who know what I'm feeling better than I know it myself.

On Friday morning, I pick up Janet and we drive over to Carson Street on the Southside. "I'm really glad you're here," I tell her as we leave the parking garage. "I want you to see why I thought all this was for real."

We step into the office, and it's all just like it was in September. Couples smile from the photographs hanging on the wall. Scented candles burn. Erica is at the desk. She greets me cordially but a bit coldly. "Hello, Cathy. First, we need you to sign this." She hands me a half-piece of paper that says: "I, Cathy Day, have received a full refund from Great Expectations Pittsburgh and have no further affiliation with this service and am satisfied with the resolution." Gladly, I sign my name. I'm not just *satisfied* with the resolution—I am amazed and ecstatic. Praise be to Great Expectations!

Erica walks away to use the Xerox machine. Janet looks at me. "How you doing?"

"I just want to get out of here."

She looks around at all the portraits of happy couples on the walls of the reception area, but then notices the big framed photograph on the wall above the couch. Janet points and whispers, "Funny that they'd pick that photo for this particular kind of office."

I look more closely. It's a black-and-white photograph by Ruth Orkin, "American Girl in Italy." The last time I was here, I sat right by this picture and only half noticed it. At first glance, you're tempted to lump it in with all the other iconic, romantic Robert Doiseneau posters that college girls put on their dorm-room walls. But nobody's kissing in this photo. A woman walks down a narrow street clutching her coat, her expression pained, while fifteen Italian men leer at her.

Janet whispers, "Everything you need to know about this place is summed up by the fact that they don't see what that picture is saying about men and women."

I've been known to make fun of the way my colleagues "read into" things. Not today.

Erica comes back into the room and hands me a check for half the

197

money I paid and a credit-card receipt for the other half. I can't even look at her. "Thank you," I say. We leave.

The first thing I do is deposit the check. Then I take Janet out for a burrito. I ask her if she and/or Jerry want to come watch *Friday Night Lights* with me, but she says they have plans.

"There's a swank cocktail party beforehand," I say. "I'm faculty, so I get to go."

"I thought you were going to go with Max?"

"I haven't heard from him," I say.

"Oh," she says. "The date went well though, right?"

"Yeah, I thought so. But what do I know?" I take a huge bite of my burrito.

"You should go anyway," she says.

"I hate going to movies by myself."

"Free drinks!"

"I hate walking into parties where I don't know anyone."

Janet frowns at me.

"Look, I'm sorry. It's just that doing this"—I point back to GE's office—"took a lot out of me. I don't know if I have anything left."

"Well, I think you're supposed to go to that cocktail party and that movie. I mean, the guy who wrote the book is doing a Q & A after, right?"

"Bissinger. Yeah."

"How freaking cool is that! Go!"

I raise my hand. "Okay, okay. I will."

I've been to many, many receptions for writers, and one thing I've learned is that the writer is usually the loneliest person in the room. People are afraid to talk to writers. Sometimes I get bored at my own after-reading receptions and walk around and thank people for coming. So when I find myself standing next to Buzz Bissinger at the cocktail party, I introduce myself. And sometime after my second Chardonnay, I decide I need to tell this man—who wrote a famous book structured around a football season—how I'm using the Indianapolis Colts' 2006 season to inspire me to have a comeback season of my own. And how love is a lot like football is a lot like a car accident. And how in both love and football, there are some things you control and some things you don't. It doesn't make much sense, but thank God, he listens to me.

Long before I knew Bissinger was coming to campus, I've had a movie clip in my head, stuck in a repeating loop. It's from the film *Friday Night Lights.* A car barrels through the Texas night driven by Coach Gaines. His team just lost a big game. Quarterback Mike Winchell sits in the passenger seat and says:

> Do you ever feel cursed, Coach, like no matter what, inside your heart you feel that you're gonna lose? Like something's hanging over you, following you, like a witch or a demon. You can't win. I feel like that all the time.

I turn to Buzz Bissinger. "Can I ask you something?"

"Sure," he says.

"Um, you know how in the movie the quarterback says that stuff about being cursed?" I repeat the above lines almost verbatim. Bissinger's eyebrows rise. Then he gives me a kindly nod. *D'oh!* Of course he knows those lines. "Well, is there a name for that? For that condition?" I don't say, *Because I think I suffer from it.*

He thinks for a second. "In golf, they call it the yips."

"Like in the movie *Tin Cup,* where he gets the shanks?"

"Pretty much," he says.

"Is this why Peyton Manning and the Colts always screw up in the playoffs? Is it like a mental block or something?"

This question appears to intrigue Bissinger. He leans on the bar. "I think a couple of years ago, no, it wasn't a mental block or the yips or anything else. But now, after those big playoff losses—the Jets, the Patriots, the Steelers—it's got to work on the team psychologically." He thinks for a second. "It's not an actual curse, but it has the same effect. Now when they get to the playoffs, there's this enormous pressure that's got nothing to do with playing the game right in front of them. They try to ignore it, but let those thoughts into your head . . ."

"And you're done for."

He nods.

As I drive home that night, a reporter sticks a microphone in my face.

**Reporter:** So Cathy, how did it feel tonight to talk to Buzz Bissinger, Mr. *Friday Night Lights* himself?

**Me:** It felt good, real good. I sure do appreciate the opportunity. If you told me when I started playing this game, way back when, that one day I'd get to play on the same field as a guy like that, well, I wouldn't have believed you.

**Reporter:** We know you weren't planning to go to the movie by yourself. Care to comment?

**Me:** Not really.

**Reporter:** We understand that you haven't heard from Max, and things didn't work out with Patrick, but hey, look what you got instead!

**Me:** I got to talk to a famous writer, but I still had to watch the movie alone.

On Saturday, I hear Bissinger speak again, and afterward I give him a signed copy of my book and shake his hand. Then I go with some friends to see the band Death Cab for Cutie, a band that Max and I both like, and I half expect to see him standing next to me. But I don't. I come home and check my e-mail. No word. I can't stand it. He hasn't answered the last e-mail, and yet I e-mail him again. I'm breaking one of the cardinal rules of old-school dating: in the early stages, a woman shouldn't let the communication count get away from her. I keep the tone of the message light-hearted and breezy, as if hey, no big deal, I just wanted to tell him about the show.

Did you ever see a band play a hockey rink? In particular, the Rostraver Ice Garden? That's where Death Cab played last night, and I have to say it's the most interesting place I've ever seen a show. We actually stood on the ice—they had it covered up with this indoor/outdoor carpeting, but the cold still got into your bones when you're standing there for two hours.

My polite poke does the trick. On Sunday morning, I open up my e-mail and—yes, at long last—there's a message from Max. I'm hopeful, because the letter is chatty, he asks about the show and talks about his week. But about halfway through, he drops the bomb. He's not sure that "the whole Match.com thing" is right for him, and his "gut" says that we're not compatible.

I go into my bedroom and throw the throw pillows on the floor. I think, *I'm alone in my lovely house. I'm alone in my lovely house which stands on my sometimes lovely street which sits on a hill overlooking this sometimes lovely city and I'm alone.* Then I cry for half an hour. It's a Pittsburgh day, gray and cold and rainy. The Colts are playing the Bills at 1:00 PM, but it's not nationally televised, so I call Scott to make sure he's taping it for me.

"Hello?!" he yells. There's a lot of noise in the background, people talking. Maybe he's still at church?

"What's up?" I ask. "Are you taping the game?"

"I'm at the game!" Scott says. "Oh, moment of silence. Call you back." Click.

"Bastard!" I yell.

My brother calls back a few minutes later, explaining that his father-in-law knows one of the refs, who gave them two seats in the end zone. "Are you taping the game for me?"

"Of course," he says, seeming to resent the fact that I'm asking.

"Well, I'm jealous. I wish I could be there."

"Uh-huh," he says distractedly.

"Did you hear I met the guy who wrote *Friday Night Lights*?"

"Really?" he says. "Well, I gotta go. Call ya later."

The Colts will barely beat the Bills by a score of 17–16, putting the Colts' record at 9–0, the first team in NFL history to go 9–0 in back-to-back seasons, but I really don't give a shit about love or football today. I'm sorry, but the best I can do for you this week is tell you that I talked to a man who wrote a really good book about watching a lot of football games.

> A player on a streak has to respect the streak. You know why? Because they don't happen very often. If you believe you're playing well because you're getting laid, or because you're not getting laid, or because you wear women's underwear, then you *are!* And you should know that.
>
> —Kevin Costner in *Bull Durham*

---

# WEEK 11: COLTS @ COWBOYS

## OR

# Curses!

---

Last night—after I stopped crying—I forwarded Max's message to my sister Andrea and my friends Sofia, Janet, and Laura. I asked:

What is he trying to say? Is he saying "It's not you. It's not me. It's Match.com"? Or is he just trying to find a nice way to let me down?

Laura says:

He seems like a schmoo-head and he obviously does not like being on match.com AND he's so busy what's the point of dating him anyway? I wouldn't pursue it and would probably write that it was nice to meet him, good luck etc. etc. Let's move on . . .

Sofia says:

I'm sorry, but, yeah, he's saying he doesn't want to go out. He's a dummy.

Janet says:

Once again I think he's confirmed his ambivalence about the whole enterprise, so you shouldn't take it too personally. (Easier said than done I know.) Chin up, little trooper! There are more Maxes in circulation out there. Better Maxes, well-balanced ones with brains and good hygiene and only a few nervous tics. You're bound to bump into one before long.

My sister says:

Maybe agree with him about the whole Match.com thing not really being for you, but maybe try one more get together and make a decision after that date. No hard feelings. Let's try for second impressions.

How can I possibly be *that* wrong about how the date went? There was some real, actual chemistry there! I log onto Match.com and look at the table that says we have twenty-five out of twenty-five things in common. Then I log onto the *Indianapolis Star* online to figure out how the 8–0 Colts almost lost to the 3–5 Bills. According to the box score, the game shouldn't have been close, and yet it was. In love and football, the stats don't lie, but they don't necessarily tell the truth either. I just want something I can count on: a fact, an indicator, a proverb, even a rule of thumb. Anything.

Finally, I write Max back.

You know, I don't know if this Match thing is for me either. I really don't like that the way I met you is that I entered in a bunch of data and hit a button called "Mutual Match" and some computer program showed me your picture and said you were a 95 percent match for me. It just goes to show it's not all about the numbers. I like to think that given our interests, we might have met each other eventually—without Match. I wish we had.

If it wasn't for the Colts, I would give up right now. Really, I'm that crestfallen. But I made a promise: *Do your best. Every day. Every week. Just one season. See what happens.*

In 2006, the NFL Network debuted the show *NFL Replay.* Four Sunday games are edited down from three-plus hours to an hour and a half. They remove all the downtime, huddles, and time-outs and insert sound from players and coaches who were "miked up" and video from the postgame press conferences. Watching *NFL Replay* is like watching a great movie on DVD: you can skip to all the best scenes and watch with the director's commentary turned on. I think *NFL Replay* is the greatest show on television. And so I'm going to give you this week's game of love in an *NFL Replay* format.

A man on Match.com winks at me. His favorite things are: "pizza, blue." Delete.

Match.com sends me my matches for the day. One of them says he's looking for a woman with cute feet who wants a male servant. I can't help it; I'm a writer and I'm curious. I e-mail him and ask if he's serious. He is, but says no one believes him. I tell him he's barking up the wrong tree; he should go post on Craigslist.com or Nerve.com, where the coupling gets a little kinkier. He says thanks. I say no problemo. Delete.

A man on Match.com sends me an e-mail written in complete, witty sentences. Marty says he's politically conservative, which is normally a deal-breaker for me, but at least he can articulate who he is in words other than "pizza" and "blue." We arrange to meet at a coffee shop in Shadyside.

**Me:** So, you have a cat, right?
*(Marty talks about his cats for three to five minutes.)*
**Me:** Yeah, I have a cat, too . . .

**Me:** So, where does your family live?
*(Marty talks about his family for three to five minutes.)*
**Me:** Well, my family lives near Cincinnati . . .

**Me:** So, do you like sports?
*(Marty talks about hockey for three to five minutes.)*

**Me:** Yeah, I like sports . . .
Delete.

The movie *Singles* is on, the Cameron Crowe flick about the dating tribulations of a group of twenty-somethings in grunge-era Seattle. One of the characters tries a dating service called "Expect the Best" and makes a hilarious introductory video profile entitled "Come to Debbie Country." I saw this movie in 1992, at a theater in Tuscaloosa with my twenty-something friends. We laughed at Debbie. I've seen it many times since and always laughed at Debbie. But now I realize that "Expect the Best" was probably Great Expectations. I am Debbie, and I'm not laughing anymore.

Match.com sends me a message. "Here are your newest matches!" Max is one of them. Delete.

It's time to say good-bye to Erik, my smoking-cessation health coach. We've been talking on the phone once a week for five months. On the off-chance that he might be single, but also because he helped me tremendously, I ask Erik if I can buy him a cup of coffee. In my previous form of existence, I would never have done this. But this is me following the Try Everything strategy. We meet at a coffee shop. Erik is wearing a ring. I give him a signed copy of my first book to thank him for his support. "You were my favorite client," he says. Oh well. Delete.

Head in my hands, I can't bring myself to check Match.com. I think, *I can't keep this up. There are five more weeks left in the regular season, not to mention the playoffs. I'm beating my head against a brick wall.* My computer dings. I look up and see that I have a new message. It's from the Colts! The subject line reads "Avoiding the Wall." It's a sign!

Since June, I've subscribed to the Colts.com newsletter. For some reason, the subject line of each missive always seems to speak to whatever I'm going through. I know this is ridiculous. It's like horoscopes; you think yours is sooooo true, until you read someone else's and realize it's just as applicable. But the part of me that knows it's ridiculous is outvoted by the part of me that truly believes that the universe is sending me pep talks via the Indianapolis Colts.

Before the Colts, it was the movie *Hoosiers*. For years, I watched *Hoosiers* whenever I began to lose faith in my dream of becoming a writer. Sometimes I'd rent the movie, and sometimes it would just appear on TNT, like a sign on my darkest days. Like when my thesis director said, "Your characters are like dolls you dress up and move from room to room." Like the day the two hundredth rejection letter arrived in the mail. Like the summer in grad school when I subsisted on corn on the cob and canned tuna. Like the years I spent trying to get my first teaching job. In 1997, I got a call from a college in Minnesota. I flew there carrying a nice suit, my curriculum vitae, and a printout of the NCAA tournament brackets. If Arizona managed to beat Kentucky, I'd win $150 in the grad-student pool. I told myself that if Arizona won, this meant I'd get the job. I was right. Arizona won, and I got the job.

I've been practicing magical thinking all my life. Such as: I'm walking along thinking about a boy I like, and boom! he drives by, which means he's going to ask me out (he did, actually). Or I'm at a music store with the Punter, and he plays the opening notes of my father's favorite song, "The Entertainer," which must mean he's The One (he wasn't). One of the reasons I chose the University of Alabama for graduate school is that their mascot is an elephant and my great-great-uncle was killed by one. It was destiny, you see.

Men may not believe in signs and magical thinking as it applies to love, but they do when it applies to sports. For years my brother Scott had to replicate the same circumstances of the Colts' first win of the season for the remainder of the season. One year that meant eating chicken wings from Ponderosa every Sunday. Another year it meant he had to drink exactly seven beers during the course of each game. The same men who mock the romantic notions of women will go weeks without shaving or washing their socks, refuse to watch a game anywhere but on a certain barstool or in a certain chair—all in the name of the team they love.

Of course, players and coaches practice magical thinking. Steelers coach Bill Cowher elected to have his team wear their white road jerseys in Super Bowl XL rather than their famous black and gold. "It's still a road game," he reasoned. But more likely, he knew that when you're on a winning streak, as the Steelers were at that point, you don't want to change anything. Call it what you will—luck or momentum or mojo or harmonic convergence—this intangible essence provides the psychological edge a player or a team desperately needs. If you believe that your road jersey brings you luck, you wear it.

Statistically speaking, you really can't win them all. You also can't lose them all. When for some reason you do—also known as a streak and/or a slump—the human mind asks, "How did this happen? Why did this happen?" Take baseball, for example. By 1918, the Boston Red Sox had won five World Series championships: in 1903, 1912, 1915, 1916, and 1918. And then nothing, nada, zilch for eighty-six years. How do you account for a concentration of championships before 1918 and the mathematically improbable drought that followed? And what about the poor Chicago Cubs, my favorite baseball team, who haven't won a World Series since 1908? We can't accept the rational answer: the world is just random, meaningless chaos, and there is no explanation. No, someone or something caused these situations to occur! But these long-running slumps cannot be blamed on a particular coach or player or owner. So of course it must be a curse. The Red Sox jinxed themselves by trading Babe Ruth to the Yankees, and the Cubs jinxed themselves by refusing to let a billy goat into Wrigley Field in 1945. I'm sure there's an algorithm or logical theory to explain the disproportionate number of championships won by the New York Yankees and the New England Patriots and *not won* by the Chicago Cubs and the Indianapolis Colts. It's naïve to assign simple explanations like Bambinos and billy goats to complex events, but we all do it, all the time.

In football, there's the Madden Curse, a supposed jinx on athletes featured on the video game *Madden NFL*. Supposedly, the season you make the cover of *Madden NFL*, you get injured or perform poorly. Victims include Daunte Culpepper, Marshall Faulk, Michael Vick, Ray Lewis, Donovan McNabb, and Shaun Alexander. There are a few rational explanations for this phenomenon. These men play football, a violent sport, so something's bound to happen to them eventually. Also, *Madden NFL* cover boys are selected on the basis of having a great season, a time when their stars have risen—there's nowhere to go but down. The scientific term for this tendency to peak, then slide, is "regression toward the mean."

And then there's the Cathy Curse: the men I date don't marry me but rather the woman they meet right after (or during) me. The third time this phenomenon occurred, I thought it was just a weird coincidence, but now it's happened *nine times*. It's hard enough when this happens once. Who can forget Sally Albright's crying jag in *When Harry Met Sally* when she finds out her ex-boyfriend is getting married? "He just met her," she sobs. "She's supposed to be his transitional person. She's not supposed to be the One. All this time I thought he didn't want to get married. But, the truth is, he didn't want to marry me." Now multiply Sally's moment by nine, and that's my story. How to explain it? The rational explanation is that people typically marry in their twenties and early thirties, including all those ex-boyfriends of mine who married right after dating me. Is this an unfortunate but completely random coincidence? Is it a curse, a case of bad luck? Or am I doing something (or not doing something) to create this situation? I wish I knew.

Which brings us to Peyton Manning. In college, he broke all kinds of records at the University of Tennessee but always lost to the University of Florida. As the Colts quarterback, he's put up amazing numbers in the regular season, but never led his team through the playoffs to the Super Bowl. How do we account for this anomaly? For the succession of failures at the hands of particular opponents, like Florida and New England? Do sports analysts say, "Peyton Manning's playoff record is the result of an unfortunate but completely random coincidence?" No, they do not. Do they say, "Any given football game is controlled by so many different variables, it's statistically impossible to pin a loss on a single individual or play?" No, they most certainly do not. No, they say Peyton is doing something (or not doing something) to create the situation.

What do Y. A. Tittle, Dan Fouts, Jim Kelly, Warren Moon, Fran Tarkenton, Dan Marino, and Peyton Manning have in common? They're all great NFL quarterbacks who—for one reason or another—never won the Big One, and thus have slightly tarnished legacies. I never realized it until now, but NFL quarterbacks and American women have a lot in common: until they get that ring on their finger, they're considered failures.

It's Sunday morning. At an undisclosed hotel somewhere near Irving, Texas, members of the 9–0 Colts are waking up. More than likely, they'll get up on the same side of the bed they always do, go through the same game-day rituals. In my house in Pittsburgh I'm waking up as well, but, unlike the Colts, I'm in a slump and not concerned about maintaining a routine. Actually, I should try doing something completely different. The phone rings. It's my mom asking me what day I'm coming home for Thanksgiving. That's when I realize I need a new goal: find myself a date with a Cincy fellow during Thanksgiving.

A reporter sticks a microphone in my face.

**Reporter:** Cathy, can you talk a little about this new game plan of yours?

**Me:** I really wanted to shift the momentum of the game, shake things up a bit. Everything seemed to be going wrong.

**Reporter:** Speaking of which, what do you think went wrong with Max?

**Me:** You know that's a really good question. I could speculate. Even though he was older than me, he seemed younger, like he might still skateboard, you know what I mean? And if I'd just given up my dream of becoming a writer, I don't think I'd want to date a practicing artist. Or maybe he just didn't like me. Who knows why?

**Reporter:** Why Cincinnati?

**Me:** I didn't go to high school in that area like my brother and sister did. I don't know anyone but my family. When I go home for the holidays, I still feel like a kid. I want to go there and go on a date, like a grown-up.

**Reporter:** I hate to ask, but what happens if you *do* meet a nice man in Cincinnati?

**Me:** I'll cross that bridge when I come to it.

I log onto Match.com and enter a new zip code into the search engine. I also narrow my search criteria and parameters. I want a smart man who is accomplished in his own right, a man who enjoys reading and talking. I name this search "Smart in Cincy." I narrowed it down to four likely candidates. Then I have to figure out what to say. How do I reach out to a man who lives five hours away—a man who won't find me unless I make the first move—without seeming desperate? I explain to each that, although I live in Pittsburgh, the Cincinnati area is where my family lives and it's the place I consider "home." I mention I'm coming home for the holidays soon.

> Sorry to be forward and say, "check me out," but I guess that's what I'm saying.

Two of these men never respond, but two of them do: Larry on the Beach (in his picture he's standing on a beach) and Quinn Holding the Cat. They're both reasonably handsome and very, very articulate. For some reason, I'm slightly more interested in Quinn Holding the Cat; his profile is funnier, and I like his smile. He wears glasses. He's bald. He's divorced. But this time, I'm not going to make the Max mistake and start imagining who they are and what they're like. I will wait and see. And so I begin the process—once again—of communicating with strangers.

At four o'clock, the Colts take the field against the 5–4 Dallas Cowboys live on national television. Everyone is watching. Well, not everyone, but a lot of people. The game will earn a 15.8 rating and a 29 share. I don't know what that means, but it's the most watched game of the NFL season so far. Everyone wants to know: Will the Colts extend their streak to 10–0, or will it end at Texas Stadium at the hands of the Dallas Cowboys, led by Bill Parcells and quarterback wunderkind Tony Romo?

I get a bad feeling in the first quarter. Marvin Harrison fumbles. Peyton gets sacked. Tight end Ben Utecht takes a big hit. Peyton fumbles. The game is still scoreless, but everything feels off, and not just because the Colts are making mistakes. Commentators Phil Simms and Jim Nantz tell the audience that they had a chance to interview Colts defensive tackle Nick Harper about the "Immaculate Tackle" in the playoff game with the Steelers. If, after picking up Jerome Bettis's fumble, Harper had managed to elude Big Ben, the Colts would have won the game. Harper admitted that he's watched and rewatched that play "at least a thousand times." He couldn't sleep for a month after that game. He didn't recover emotionally for three months, Simms and Nantz report.

Whose fault is it that the Colts lost against the Steelers? Some said it was Peyton's fault. Some pointed to Harper. Even Harper pointed to Harper. But the easiest person to point a finger at that day was Mike Vanderjagt, once the most accurate kicker in the NFL, who shanked the ball right and sent the Steelers on to the Super Bowl. The Colts traded their kicker after that, and now, in the second quarter of the Colts @ Cowboys game, Vanderjagt takes the field wearing a helmet emblazoned with a blue star instead of a blue horseshoe. Phil Simms says, "There's gotta be a few nerves involved here." Vanderjagt kicks, but the ball hits the right upright of the goalpost and bounces away. I laugh gleefully in front of the television, enjoying Vanderjagt's shame. In the locker room after the game, Vanderjagt will say: "It was just six inches from being a great kick." And he's right. Football is a game of inches. Six inches one way, you're a hero. Six inches the other way, you're a goat.

With three seconds left in the first half, Vanderjagt trots onto the field to redeem himself. The Cowboys need him to kick a 46-yard field goal. With his former teammates rushing toward him, he kicks again—and the ball sails wide right. Vanderjagt kneels on the turf, hitting the ground with his hands. He walks off the field all alone with shoulders slumped, shaking his head. It's his fifth miss of the season—this from a man who holds an NFL record of forty-two successful field goal attempts in a row, the man who did not miss a single field goal or extra point attempt during the entire 2003 season. Later, columnist Bob Kravitz of the *Indianapolis Star* will write, "He used to be the cockiest guy in the building. . . . There can be absolutely no question that the playoff miss last season against Pittsburgh . . . planted a seed of doubt that has germinated into fully-blown anxiety." In an interview Bill Parcells says, "He keeps telling me that I don't have to worry about him. Well, *I am* worried about him now. That's all I'm going to say."

Even I'm worried about Vanderjagt, and I think he's a jerk. My television screen may only be nineteen inches wide, but it's big enough to see he's in full-blown meltdown mode, and I can't bring myself to enjoy his misery. I've never kicked a football in my life, but I know how he feels:

emptied out, like something vital within you is suddenly gone, something you never thought about because it was always just there—until it wasn't anymore.

By 7:00 PM, I get e-mails from both men in Cincinnati, and I'm happy. I feel like my slump might be over. By 7:30 PM, the game is over, and the Colts have lost. Their streak is over. A reporter sticks a microphone in my face.

**Reporter:** Cathy, do you believe there might be an inverse relationship between your love life and the Colts' season?

**Me:** No comment.

**Reporter:** If it comes down to it, are you willing to sacrifice your ring so that the Colts can win theirs?

**Me:** No comment.

Thanksgiving Day is no longer a solemn festival to God for mercies given. It is a holiday granted by the State and the nation to see a game of football.

—*New York Herald,* 1893

---

# WEEK 12: COLTS VS. EAGLES

## OR

# What Would Peyton Manning Do?

---

My credit-card bill drops through the mail slot, and there's another $99 charge from Chemistry.com. How can this be? The last time I talked to them, I said I wouldn't be renewing my membership. So I get on the horn to Chemistry.

"How may we help you today?"

"Yes, I'm calling about an incorrect charge."

The customer-service concierge looks up my account information. "I see that you were charged for another three-month membership."

"Yes, well, I called you guys a few months ago to complain about the lack of response I was getting, and at that time I told you I didn't want to renew my membership."

The concierge explains that this is not the proper procedure to cancel a membership.

I ask, "So calling Customer Service and saying, 'I don't want to renew,' isn't the right procedure?"

No, it is not. Apparently, when I joined Chemistry in July, I agreed to their automatic renewal terms. Apparently, I was supposed to cancel my membership *online,* not over the phone. And I cannot cancel my membership now, today, and receive a prorated refund. There's a deadline after which you're locked in for the full three months, and that deadline came and went—two days ago.

The concierge says, "Also I see that, since the automatic renewal went into effect, you *have* used our services."

I laugh. "No, I haven't."

"Yes, ma'am, you have," the matchmaking concierge insists. "I see here that you logged on a few weeks ago and communicated with a Robert?"

Robert the Gambler! I forgot about that. I wanted to ask him a dumb question: "When you say that a woman must love to gamble, do you mean that literally or figuratively?" The answer—literally—is going to cost me $99.

"Look," I say, "I wouldn't have logged on if I thought it was going to cost me anything. I assumed you were giving me free time on my membership, like you do for men."

Silence. "Ma'am, I don't know what you're talking about."

"I would like to ask you one question. How many male members do you have within a twenty-mile radius of Pittsburgh?"

"I'm sorry, but I don't have that—"

"No! Strike that! How many *active* male members do you have within a twenty-mile radius of Pittsburgh?"

"We don't have that information available."

"Oh, but I'm sure you do! Somewhere in that computer of yours, I'll bet you know *exactly* how many men use Chemistry in the Pittsburgh area. I'm a consumer, and I deserved to know that information so I could decide if I was going to get my money's worth, because let me tell you, I did *not* get my money's worth from your service."

Pause. "I'm sorry you're disappointed, but we can't make any guarantees. Basically, we only provide a means for people to communicate with each other."

"*Communicate . . . with . . . each . . . other,*" I say, drawing those words out. "Exactly. Look in your computer there and see how many men actually responded to my profile."

"I see a Rick—"

"Yes, Rick, who informed me that he hasn't paid for his Chemistry membership in a long time. He told me that he thinks you guys don't have enough men on your roll to satisfy female customers, so you just keep giving men like him free renewals!"

"No, ma'am. That is not our policy."

"Aren't you owned by the same company as Match.com?"

Pause. "Yes."

"Well, here's what I think. I think you guys were sending me profiles of men who don't actually *subscribe* to Chemistry. They subscribe to Match .com. You borrowed their information from Match to artificially inflate your rolls and keep women like me happy!"

"No, ma'am. That is not our policy."

"Why should I have to pay $99 . . . *twice* . . . when Rick didn't have to pay anything? That is *discriminatory*. You're taking advantage of women."

"No, ma'am. That is not our policy."

I'm so mad, I don't know what to do with myself. I could buy a pair of shoes, a book, a television, a dining room table and get better customer satisfaction than this. "You're not going to do anything to help me, are you? You're going to charge me another $99 and there's absolutely nothing I can do about it?"

The concierge maintains a neutral tone. "There's nothing I can do."

"Put this in your computer. When this three-month membership is over, it's over. Got it?"

"Yes. I'll take care of it."

"Good!"

I hang up the phone and scream so loud that my cat jumps straight up in the air. Then I call my mom. "These people . . . these people!" I stammer.

"Cathy? What's wrong?"

I tell her exactly what's wrong.

Mom sighs. "You know, when you started doing this, I was afraid for you. I thought the men you met might turn out to be bad people. But so far, they've turned out to be pretty normal. Pretty nice."

"I know! It's these snake-oil salesmen who're driving me crazy!"

"They should be ashamed of themselves," Mom says.

"I don't think they give a shit." I sigh. "You know what I'm going to do?"

"What are you going to do?"

"I'm going to prove I was right. I've seen guys on Match who *I know* I saw on Chemistry. I'm going to contact them and ask if they really joined Chemistry or not."

"You go get 'em!"

"Thanks, Mom."

I log onto Match, but quickly realize all the names and faces have blurred over these past few months. The only man I know for sure I saw on both Chemistry and Match—because he had a unique profile picture—is Chris the Rocker, the man I met on Match currently enrolled in a class with my former Pretend Boyfriend, the Punter. I search for Chris's profile on Match so I can send him a message. Damn! He's taken himself off Match. I have no other way to contact him—except one. I haven't talked to the Punter since that horrible dinner, the day I cried about the dumb pipe. Damn! I don't want to talk to the Punter, but I really want to know if my suspicions about Chemistry are right or not. So I pick up the phone.

"Um, I need to get in touch with one of your students," I tell the Punter. "He's older, probably. In his thirties. His name is Chris, I think."

"You think?" I can hear him grinning at me.

"Do you know who I'm talking about or don't you?"

"Tell me why you're asking."

"I can't," I say. "It's this project I'm working on. It's a secret."

"Oh! Top-secret stuff, huh?"

"Shut up."

"It seems to me that if you knew him, you'd know his name."

*Good point.* "Look, I met him in a coffee shop," I lie. "He was reading that book you teach, and I started talking to him, and now I need to talk to him again, okay?" This is a fairly plausible lie.

The Punter chuckles and tells me the Rocker's full name. "Do you want his e-mail address?"

I consider this. What's the least creepy way for me to contact this student? "Why don't you just bring him by my office next week, after break?" I tell him when my office hours are.

"Okay. Sounds good," he says. "Seriously, you're not going to tell me what this is about?"

"Maybe later."

"Happy Thanksgiving, Cathy."

That's when it hits me. It was exactly a year ago that the Punter e-mailed me from his then-girlfriend's place in New York to wish me a happy holiday. The day after Thanksgiving break, the Colts played the Steelers on *Monday Night Football*; I made a bet with my workshop, took the bus home to my apartment, and spent the whole game fighting with the Punter on the phone. So much can change in a year's time. It's a brand-new season. The Colts are 9–1 and the Steelers are 5–4. I own my first house and I have friends. And I hardly ever think about the Punter anymore.

For the last few days, I've been communicating with Larry on the Beach and Quinn Holding the Cat. I want one of these men to suggest we meet while I'm in the Cincinnati area for the holidays. I can see it now: the day after Thanksgiving I put on some grown-up clothes (instead of my usual holiday attire of sweatpants) and offhandedly say to my family playing cards at the kitchen table, "Oh, hey, I've got someone I need to meet. See ya later." Their eyes will grow wide with wonder, and I will get in my car and drive forty miles east just to drink a cup of coffee.

I hear from Quinn first, who asks if he can call me tonight. Immediately after setting up this phone-call appointment, Larry e-mails to suggest we meet for coffee while I'm home for the holidays. Sigh. I tell Larry that unfortunately, I'm going to be too busy with family to meet him during Thanksgiving, and he writes back to say in that case, he's going to drive to Chicago to spend the holiday with an aunt and uncle. Larry on the Beach was willing to cancel these plans in order to meet me, which makes me wonder if I've made the right choice. Hmm . . . If Larry had contacted me ten minutes sooner, would it have made any difference? Don't I like Quinn better anyway? *Stop!* I tell myself. *You can't second-guess every move, every decision.*

Quinn calls that night at eight, right on time, but I'm in line at the grocery store buying cat litter. "I'm so sorry, but I'm in the middle of something right now. Can I call you back in fifteen minutes?"

"Sure," he says.

When I get home, I call Quinn back, but I get his voice mail. I leave a nice message, apologizing. "I'm leaving for Cincinnati first thing in the morning, but I'll be up late packing, so feel free to call me tonight."

He hasn't called by 12:30 AM. *Oh well, I guess maybe he got busy, too.* I send him an e-mail to say, "Sorry I missed you! Call me tomorrow!" Then I go to bed.

I leave for Indiana before the sun comes up. All morning, as I make my way through the Fort Pitt tunnel and West Virginia and Ohio, my cell phone rests between my legs. It does not ring. All day, as I help my mom cook and read a story to my nephew Clay and rub my pregnant sister's aching back, my phone does not ring. All night, as I watch *Hidalgo* with my grandma and drink a beer with my dad, my phone does not ring.

It's Thanksgiving Day, bright and beautiful. The women are in the kitchen peeling potatoes and things like that. The men are outside smoking the turkey and drinking. Plus, they've got a TV set up outside on the patio so they can watch the Dolphins versus Detroit game *while* they smoke the turkey and drink. Hmm . . . inside or outside? I don't know about you, but I know where I'd rather be.

I ask my brother Scott for his opinion about this Quinn situation. We're sitting in lawn chairs in front of the TV. He asks, "Why didn't you just talk to him when he called you?"

"I had my hands full. I was at the store."

"Did you tell him that?"

"What am I supposed to say? *Hi, nice to meet you, I'm holding a giant bag of cat litter, can I call you back?*"

Scott takes a sip of beer. "Maybe he thought you were with another guy."

I throw up my hands. "Oh! What? I'm also supposed to reassure these dudes that I'm really and truly single? Jesus!" When I say that word, Scott gives me a hard look, which I ignore. "I'll bet *he's* married. I'll bet he snuck out of his house to call me that night."

My brother shakes his head. "I don't know, Cath. Look, if it was meant to be, it would happen."

I snort. "I don't believe in that crap anymore."

Scott gives me a disgusted look, stands up, and walks into the house.

My dad's been sitting nearby, listening to us. "What do you mean by that?" he asks.

"The only people who say, 'It will happen if it was meant to happen,' are the happy ones. The people 'it'—whatever it is—already happened to."

My dad lights a cigarette and stares at me.

I say, "You can't just sit around waiting for God or fate or whatever to give you what's 'meant to be.' What if I'm making mistakes that are hurting my chances of finding someone? Am I not supposed to work on those things? I'm sick of sitting around waiting for things to happen. Nothing's happening. I guess I have to make things happen!"

My mom is standing at the screen door with a concerned look on her face, listening to me rant. My brother-in-law John leans over. "I'll bet that most of the guys online are either already married or just divorced." John lowers his voice. "They just want to get laid."

I don't lower my voice. "So you're saying they see my picture and *don't want* to sleep with me?"

My dad gets up out of his chair to check on the turkey.

John laughs. "No, what I'm saying is that they probably see your picture and think, 'She's cute,' but there's probably something in what you've written that makes them think you're after a commitment."

"Well, yeah!"

"And if I know you, and I think I do a little bit," he says, leaning over the arm of the chair, "I'll bet you really lay it out there real clear, so they probably figure, 'Why bother?' and don't contact you. You should be glad, actually."

I look into my lap. "I don't even care about getting married anymore. All I really want is someone to watch TV with."

My dad returns from his trip to the smoker. John laughs and says, "Relax, Cathy, it'll happen when it's supposed to."

"That's it!" I stand up, although I don't know where I'm going. "All you married people keep saying that! I'm sick of hearing it!"

I go inside, walk past my mom, through the kitchen, where my grandma is doing dishes, and march upstairs to my room. Andrea is in there, changing Clay's diaper.

"I heard," she says, pointing to the open window.

"Whatever." I lie down next to Clay and tickle his belly. He smiles at me, and it's the best thing that's happened all day.

"That guy hasn't called you, has he?"

"No." I hand her a fresh diaper. "I should have picked the other guy. Larry. I'll bet he would have called."

Clay kicks Andrea in the belly. "No no no," she says. "Baby." He tries to say the word, but it comes out like *bye-bye*. "Are you mad at John?"

I take a deep breath. "No, I'm just frustrated."

Andrea folds up Clay's diaper and hands it to me. "You know what I think? Would you throw that away for me? Thanks . . . I think you think too much. You analyze everything *way* too much."

There's a pause. "You know what, Andi? I get *paid* to think." I point to myself with Clay's poopy diaper. "That's my job. That's what I fucking do!" I turn around and walk to the bathroom. "I'm me! I'm not you."

Behind me, my sister mutters, "I know."


At four, the whole family gathers around the table. My dad leads the prayer, a subdued one this year. I've never seen my father this down. Now that the settlement has been . . . settled, he has to figure out what to do with the rest of his life. When he retired, he wanted to see the West, work on cars, fish for blue gill, but pretty much everything—standing too long, sitting too long—brings the pain. And now, Dad's in a bigger funk since Scott and Sara announced they're moving to Missouri. It's a good career opportunity, my brother told me a few weeks ago. "I used to have head-hunters call me about jobs like this, but I always told them I wasn't interested. I guess I couldn't imagine living that far away from home all by myself." Scott's a lot braver since he got married. All day, as we smoked the turkey, drank beer, and ate cheese, Scott and Sara have been trying to mention his new job and the houses they've looked at online, but when they do, everyone gets really quiet and changes the subject. After we say "Amen," Scott says, "You know what? The day they called me about the job, I saw a car in Shelbyville with Missouri license plates. You never see Missouri plates around here. It's a sign, a God thing."

I have to fight the urge to yell, *You're basing your decision to move to*

*Missouri on the fact that a car drove by!* But I don't say anything, because my brother could counter with, *So what? You're basing your decisions about dating on the outcome of football games!*

My sister spoons some mashed potatoes into Clay's mouth and says, "I think we should play this game. Let's go around the table, A, B, C, you know, and say something we're thankful for that starts with that letter."

Did I mention my sister teaches third grade?

"Fun," I say.

She gives me a hard look. "I'll start. I'm thankful for . . . apple pie." She nudges John. "Your turn."

John grins. I know there's quite a few B words he'd say (and fondle) if my grandma wasn't at the table. "Buns," he says, picking up a roll out of the basket.

"What about babies?" my grandma says in her quavering voice.

"Buns *and* babies," he says, recovering quickly. He pats Andrea's stomach.

It's my grandma's turn. "Clay," she says. "I'm thankful for you." She points at him and he laughs and claps his hands.

"Our dogs," Sara says. She and Scott have two.

"E?" Scott says. "What starts with E?"

I strum an air guitar.

"Oh yeah, Eddie," he says.

Grandma looks puzzled.

"Eddie Van Halen," I tell her. "He plays in a band Scott likes."

"Oh," she says. "Right."

I can tell that Scott is trying to come up with something else—being thankful for a rock guitarist doesn't really match the sappy tone of this game—but he can't think of anything else. He shrugs and we move on.

It's my dad's turn. "Family," he says without hesitation. "I'm thankful for my family."

"G," Andrea says, looking at me.

My turn. *Goober peas,* I think. *Gomer Pyle.* Andrea gives me a look that says, *Don't you dare say Gomer Pyle. Knock it off.* In Indiana (and in my family) nobody likes a smart-ass.

"Grandma," I finally say.

Grandma smiles at me from across the table.

My mom puts down her fork. "Home," my mom says. "Our happy home."

*God!* I think. That should have been my G word, but everyone would still think I was being a smart-ass.

During my first year in Pittsburgh, everyone in my family came to visit me at least once. Dutifully, I drove my family members around, showing off the views, taking them on tours of the Cathedral of Learning and Heinz Chapel, through the open-air markets of the Strip District, where we ate fries-and-slaw-laden Primanti Brothers sandwiches and tried Iron City beer. In my family, vacation is a broad term that means you go somewhere that's not your house in order to sleep in, eat different food, and watch the sun set in a new landscape. Absorbing arts and culture isn't high on the family fun list—unless it's me and my brother. Scott is a product engineer, which I understand to mean that he designs and manufactures big, complicated metal stuff, like transmissions. But he also has a visual artist's eye. I love to show him beautiful things and see those things through his eyes (or the lens of his camera). The Guggenheim's gyred walkway. Light reflected off a freshly caught fish. The snowing flower petals in a Japanese print at the Met. The torpedo tubes inside a decommissioned submarine. A blue sea surrounding a rectangular green island called the RCA Dome.

During my first year in Pittsburgh, Scott and Sara came to visit me. They'd only been married for about eight months, still newlyweds, really. As the weekend went on, I felt a seismic shift I couldn't name—until I took them to the Carnegie Art Museum. Then I got it. I don't think one is the loneliest number at all: it's three. Now it was Sara and Scott walking down corridors, talking softly together, while I stood off to the side a little. I'd gotten used to this triangular arrangement in my life. Me plus couples. My brother had been alone for a long, long time, too, my partner in singleness, but now it was just me.

We consulted our maps. "Well, if you want to see the paintings chronologically, you start with the medieval stuff." I waved my hand dismissively. "But it's all Jesus and Mary. Jesus and Mary. Don't you think they could've painted a fucking tree?"

222

Now, I knew that Scott and Sara were pretty devout Christians. I also knew that Scott had recently stopped swearing. For these reasons, and because I was feeling petulant and jealous, I transformed into this potty-mouthed blasphemer. I don't know why. Well, now I do. I didn't then.

Scott and Sara looked at each other. "We kind of like that old religious stuff," he said.

"Whatever," I said.

I stood around for a while, then I said, "Well, I'm going to head to the more contemporary stuff. You know I love Jesus, but this shit really bores me."

My brother stepped away from Sara and looked me straight in the eye. "Do you love Jesus?" he asked.

I stared at him. "Are you kidding me?"

Sara ambled away, pretending not to notice we were having a fight in the middle of the exhibit hall.

"The way you talk sometimes," Scott said. "The foul language. It makes me wonder."

I lowered my voice. "You think because I use the f-word, I don't believe in God? How can you even think that? You're my brother. Don't you know me at all?"

He shrugged his shoulders.

"You know what?" I said. "Most of the people I know are atheists!"

"Really!?" he asked. I don't think my brother's ever met one.

I stomped off. An hour later, we met by the entrance and went back to my apartment. We pretended like the whole thing never happened.


After dinner is over and all the dishes are washed and put away, half the family piles into the Jeep. My mom calls these trips "outreach projects." Basically, she's embraced "Practice random acts of kindness." During the holidays we drive around giving candy to strangers. It's a warm, rainy night, but we've got the heat on for Grandma. Sara's sitting next to Clay's car seat singing "Old McDonald" with him. I'm sitting by the window, staring at the streaks of light shining on the asphalt. I still have my cell phone with me, just in case stupid Quinn ever calls. My mom drives to the hospital's emergency room, and then a grocery store, the police station, a convenience store, a gas station. Then we see the light on inside a local bar.

Mom and I walk inside. It's smoky and extremely well lit for a bar. Everyone turns around on their barstools and stares at us. We walk up to the bartender, a short woman wearing a Harley Davidson T-shirt and smoking a cigarette. She eyes my mother, who's holding out a paper sack.

"Who's this for?" the woman asks.

"It's for you."

"Why?" she asks. "I don't know you, do I?"

Mom smiles. "It's because you're working tonight."

The woman takes a drag on her cigarette. "Who do you work for, lady?"

"Nobody," my mom says. "I just do this . . . with my family." She nods at me. I give a dumb little wave.

By now, everyone in the bar is staring at us. "What's in the bag?" an old man asks. "A sandwich?" He looks excited about this possibility.

"It's candy," I say. I take my mom by the elbow and steer her toward the door.

The woman sets the bag on the bar. "Well, thanks, I guess."

"Happy Thanksgiving," my mom calls out.

We step outside. "Geesh," she says. "You think nobody ever did anything nice for her before."

"Maybe not," I say.

We get in the Jeep and tell Sara and Grandma what happened. "Maybe you should make little tags that say, 'Thanks for working on Thanksgiving,' so you don't have to explain what you're doing," Sara says.

My mom's cell phone rings. A minute later, she says, "It's Andi. Her blood pressure's up, and she thinks she's having contractions."

We're only five minutes away, but we race back to the house anyway. The baby's not due for another month. Thankfully, it's a false alarm. "I think I just ate too much," Andi says. John packs up all their stuff to head home. He pats Clay on the butt. "Go give Aunt Cathy a kiss bye-bye." He runs over and kisses me with an open mouth.

"Ooh, a French kiss!" I laugh.

Andi gives me a hug. "Promise me you'll try and have a good time tomorrow," she says. "I hate it when you're sad."

"I don't like it either," I whisper in her ear. "But I'll try."

After everyone's gone to bed, I check my e-mail. Still nothing from Quinn. Then I see I have a message from Chemistry. "Jake in Pittsburgh is interested in you!" the message says. Oh well. I have to pay for the next two months anyway; I might as well use it. I log in and read his profile. He describes himself as "an artist with a day job who rarely takes himself seriously."

Despite disappointments and heartache, we somehow hold on to our romantic impulses, or at least, we bring those impulses out in each other. We sleep late on a cold Sunday morning. We TAKE CARE of each other.

I like that he put those two words in all caps, so I click the Yes buttons and close my laptop for the night. Maybe this holiday isn't going to be a bust after all.


The next morning over breakfast, my grandma says, "You know, Cathy, I read that story you published. That last one."

Grandma subscribes to the announcement list on my Web site; this is how she keeps up with my doings. "Uh-huh. Thanks, Grandma."

"Well, I noticed you used some words in there . . . you know . . . cuss words."

My mom is making toast at the counter. She's listening in but not getting involved.

"I'm sorry if it bothered you, Grandma."

"Oh, heavens, it doesn't bother me." She waves her hand. "It's just . . . I wonder if you've thought about Clay reading that story someday. Is that really the kind of language you want that poor child to be exposed to?" My grandma frowns, shaking her head at the hypothetical tragedy of exposing my nephew to the word "ass."

I put my cup of coffee down. "Grandma, I don't write for kids. I write for adults. And I think that by the time Clay is old enough to read anything I've written, he'll have been exposed to plenty worse than what's in my stuff."

"Oh, I know," she says. "All I'm saying is—"

"Why are you getting upset on Clay's behalf, Grandma? He's not even two years old. If it bothers *you* that I use those words, then just tell me. Don't say you're worried about Clay. Say it embarrasses *you*."

My grandma just sits there with a shocked look on her face as I stand up from the table and stomp upstairs to my room.

A few minutes later, my mom knocks on the door and comes in with my coffee cup and something else in her hand. Sitting on the edge of the bed, she says, "I want to talk to you." She tells me she's proud of me for all the effort I've been making lately, but maybe I need to take a break. Yesterday she heard me say I no longer believe that things work out the way they're supposed to. "You're so worked up about this. So frustrated. I hate to see you like this."

I burst into tears, and I can't stop. It's like the pipe all over again. For a long time, my mom just hugs me. Then she hands me a small pocket-sized booklet titled *How Does God Guide Us?* It's the same shape as the daily devotional, *Our Daily Bread,* which everyone I know in the state of Indiana keeps next to the toilet.

I blow my nose. "Mom, why are you giving me this?"

"I think you need to trust that God has a plan, that all of this is part of a plan."

"What kind of stupid plan says I get ripped off? What kind of plan says I have to end up all alone, huh? I think that plan sucks." I roll over on the bed, putting my back to my mom. "I . . . just refuse to accept that this . . . situation . . . is of my own making or that the universe has a point."

"Why do you say 'universe'? Why can't you say God?"

I sigh. "I don't know, Mom. Because I just feel more comfortable calling it something else, okay?"

"You need to find a way to give some of this to God and just trust that he'll take care of it," she says softly.

My mom can't see me roll my eyes. "Okay."

Then we go downstairs together and find my grandma crying at the kitchen table.

My mom puts her hand on Grandma's shoulder. "Mom? What's the matter?"

She looks up at me through steamed-up glasses. "Cathy, I'm . . . just so sorry . . . you thought I was criticizing you!"

"Oh, Grandma." I sigh. I kneel down and give her a hug.

"I'm your number one fan! You know that, don't you?"

"Yes, Grandma. I know."


Growing up, I felt so different from my family that I sometimes wondered if I'd been born on another planet. Maybe this is why I loved the movie *Superman* so much. Maybe I'd been adopted by a couple of recent high school graduates from Smallville, Indiana. Maybe one day my true identity would be revealed. I'd throw a rock into a pond and Marlon Brando's head would appear and tell me who the heck I was. "Even though you've been raised as a human," he'd say, "you are not one of them."

In the fifth grade, I escaped to the garage, sat on a stool at my dad's reloading bench, and wrote my first story. It was called "Superfrog." Basically it was the plot of *Superman* with frogs instead of people. I must have shown the story to my mother, because sometime later we were at a store and she said, "Cathy! Look at this!" It was a Superfrog pin! Something from my imagination had become real. We were both a little stunned. My mom always nurtured my obsessions, which is extraordinary, considering what I've always been obsessed with. A lot of mothers might say, "You're not adopted! Why do you keep writing these stories about leaving, about becoming a different kind of person, a different kind of woman? Aren't we good enough for you? Aren't I?"

No, my mom said what Superman's adopted father said: "You can do all these amazing things, and sometimes you think that you will burst wide open unless you can tell someone about it, don't you? There's one thing I know for sure, and that is you are here for a reason." My mother didn't try to talk me out of becoming the person I wanted to be. She gave me a great gift: she let me go and didn't take it personally.

Whenever I see *Superman*, I always tear up during the scene when the actor playing the younger version of Christopher Reeve says good-bye to his mother. I always see myself as the young Clark Kent and my mom as Martha Kent.

*(Martha Kent sees her daughter Clark standing outside in the vast wheat field, and she approaches her.)*

**Me:** I have to leave.

**Mom:** I knew this day would come. We both knew it from the day we found you.

**Me:** I talked to Ben Hubbard yesterday and he said . . . he can come around to help.

*(My composure is rapidly breaking down.)*

**Me:** Mother . . .

**Mom:** I know, daughter. I know. Do you . . . know where you'll be going?

**Me:** South. Then North. Then East.

**Mom:** Remember, daughter. Always remember.

*(We embrace and watch the sun rise over the beauty of the Smallville countryside.)*

On Saturday I say good-bye to my family and to the state of Indiana and drive back to Pittsburgh. My quiet house and my lonely cat greet me. When I wake up on Sunday morning, I'm not sure where I am at first, but I quickly reenter my familiar morning routine: make a pot of coffee, empty and/or fill the dishwasher while the coffee drips, take my pills, check my e-mail. And then, because it's Sunday, I get back into bed and read the *New York Times.* Everything's silent. There's no crying grandmother downstairs. No mother pushing religious tracts into my hands. My dad's not down in the basement smoking his morning cigarettes, filling the house with the one smell I'm trying hard to forget. An empty day stretches before me, waiting to be filled. No one expects anything of me, except my cat. Well, that's not true. I have a hundred pages of student work to read and respond to, but I have all day to accomplish this. I can work uninterrupted. I can watch a movie, too. Eat popcorn for dinner. To shower or not to shower? To nap or not to nap? These are the questions that plague me. Sometimes, Andrea will call me and ask, "What are you doing?" and I'll say, "Nothing." And she'll say, "I wish I could be doing nothing, too," and I'll say, "No you don't."

That night my friend Laura calls to ask if I'm going to watch the Colts versus Eagles game. "I don't think we should watch it together," she confesses. "I can get a little intense sometimes."

"Me, too."

"This week I need to watch them alone." The Eagles are Donovan McNabb–less; their star quarterback is out for the season with a knee injury, and the backup, Jeff Garcia, is starting.

"I don't even want to think about Peyton getting hurt."

"Don't even say it," Laura says. "God, I hate being an Eagles fan sometimes." She sighs.

"Call me at halftime," I say. "It'll sort of be like watching the game together!"

So I watch the game alone and put up my Christmas tree. In the first half, the Colts steamroll the Eagles; I almost hope Laura has fallen asleep and isn't watching. Joseph Addai scores three touchdowns—in the first half. There's thirty-four seconds left before halftime, and the score is 21–7. John Madden and Al Michaels are extolling the virtues of tight end Dallas Clark when Clark's tackled at the knees by the Eagles' Sean Considine and dragged down at the 25-yard line. Clark grabs his right knee and writhes around in agony. The camera shows Peyton's "Oh no!" look. A resounding hush falls over the RCA Dome. Up in the box, Colts' president Bill Polian shakes his head. Finally, Clark stands up and limps off the field. The assembled crowd rises and gives him a standing ovation. It's not halftime yet, but my cell phone rings.

"It's the curse," Laura says. "The Madden Curse."

"What are you talking about?"

"Haven't you seen that commercial for the football video game? The one where Dallas Clark takes this huge hit?"

Then I remember that yes, I have seen it. "Oh my God! In the commercial, aren't the Colts playing the Eagles? Is it the same guy who just tackled him?"

Laura says no, in the commercial it's Darren Howard and Brian Dawkins. "But still, this is a really weird coincidence."

"I'm sorry your team is losing," I say.

"Did you know that the guy who just tackled Dallas Clark, Considine? Those two used to play together at Iowa."

"How do you know that?"

"I know my Eagles. Plus, I went to Iowa for undergrad. Go Hawk-eyes."

"Do you believe in curses?"

Laura considers this. "When I played field hockey, I was really super-stitious. I had a lucky scrunchy and lucky socks. I ate the same cereal every morning. Stuff like that."

"I think there's an inverse relationship between the Colts games and my love life."

Laura laughs. "What do you mean?"

I sit down on the couch. "When they win, I lose. When I win, they lose."

"So I guess you're not having a good week then, huh?"

"You could say that, yeah."

On TV, Adam Vinatieri kicks a 44-yard field goal to end the first half. The score is Colts 24, Eagles 7.

"I can't stand to watch this anymore," Laura says. "I'm going to bed."

And in the fourth quarter with the Colts up 45–21, my cell phone rings again. Finally, it's Quinn from Cincinnati.

# Push to the Playoffs

> I wanted to use sports for social change.
>
> —Billie Jean King

---

# WEEK 13: COLTS @ TITANS

## OR

## *Def*ense! *Def*ense! *Def*ense!

---

A reporter sticks a microphone in my face.

**Reporter:** Cathy, can you tell us what happened when you finally spoke with Quinn from Cincinnati? What did he have to say?

**Me:** He said he fully intended to call me back, but things just kept getting in the way. He seems nice. He's not as funny on the phone as he was in his profile. He's a doctor. He has a cat. He's divorced. That's what I know.

**Reporter:** What about Jake?

**Me:** Who's Jake?

**Reporter:** The one from Chemistry. The artist with a day job.

**Me:** Oh, the one who wants us to TAKE CARE of each other. I'm sorry. I get confused sometimes.

**Reporter:** It's understandable.

**Me:** He has a rather dangerous hobby. Parachuting. I don't have a problem with that—as long as I don't have to jump out of a plane.

**Reporter:** And aren't you meeting Chris the Rocker this week?

**Me:** Oh shit! Sorry . . . yeah. I almost forgot about him. Thanks for reminding me.

**Reporter:** No problem.

**Me:** Hey, can I ask you something? How did you get this job? Do you think the NFL needs any more women to be sideline reporters?

Man, I'd love to do this . . . walk around on the sidelines and ask the questions the people watching on TV want to ask but can't . . .

**Reporter:** Well, you need a background in television broadcasting.

**Me:** Oh. Well, is this where you want to be? Wouldn't you rather be doing play-by-play or color? Or sitting at the desk with the big boys?

**Reporter:** Sure, I would. But America likes to see what Howard Cosell called "the jockocracy," former players and coaches sitting at the big desk calling the games. It's the perception that those guys know more about football because they played it or coached it.

**Me:** But not all TV broadcasters are former players. What about Al Michaels? He never played sports. The Gumbel brothers? Bob Costas is shorter than me! Doesn't it bug the crap out of you? Men see you on TV doing your job, they see your fuzzy hat and your long hair and your eyelashes and they think, *That chick doesn't know football. She's just there because the network has to hire women.*

**Reporter** (*Sigh.*): When I'm doing my job, I don't think about being a woman. I don't think about what I look like standing there. If I did, I don't think I could go on camera.

**Me:** All I ever wanted was to be taken seriously, and the only way I saw to do that was *not* to be a woman. I think I forgot I *was* a woman until I turned thirty-seven.

**Reporter:** I know what you mean. But the kicker is that men never stop seeing you as a woman, as *not* them.

**Me:** I remember one time, some guy said, "You're not a real professor. You just got this job because they needed to hire a woman."

**Reporter:** Really? He said that? To your face? That's fucked up.

**Me:** Once I got an e-mail from a guy who said, "Ms. Day, I never read women writers. I have no idea why I picked up your book, but I'm happy I did."

**Reporter:** Why couldn't he just say, "Hey, I liked your book"?

**Me:** I think he thought he was giving me a compliment. He thinks men write about big important things—like America and History and Ideas—and women write about little things—like gardens and babies and *feelings.*

**Reporter:** And dating.

**Me:** Shut up. Dating is just a word we came up with to describe a complicated equation. Sociocultural forces plus fate and/or chance equals love. It's a very serious subject, or haven't you ever heard of Jane Austen? Besides, what I'm really interested in is sports.

**Reporter:** Honey, I hate to be the one to break it to you, but no, you're not.

**Me:** Yes I am!

**Reporter:** Seriously. No, you're not.

**Me:** Maybe not in the same way guys love sports. I don't memorize data. I love the drama, the stories. Why is the way men talk about sports the "serious" way?

**Reporter:** Let me tell you something. You think that saying "I love football" means that men will take you seriously, that your ability to discuss the Colts run defense obliterates the fact of your female-ness. But it doesn't. When you say that you love football, deep down, men think, *Great! Maybe she'll give me a blow job while I watch the game.* Or they think it means you won't nag them about watching football games all day on Sunday.

**Me:** Why can't we watch the games together?

**Reporter:** You can! But let's say you have a baby. The kid's two years old and has a cold. It's Sunday. Who do you think's gonna do most of the baby-watching that day, and who's gonna do most of the football-watching? Men love sports because it's a way to *escape* domestic life, either physically or mentally.

**Me:** This is why a lot of women hate football, isn't it?

**Reporter:** You got it. Football, it's like a culturally sanctioned mistress. Men want to sneak off to meet her because when they're in her arms, they're free.

**Me:** You know what? I understand that. Completely.

**Reporter:** Tony Kornheiser from *Pardon the Interruption* said, "Men are clinging to football on a level we aren't even aware of. For centuries, we ruled everything, and now, in the last ten minutes, there are all these incursions by women. It's our Alamo."

**Me:** Wow.

**Reporter:** Hey, what do you mean you love "the stories" in sports?

**Me:** Men stand around watercoolers, talking about how the Colts' run defense sucks, but most of those guys couldn't explain exactly *why* it sucks. See, men just need something to talk to each other about. Something that's not gardens or babies or feelings. So they talk about, they gossip about football. They say they're comparing field-goal percentages. They say they're talking about whether the Colts should have traded Edgerrin, but they're really talking about characters in a big, complicated story.

**Reporter:** Cathy, do you still want my job?

**Me:** Nah. I'm really very very shy. But you know, I just want to say what a great job you're doing out here, asking these prompting questions. Without you to put it all in context for us, a football game would just be a bunch of random guys in tight pants running into each other.

**Reporter:** Thanks, Cathy. Good luck this week. Back to you, Bob.

Two people are waiting for me outside my office: the Punter and Chris the Rocker. I put a smile on my face and shake Chris's hand while the Punter officially introduces us.

"Chris," I say, "I wonder if I could borrow a moment of your time?"

Ever since I walked up, Chris has had a bewildered look on his face. "Sure," he says.

"Wanna have dinner tonight?" the Punter asks me out of the blue.

"Sorry! I've got class tonight. Maybe another time!"

Chris and I go into my office. He quietly shuts the door behind him. "You're from Match, aren't you?"

I set my bag on my desk and shrug out of my parka. "Yeah, that's sort of why I wanted to talk to you."

His eyes get wide. "Am I in trouble or something?"

"Oh my God, no!" I raise my hands. "Please, sit down and let me explain."

Chris takes a seat. He's wearing sweatpants, a baseball hat, a backpack, and a two-day growth of beard. It's the end of the semester, after all. All my students look a little haggard and smell like ashtrays and old sheets. Chris is almost as old as I am, but he could pass for a twenty-year-old undergrad as long as you don't look too closely at the crows' feet around his eyes.

"First off, I want to apologize for how strange this must feel to you. We initially met in a completely different context. I'm so sorry that in order to find you, I had to go through your professor, but I hope you'll allow me to explain. I want to ask you some questions about your online dating experiences. I guess you could say I'm sort of doing a study."

He tips his baseball hat back. "Is that what you were doing on Match?"

"No, I was just trying to meet someone nice. Probably just like you." I wipe my palms on my corduroys. I'm not prepared for the weirdness of this moment. "But during that time, I started to suspect that some of these companies are engaging in what I think are unfair business practices, and the only way I can prove it is to talk to other parties involved." I hold out my hands. "That's where you come in."

"I've never been involved in a study before. That's cool." He leans his elbows on his knees. "Do I have to sign anything?"

"No, no," I say. "This isn't like a formal study or anything. It's more like a personal project of mine. Okay? Let me show you something." I turn to my computer and go to the Chemistry Web site. "Do you subscribe to Chemistry?"

"No."

I laugh out loud. "That's what I thought! Let me show you something." I go to my list of Active Matches, turn the monitor so he can see, and point to his picture. "Then how did you end up here?"

Chris and I both stare at the computer screen, a small window into my private life—and into his private life, too. He leans forward in his chair and squints. "That's me all right. Wait, isn't this the one that's, like, owned by Match.com?"

"Yeah. See, I actually was sent your profile back in July or August."

Chris's eyebrows furrow as if to say, *Really?*

"And I clicked that I was interested in you."

Chris's eyebrows rise, as if to say, *Really!*

"But I never heard from you, so I thought you'd seen me and weren't mutually interested."

Chris's eyebrows furrow again.

"But then I went on Match a few months later, and you contacted me, which made me think two things. Either you were never actually on Chemistry, or you were and there was some glitch in the system and you and all the men I clicked Yes on were never notified."

Chris scoots his chair closer to mine. "Excuse me . . ."

"Sure, sure," I say, handing him the keyboard and mouse.

He reduces the window and opens another, back to Chemistry. "I don't know if I've ever checked this account," he says, pecking at the keyboard.

"So you do subscribe?"

"I think I remember them trying to get me to sign up for this site. They offered me a free membership, so I started to do it, but they were going to make me take this really long test or something, so I bailed and never finished." He pecks away a few more times. "Yeah, look, there you are!" There's a long list of women's names on the screen, and sure enough, there I am. "I never saw this. Let me see how far I got . . ."

I lean back and give him some space. "When I was signing up, there was this little meter, like a download gauge, that told you how far you were into the enrollment process."

"Yeah, look," he says. According to the meter, Chris has completed 9 percent of the process.

"And you never paid a dime?"

He laughs. "No way."

"They sent me your profile, so I thought you were really a member. You never even finished the test!"

He shrugs. "I guess they figure 9 percent of me is better than 100 percent of other guys!"

I politely ignore this. "How can they say that we have chemistry if you never took the dumb test! Can I see that for a minute, please?" I take the keyboard and mouse and open up the window into my Chemistry account. At the bottom of the profile is a button to find out how our personalities compare. It's only when I click on that button that I get this message:

Chemistry has selected Chris as a match for you based on the pro-file information we have received at this point. You can see how you match at this stage in the chart below. When he completes his entire Chemistry Profile, you'll be able to learn more about him.

"That must be their out," Chris says. "They can say I haven't completed my profile yet, but honestly, if you hadn't contacted me, I wouldn't have thought about this ever again. Umm . . . can I ask you something?" he says. I say, "Sure," and he asks me if I'm dating the Punter.

I smile serenely. "No, he's just a friend."

"Because out in the hallway, he just asked you to dinner, and you know, I don't want him to think I'm putting moves on his woman."

"No. Seriously, there's absolutely nothing to worry about." That's when I see the look on his face, like he's going to ask me out. I stand and stick out my hand.

"This was interesting," Chris says.

"Likewise," I say.

Now I have my proof! I was right about Chemistry! But you know what? I'm still single.

For the next few days, I correspond with Jake the Parachutist. He stresses his loyalty, his generosity, his stability. He promises that he will take my face in his hands and lavish me with love and draw me bubble baths at the end of my long workdays. I think it sounds canned and absolutely ridiculous until he goes on to say that he's learned from past relationships that he needs an intellectual equal, a woman he can really talk to. And that in order to keep an intelligent, independent woman in his life, he's going to have to give *her* as much emotional support as he wants in return.

Oh my.

When I tell him that I am a writer, he says, "I think I have a 'thing' for writers, something about intelligent women who can communicate with the written word or spoken word, women who are thoughtful and articulate are very attractive." He leads a quiet life except for the parachuting, which he hopes will not be a deal-breaker. He signs his e-mails to me, "yours faithfully . . . . . . . jake." Always lower case, always seven periods, always faithfully. The supersappy lyrics from "Faithfully" by Journey waft through my head. Maybe I've finally found the right guy for a girl like me.

I'm in my office when I get a new e-mail from Jake. He wants to know if we can talk on the phone, and offers up his number. He signs off with his full name for the first time: "yours faithfully . . . . . . . jake oregon."

"Is that him?" Laura asks. She and Janet are in my office.

"Yeah. What do you think?"

They scan through his profile and pictures. They approve.

"Wait," I say, plugging his first and last name and "Pittsburgh" into

Google. The first link that pops up says: "Beware Jake Oregon of Pitts-burgh, PA. Chronic Cheater. Pays Hookers."

"Oh my God!"

"What?" Janet and Laura step behind me and look at the screen.

I click on the first link and am taken to some sort of support group's message board.

> I am writing this to protect one of you from becoming this man's next victim. I lived with this man for two years. Jake said I was the most important thing in his life and that he loved me more than anything. Every day, he took my face in his hands and said he loved me. Some-times he'd declare that a normal day was "Sandy Appreciation Day" and buy me flowers and a card for no reason. We were best friends and lovers, but I didn't know he had a secret: sexual deviancy. I re-cently discovered that he slept with prostitutes before and during our relationship. And he still is. I've found his profile on match.com and other dating sites. His profile spells out what he is looking for, which is everything he and I had together. Don't believe his lies like I did. I can prove that I'm telling the truth.

The text that follows is cut and pasted, a series of e-mails between Jake and a woman who signs her name "Trixie." First Jake sends her an e-mail seeking an "extended appointment," he says, signing his name, "yours faithfully . . . . . . . jake."

Oh my.

There's some back and forth as they settle on the day and time. Then there's some cut-and-pasted MapQuest directions to Trixie's home, along with her address and cell phone number. She warns him to call only if he needs to cancel or he gets lost.

My office is very quiet.

Finally Janet says, "Do you think this is for real?"

I point to "yours faithfully" and the seven periods. "That's how he signs his name."

Laura says, "Maybe a bitter ex is spreading lies about him on the Internet?"

I consider this. "Do I want to go out with a guy who would piss a woman off this badly?"

"Good point," Laura says.

"Oh, Cathy," Janet says, putting her hand on my shoulder. "I'm so sorry."

"Look at some of the other links," Laura says. "What else did this guy do?"

Apparently there are quite a few Web sites that specialize in the exchange of this sort of information—TrueDater.com and DontDateHim Girl.com, whose founder, Tasha C. Joseph, likens her site to "dating credit reports." In any case, Jake's girlfriend has gone onto a few of them and told the same story numerous times, always attaching her "evidence," the cut-and-pasted e-mails and directions to Trixie's house.

"Do you believe her?" Laura asks.

"Look at the e-mail address he used to contact the hooker," I say. It's gobbledygook, a bunch of letters and numbers that don't seem to have anything to do with his name, his address, his zip code. "Like he has so many addresses, he just has to generate them randomly. Now look at the e-mail address he wrote to me from." Again, the address seems like jabberwocky. "I remember thinking that was a really strange e-mail address, you know?"

"What gave you the idea to Google him?" Janet asks.

"What is it they say? The best offense is a good defense?" I turn my computer off. "I don't believe anybody anymore." Then I go straight home and throw up. I climb into my bed. I don't leave the house for two days.

Late Friday night, my sister Andrea gives birth to her second child, a boy. Daniel. He's a month early but plenty healthy. On Saturday night, Andrea has recovered a little from the C-section, and Clay is brought to the hospital to meet his little brother. Everyone in my family is at Good Samaritan Hospital—except for me. My brother calls. "Send me a picture," I say. "I want to see this!" But apparently I can't get pictures sent to my phone. My mom and sister have a ton of pictures on their cameras, but there's no way to e-mail them to me. I can't believe this. This is the information age. If I can get the phone number, e-mail, and mailing address of the prostitute frequented by Jake the Parachutist, why can't I see my newborn nephew?

Scott hands the phone to Andrea. "I wish I could be there," I tell her. "If he'd come just a week earlier, I would have been there when he was born!"

"Why don't you come?" she says tiredly.

"I teach on Monday and Tuesday. It's finals time. I'd get there, meet the baby, and have to turn around and drive back again."

She yawns. "When are you coming home for Christmas?"

"Two weeks."

"It's okay," she says, "he'll be cuter by then anyway. Maybe by that point you'll be going out with this Quinn guy and you'll just move to Cincinnati and you can see us whenever you want!"

"He's supposed to call me tonight. We'll see." I decide not to tell her about Jake the Hooker-Loving Parachutist. She just had surgery.

"I miss you," Andrea says tiredly. "Call me later."

And magically, Quinn does call. I tell him my whole family is at Good Sam Hospital. "You're a doctor, right? Is that where you work?"

He says no, he's got a private practice. "You didn't tell me you were famous," Quinn says.

I laugh. "Probably because I'm not."

"Well, don't take this the wrong way, but I Googled you and found your Web site."

"Well, anybody can get a Web site," I say. I don't tell him that I Googled him, too. He's clean—thank God. "I told you I was a writer."

"But you've published a book! I went out to the bookstore and bought it."

"Thanks. That's very sweet of you." It's a cold night in Pittsburgh, and I haven't left my bed all day except to make coffee and use the bathroom. I ask Quinn, "Why didn't you call me when you knew I was in Cincinnati?"

He hmmms a bit, but then he says that he thinks women on Match.com move way too fast. "I like to take it a bit more slowly."

"I think women are just anxious to get the ball rolling, you know?"

Quinn laughs. "What's the hurry?"

"Maybe you're worried women just want to hurry up and get married."

"As if that's the answer to everything." He sighs.

"What do you mean?" I ask.

"Marriage isn't some ticket to happiness."

I snort. "I wouldn't know."

"Look, being single isn't the greatest thing in the world, but most of the people I know who're married are pretty miserable."

"Really? Most of the married people I know seem happy."

"That's what they tell you anyway. Trust me. I was married, and I think a lot of married people stay together because they fear the alternative—the stigma. They don't want to be alone. They'd rather have someone around, even if they never really talk anymore, or all they do is yell."

For months, people have said to me, "It's not like being married is the answer to all your problems, Cathy. It might just create new ones." But for some reason, Quinn's words sink in.

"So being single is like a badge of honor," I say. "We're saying we refuse to accept an unacceptable partnering."

"Exactly!"

Maybe the man's got a point.


But he still hasn't asked me out on a date. Talking's fine. Talking's great. Especially when the person exists in physical reality and not just on the sidelines of my subconscious. So I keep looking on Match. It's Sunday, but there's a whole lot of nothing. I delete an e-mail from a twenty-three-year-old man who says he likes "older women" (please don't let me hurt him). I wink halfheartedly at a cute guy named Dennis who says he's from New Jersey. Whatever. I can hear my own excuses starting to form: I'm busy, I'm coming down with something, there are white spots on my tonsils, it's almost finals, I have papers to grade. I want to give myself an excuse, any excuse, to just stop this madness and resume my dull and solitary existence.

I take a nap during the Colts game against the Titans. I can't watch the game anyway, so I might as well. The Colts are going to win; the Titans are 5–6. But when I wake up and check the box score online, I discover that the Colts have *lost* 17–20! I call my brother Scott in Batesville. "What the hell happened?" I yell.

"Calm down," he says. He's outside putting up Christmas lights. "The Colts blew a 14-point lead. They had four false starts. Penalties. Then some guy on the Titans . . . Bironas . . . kicked a 60-yard field goal at the very end. Sixty yards! It set some record or something. That game really sucked."

"Sorry."

"I'm in a bad mood right now."

"Me too," I say, but inside, I feel this weird flicker of hope, too. If the Colts just lost, maybe that means something good is going to happen in my love life.

And guess what? For once, I'm right.

*Playoffs? Don't talk about—playoffs! You kidding me?*
*Playoffs? I just hope we can win a game!*

—Jim E. Mora, Indianapolis Colts head coach, 2001

---

# WEEK 14: COLTS @ JAGUARS

## OR

# Do You Believe in Miracles?

---

Quinn from Cincinnati sends me an e-mail. One of his patients is dying, and there's nothing more he can do. He writes about one of his best friends who died of cancer a few years ago, and how it's all coming back: feeling helpless and frustrated and angry. This is the first time Quinn has really opened up to me, so I write him back and say it must be hard to be a doctor. I tell him about my mother, a hospice nurse, about how she's taught me that helping someone doesn't have to mean you fix them; sometimes it means you just say, "I'm here. I'm listening."

A few hours later, my computer dings to tell me I have a new e-mail. It's from Buzz Bissinger! He thanks me for giving him a copy of my book when he was in Pittsburgh. He read some on the plane and says he's enjoying it a lot. I'm so excited, I yell. I'm in my office at school, so Janet comes running in to ask what's wrong.

"Nothing's wrong!" I say. "Buzz Bissinger liked my book!"

"Wow, that's awesome!" she says. Then she cocks her head a little. "Hey, that's nice. I came in here because you got some *good* news via the Internet!"

I write Quinn back. "Hey, guess what? I just got an e-mail from Buzz

Bissinger, the guy who wrote *Friday Night Lights.* He was in Pittsburgh a few weeks ago. Check it out!" I forward the message to Quinn and hit Send.

And that, folks, is the last time I ever hear from Quinn in Cincinnati.


A reporter sticks a microphone in my face.

**Reporter:**  Cathy, what went wrong?

**Me:**  I don't know. I don't know. Fuck!

**Reporter:**  I could speculate, but—

**Me:**  Let's talk to a guy then. I'm sick of trying to read their stupid minds.

**Reporter:**  Well, my husband's here . . . *honey!* Could you come over here for a sec?

**Reporter's Husband:** What's up?

**Reporter** (*Explains the situation with Quinn, from the picture holding the cat to the Thanksgiving Date that Never Was to the recent e-mail exchange and the ensuing radio silence*):  So, what do you think?

**Reporter's Husband:**  Well, if I was this Quinn guy. . . . What did you say he does?

**Me:**  He's a doctor.

**Reporter's Husband:**  Still. I'd be a little intimidated. . . . You got an e-mail from the guy who wrote *Friday Night Lights.*

**Me:**  If I was a guy and I met a woman who knew Buzz Bissinger, I'd think that was cool!

**Reporter:**  Cathy, need I remind you? You are not a guy.

**Reporter's Husband:**  Maybe Quinn thinks he'd have to compete with Buzz Bissinger.

**Me:**  Who said anything about a competition? I'm not pitting them against each other, for godssakes! Why can't it just be one writer telling another writer that he likes her work? What if the e-mail was from Laura Hillenbrand?

**Reporter's Husband:**  Who's that?

**Reporter:**  She wrote *Seabiscuit.*

**Reporter's Husband:**  Okay, then here's what I think. Bottom line. You scared the guy off. Maybe you should be more modest.

**Me:**  Ouch. (*I blush, and my eyes well up with tears.*)

**Reporter:**  Uhh . . .

**Me** (*I gather my senses.*):  Now wait a minute here. I'm a Hoosier. We're a very modest people. And this wasn't a First Meeting Coffee Shop Date and I said, "Oh! Guess what? I got an e-mail from Buzz Bissinger today!" Quinn and I had been e-mailing and talking on the phone for almost two weeks.

**Reporter's Husband:**  You asked for my opinion . . .

**Me:**  I can't believe it. I work all my adult life so that I can walk in the tall grass with the big dogs, and now none of the other dogs will play with me.

**Reporter:**  Cathy, I know you weren't bragging. You were just really excited.

**Me:**  Yes! I was!

**Reporter:**  Once John Madden said, "Nice job, Suzy," and I glowed for a week, didn't I, honey?

**Reporter's Husband:**  You wouldn't shut up about it.

**Reporter:**  And this time you searched for a man who wouldn't be intimidated, another "big dog," professionals only!

**Me:**  If a doctor who makes triple what I make is intimidated by me, who's left? Captains of industry?

**Reporter's Husband:**  Maybe Quinn stopped calling because he met another woman, or because he decided to move to Alaska. It might not have anything to do with Buzz Bissinger. Why don't you just ask the guy?

**Reporter:**  Honey, if you stopped communicating with a woman, would you want her to ask why you stopped communicating?

**Reporter's Husband:**  Good point.

**Me:**  What's he going to say if I ask? "Deep down, you make me feel inferior."

**Reporter's Husband:**  Um . . . are we done here? Because I'd like to get back to the game.

**Reporter:**  Sure, honey. I'll see you later.

**Me** (*Pause.*): He's nice.

**Reporter:** Thanks.

**Me:** You know, the first question you asked me today was "What went wrong?" The implication is always, "What did you—sorry-ass single person—do wrong?" Have you seen this show on A&E called *Confessions of a Matchmaker*?

**Reporter:** The one set in Buffalo? I love that show!

**Me:** Here's the premise: everybody who walks in her office door has some personal flaw that's keeping them single. They have too many pets. They're too close to their mother. They wear weird clothes. The assumption is that if you're still single, there must be something wrong with you. It's hard enough to get out there and date, let alone having to constantly worry if your glaring defect is showing.

**Reporter:** But, Cathy, um, you do have flaws . . .

**Me:** Don't you think I know that? Don't you know me at all by now?

**Reporter:** Okay, I won't ask you, "What went wrong?" anymore.

**Me:** Thanks. That would help a lot.

**Reporter:** Reporting live from the sidelines of this battle taking place inside Cathy Day's head, this is Suzy Hightop. Back to you, Bob.

On Saturday night, I go out to dinner and a movie with Ben and Laura, Janet and Jerry. We go to Fuddruckers, where I order nachos and a milk shake. These days I'm all about comfort food. While Jerry and Ben discuss who should win the Heisman Award, Janet asks, "Hey! You have a date tomorrow? Who's this guy?" So I tell them about Dennis, the cute guy I winked at a week earlier. We started e-mailing and discovered an interesting coincidence: I moved from New Jersey to Pittsburgh to be closer to my family in Indiana, and he just moved from Indiana to Pittsburgh to be closer to his family in New Jersey.

Laura's eyebrows raise. "That's soooo weird."

"I know," I say. "What are the chances? We talked on the phone last night for over an hour." We had a lot in common—geographically at least. Two years ago, each of us was stranded in the other's home state, feeling that salmonic drive to swim upstream. Separately but simultaneously we moved closer to home, but our jobs dictated how close to home we could get. And that's how we both ended up in Pittsburgh.

"What's he do?" Janet asks.

"He's a CNC operator." Janet and Laura both look at me blankly, waiting for me to translate. Truth is, I had had to ask my brother Scott to translate. "It means computer numerically controlled," I tell them, explaining that these days, most high-powered machines are controlled by computers with programmed instructions. "He's sort of an IT guy for huge-ass machines and engines."

"Oh," they say, nodding their heads. "IT guy" is a job title we all understand.

Perhaps you're wondering why I'm out on a Friday night with two married couples instead of my many single friends. And I say, I would love to be a member of one of those New Urban Families the media keeps yammering about, just like the ones on TV and in the movies. Tell me where to find Joey and Rachel and Phoebe! (But don't tell me where to find Carrie, Samantha, and Miranda—they scare me a little.) How can I get in touch with Bridget Jones and her friends Shazzer and Jude and Tom? For now, my urban family consists of these two couples who—thankfully—are not like Bridget's smug marrieds. When I'm with this group, I feel like I'm simply out with four people I know, and that's a blessing when you're a person like me: a Lone Single.

I need to say some things now about what it's like being a Lone Single. I speak from my own experience and those of my fellow Lone Single friends all over the country, but to be on the safe side and because I really do like to be invited to parties, I'm going to address my comments to fictional characters. You know that scene in *Bridget Jones's Diary*, when she walks into that dinner party with all the couples? The one where they ask her why there are so many unmarried women in their thirties, and she takes a big, big drink of wine and says, "Oh, I don't know, maybe because underneath our clothes, we're covered in scales." These comments are for the hosts of that little soiree.

I know, I know, you don't want your Lone Single friend to feel uncomfortable at your dining room table. You want everyone to have a good time—but what to do about Bridget. . . . Maybe you should invite that chum of your sister's, Barry, you know, the one who drives the Miata? But maybe that will seem too much like a setup. Hmmm . . . who else do you know who's not coupled up? Isn't George's wife at her mother's for two weeks? Maybe he'd like to pop over and keep Bridget company. Or there's Ramona. She's going through that nasty divorce . . . maybe she and Bridget will hit it off? Oh, crikey! Why can't Bridget have a husband or a boyfriend like a normal person! This is impossible! You're just trying to have a simple, balanced dinner party. Well anyway, she probably has better things to do on Saturday night than hang out with a bunch of old married couples. She's probably out at one of those clubs, dancing and having the time of her life!

Oh, host and hostess, don't *not* invite Bridget. See, it's moments like this when being single feels like having cancer or being extremely obese, because we know you don't know quite what to say or not say, what to ask or not ask. A social gathering needn't look like Noah's Ark. Why not invite Bridget and George *and* Barry *and* Ramona? And why not seat everyone more randomly? Maybe everyone is sick of talking to their spouses all day. But please, don't feel like you have to go in search of a right shoe to pair up with Bridget, who is left. It's a party, not a shoe store. Oh, gracious host and hostess, keepers of invitations, when you're creating a guest list or perhaps musing about seeing a movie and grabbing a drink afterwards, don't think in terms of pairs. Think *household.* For now, Bridget is a household of one. Don't forget her. She is not out dancing. Bridget is at home right now, sloshed on Chardonnay, lip-synching to Céline Dion.

After the movie we walk to our cars in the parking lot, dusted now with snow. Ben and Laura give me hugs. "What are you two doing on your date tomorrow?" Janet asks.

"Well, he says he likes art." I roll my eyes. I figure this was just his attempt to seem sensitive and cosmopolitan. "So we were going to go to the Carnegie Museum, but then I remembered that the Colts are playing the Jaguars tomorrow, so we're going to a sports bar to watch it."

Janet and Jerry give me hugs. Laura says, "You never know, Cathy. This might be the one you've been waiting for."

I roll my eyes again. "You know, after the whole chronic cheater, pays hookers thing, I've decided to keep my expectations low." But I'm lying. That hopeful feeling is still there, even though I've tried to suppress it with a milk shake and nachos.

It's Sunday, December 10, 2006, and I wake up in a foul mood. It's finals week, and I have a ton of work to do. My hopeful feeling from last night is gone. In its place is a growing certainty that this date is just going to end up being a big waste of a perfectly good afternoon, time that would be better spent attacking my huge grading pile. The Indianapolis Colts are in Jacksonville, Florida, preparing to take on the Jaguars at 1:00 PM, and I am in Pittsburgh, parked outside a sports bar in the Strip District, preparing to take on this Dennis character. He's sitting at the bar when I walk in, staring at me with a deer-in-the-headlights look on his face. I walk right up to him and stick out my hand. "Dennis? Hey, I'm Cathy. Excuse me. I really have to use the restroom."

"Sure," he says, looking a little shocked.

I turn and walk away. As I use the bathroom, I have to remind myself: *Be nice, Cathy.* Dennis seems like a good egg, so why do I feel mad at a man I've spent two seconds with? He's tall and blond and nicely dressed in cargo pants and a sweater. Dennis isn't the Punter. He's not Jake the Parachuting Hooker-Lover. He's not Max or Quinn. Dennis is a brand-new ball game. I can't walk into that bar thinking about the games I've already lost. I can't walk out there thinking I'm probably just going to lose this game just like all the others—or that's exactly what will happen. If it hasn't happened already. I probably didn't make a very good first impression, storming in like this was some annoying meeting to be gotten through. *Come on, Cathy. Man up. Smile and at least act like you're having a good time. The Colts are playing a division rival, and you get to watch it on a large screen and drink beer.* The guitar intro from Golden Earring's "Twilight Zone" plucks its way through the bathroom, carried by an invisible sound system. I yank the bathroom door open and walk down the dim, tunnellike hallway. The sports bar opens up before me—an enormous space full of big screens and neon beer signs. Dennis is still seated at the bar, and I slip into the stool next to him. "Sorry," I say, smiling. "Let's try this again."

Dennis smiles back. "It's really nice to meet you." He's already finished his beer. "I asked the bartender where they'll be showing the Colts game." He points to one of the small televisions situated above the bartender's head. "That's it. You're the only one in here who wants to watch that game."

This is when I finally notice that the bar is almost empty. "Where are all the Steelers fans?" I ask.

The bartender says, "They played the Browns on Thursday."

"Oh, right. I forgot."

Today, the Sports Rock Café in Pittsburgh resembles a Lost Generation café in France: most of the patrons are expatriates. The bar has four superlarge screens showing four different games. There are no black-and-gold bumblebees on any of the screens. Against the brilliant emerald turf I see Packers green, Vikings purple, and Falcons red. Families sit at the tables before each screen, eating chicken wings and burgers, drinking pitchers of Coke and beer. A few are wearing non-Pittsburgh sportswear: a Lions jersey, a 49ers baseball cap. With no Steelers game to watch, native Pittsburghers are likely out Christmas shopping or putting up holiday lawn decorations, which makes it safe for the rest of us to enter sports bars not wearing a Steelers jersey and cheer for a team that's not the Steelers.

"So I'm the only one in here who wants to watch the Colts game?" I ask.

"Yep," the bartender says with a smirk.

"Nope," Dennis says. "There's two."

As it turns out, arranging a football date rather than your standard coffee first date was a stroke of genius, because if I'd met Dennis for only forty-five minutes, I would have walked away thinking, *This guy isn't interested in me at all*. He's very quiet for most of the game and seems a tad nervous and jumpy. When he's not peeling off his beer label, he's holding on to the bottle as if for dear life. But I don't care. I understand social anxiety. As Jacksonville's Maurice Jones-Drew runs for yet another first down against the Colts, I realize that if this date is going to work, I'll have to keep the conversation going, which is fine by me. Most of the men I've met on first dates won't shut up long enough to even ask me a question.

At one point, Dennis gets up to use the restroom, and my cell phone rings. It's my sister Andrea. She's nursing, but she wants to know how the date is going. "Not too good," I tell her. "I don't think he's that into me. He barely even looks at me." But then I tell her about his good points: he drinks Miller Lite (my family's beer of choice), laughs at my jokes, and rebuilds car engines in his spare time. He likes art, museums, *and* football.

"No way," she says. "And you have that connection with the whole Indiana, New Jersey, Pittsburgh thing. Wait. Do they have Trivial Pursuit at that bar?"

I look around. "No, I don't think so."

"Good. Don't play Trivial Pursuit. You'll beat him and it will make him feel bad. That's my opinion."

I roll my eyes. "Will do, Andi." I see Dennis coming back from the bathroom. "Call ya later," I whisper, clicking my phone shut.

After a while, I wish I *weren't* watching the Colts game, which just gets uglier and uglier. They lose 44–17, their second loss in a row. The Jaguars rush for 375 yards, tied for the second most in an NFL game since 1970. "That was the worst football game I've ever seen," I say to Dennis when the game is finally over.

"Yeah."

I figure he's probably itching to go home. "Well," I say, "we could leave or go ahead and watch some of the Jets game. You said you liked the Jets."

"Okay," he says.

Later, I say, "Well, if you need to go home, that's okay, or I could show you around Pittsburgh a little."

"Okay," he says.

We walk across the street to the nearly empty parking lot. Dennis points. "That's my truck over there," he says.

"Oh, that's the same kind of truck my brother used to drive." When we climb inside, I see that's exactly the same interior, too. I direct him back up Liberty Avenue and through Shadyside to Oakland, toward the University of Pittsburgh's campus. From a distance, I point out the Cathedral of Learning, lit up white against the blue-black night sky.

"That's where I work," I say. *Watch out,* I think. *This is where he gets freaked out.*

"Wow," he says. "That's really cool." He says he'd love to see the inside.

We park on Forbes and walk through the revolving doors into the four-story Gothic Revival Common Room, decorated for the holidays with ten-foot Christmas trees twinkling with white lights. It's like walking into Notre Dame, but instead of pews or altars, there are tables crowded with students studying for exams and six-foot limestone hearths ablaze with crackling fires. *Here it comes,* I think. *He's gonna freak out now. He's going to think, "I can't go out with a girl who works here."*

"Wow," he says. "This is amazing."

We explore the first floor together and discover that the Cathedral of Learning is made of Indiana limestone. I find this fact enormously comforting, like nachos and a milk shake.

Dennis and I take the elevator to the fifth floor so I can show him my office. "I'm telling you, it's not nearly as impressive as the ground floor," I say.

When I unlock the door and turn on the light, Dennis says, "Look at all those books!"

"Yeah," I say. "I just keep them there because it makes me look smart."

Dennis sees that on the bottom shelf there are some paperback copies of my book. "Is this yours?" During the game, I told him I wrote a book, but didn't go into much detail.

"Yeah," I say. *Here it comes,* I think. *He's gonna think, "I can't go out with a writer."*

"Wow. Can I buy one from you?" He has this sparkle in his eye, a look that definitely says "I like you."

*Zing!*

I can scarcely believe it. He still likes me! I'm amazed.

As we walk back to his truck, I get nervous and reach for the candy I keep in my coat pocket. "I used to smoke," I confess, worried what he'll think of this. Dennis seems like a straight-arrow kind of guy.

Instead, he sighs. "So did I. Quit a few years ago."

*Zing!*

We talk about how hard it was to quit smoking, and I hand him some candy.

"Spree," he says. "I love Spree."

"Me, too."

*Zing!*

Dennis drives me back to my car in the Strip District. Even though it's our first date, I feel like I can trust him enough to show him where I live, so I take him through Polish Hill.

"Oh, this is where you live?" he asks.

"Yeah, it's kind of a unique neighborhood." I direct him to my house and point it out as we pass. "It's a lot different from Indiana, isn't it?"

"Yeah."

"Sometimes in Pittsburgh, I feel like I'm in another country."

"I know what you mean," he says, "and I've never even been to another country."

When we get to the Sports Rock Café parking lot, he pulls up next to my car. I look down at my watch. "Well, our first date lasted six hours. That's pretty good."

"Yeah," he says. "I hope I can see you again."

"Well, I'm leaving on Wednesday or Thursday to go back to Indiana. And Tuesday I'm having my students over to my house for class. That leaves Monday."

"That's tomorrow," he says.

"Oh," I say, looking at my hands. "Well . . ."

"Why don't you come out to where I live?" he asks.

This is what we decide to do.

Now all that's left is our parting, and he's leaning over the console toward me. Sure, this is our first date, but I don't even think twice before I kiss him good night.

*Zing!*

On the way home, my cell phone rings. It's my brother Scott. I talk in a mad rush, telling him all about Dennis. "Wow," Scott says. "This guy seems real nice. Sounds a little like fate brought you together."

"Oh fate schmate," I say, but inside I'm thinking, *Yes it does sound a little like fate, doesn't it?*

> It was TV. It changed everything, changed the way we think. I
> mean the first time they stopped the game to cut away to
> some fucking commercial, that was the end of it. Because it
> was *our* concentration that mattered, not theirs, not some
> fruitcake selling cereal.
>
> —Al Pacino in *Any Given Sunday*

---

# WEEK 15: COLTS VS. BENGALS
# WEEK 16: COLTS @ TEXANS
# WEEK 17: COLTS VS. DOLPHINS

## OR

## Are We There (at the Playoffs) Yet?

---

The rhetoric of dating has become so silly and debauched that I'm
forced to use the rhetoric of sports to talk about it. For example:
not even for research purposes can I bring myself to watch an entire episode of most reality dating TV shows. You know, *Blind Date* (the one with
the thought bubbles), *elimiDATE* (the one with four competing suitors),
*The Bachelor* and *The Bachelorette* (oh those horrible rose ceremonies!),
*Average Joe* (the one that asks female contestants to choose between certi-
fied hunks or obvious geeks), not to be confused with *Joe Millionaire*—
the one where a poor guy pretends to be a rich guy. I stumble across
these shows sometimes, stare in horrified fascination, think *Paddy
Chayefsky was right! Network isn't even a satire anymore!* and quickly turn
the channel.

However, reality TV doesn't have to be a sign of the Apocalypse. When
it wants to, it can approach documentary filmmaking in the spirit of

*Roger and Me* or *Supersize Me*. Singer Lisa Loeb's reality dating TV show *#1 Single* on E! was like that. Here was a professional woman my age searching for a true partner. It wasn't a thinly veiled Helen Fielding posing as Bridget Jones or a thinly veiled Candace Bushnell posing as Carrie Bradshaw, but Lisa Loeb posing as a public version of herself. The premise: she's been in two six-year relationships that didn't work out. She's thirty-seven. Time's awastin'. So she moves from LA to New York City. She enlists the help of friends and family. She tries all sorts of ways to meet men, using both virtual and actual social networks. Lisa tries one service that introduces her ahead of time to a single guy on her already scheduled plane flight, an ingenious service that allows busy professionals to travel and date simultaneously. Lisa borrows a dog and walks it in the park. Lisa's sister walks up and down the street asking men "Are you single?" Lisa asks a male friend to be her wingman, but then ends up dating the wingman briefly, until he seemingly parlays his fifteen minutes of fame into an acting job and takes off for LA.

The question you're asking (and I asked too) is: "Why did she do this?" To promote herself? Why not conduct her search for love privately like everybody else? However, I am enormously grateful that she allowed some documentary filmmakers into her "life project." Bless her little bespectacled heart, she inspired me. Unfortunately, Lisa didn't find love at the end of season one, and there's been no season two (probably because her show didn't provide the cheap thrills of *elimiDATE*). If you rounded up a group of people and put them in five groups (teens, twenties, thirties, forties, fifties, and up) and showed them an episode of *#1 Single*, here's what I'll bet they'd say:

**Teens:** Who the hell is Lisa Loeb?

**Twenties:** Who cares if there's a camera with her on dates? People film themselves all the time. Hello . . . YouTube! Anyway, the show's kinda boring. She needs to get in a hot tub or dump a drink on some guy.

**Thirties:** Isn't that the girl who wrote that song from *Reality Bites*? *(The person starts wistfully singing the lyrics to "Stay [I Miss You]."*) Wait! Oh my God! Is she really going on dates on television?! Is this woman insane?

**Forties:** A desperate move to kick-start her career, plus she's desperate to get married and have children. Desperate, desperate, desperate.

**Fifties and up:** If she hadn't been so selfish and hungry for fame and pursued a singing career, she'd have a husband and babies by now. She's a narcissist, just like all the other kids today!

Replace "How do you feel about *#1 Single*?" with "How do you feel about online dating?" and you're likely to hear these same generational reactions, which are based on that age group's comfort with communication tools such as e-mail, webcams, MySpace, AOL Instant Messenger, text messaging, blogs, and YouTube.

In both dating and football, technology has changed everything—how the game is played and how we experience the game itself. First, of course, radio and then television allowed us to experience football games without being physically present. Then technology changed how we watched football on TV. The first use of instant replay during a televised football game occurred on December 7, 1963, during the Army-Navy game. The TV announcer felt the need to explain to the potentially confused viewing audience, "This is not live, ladies and gentlemen. Army did not score again." It's hard to imagine watching a televised football game in the low-tech days, before instant replay and Skycams, when there was no box in the corner of the screen to tell me instantly the score, the quarter, the time remaining, and before the "crawl" feeding me statistics and scores from other games. I know I'm not the only person who has trouble following live football games now because I keep looking for that magical yellow first-down marker. Some of the impediments (like space and time) that once stood between a football fan and the game itself are being obliterated. We can DVR games and watch them later. We can root for teams outside our region. We can connect to our favorite team via Direct TV, online hometown newspapers, and Internet fan forums, where we can sit on virtual barstools and virtually cheer and chat with fellow fans before, during, and after games.

Technology has changed how we experience football games that have already been played. There's a big difference between watching a Colts game live on national television and watching the NFL Films production of that game on Wednesday night on HBO's *Inside the NFL*. Using multiple cameras (one devoted exclusively to that now ubiquitous, slow-motion "tight-on-the-spiral" shot), manly background orchestration, and the deep, deep voices of narrators like John Facenda (who some call "The Voice of God"), the editors and producers at NFL Films can transform a mere gridiron game into a gladiatorial battle of colossal and epic proportions. Did you know that the NFL is the second-most filmed subject, behind World War II? Watch a History Channel documentary about D-Day and then watch *NFL Films Presents,* and you can't help but get swept up in the unfolding historical drama unfurling before you.

And technological progress has changed the way football players play the game. Take the football helmet, which was once nothing more than a leather head harness. Then the helmet went plastic (like everything else in America) with a chin strap and a single-bar face mask. Scientists speculate that someday in the not-so-distant future, the football helmet will become a one-piece helmet and shoulder pad combination. Can't you just hear your dad saying, "In my day, we didn't even play with helmets! These guys are soft, I tell you! Soft!" And haven't you already heard him say, "In my day, we didn't meet girls on the Internet! We met them in bars, the old-fashioned way!"

What kind of old-school Luddite would argue against using technology that helps people? That saves the lives of football players? The NFL is always weighing whether a technological advancement is "good for" the game of football or not. Is instant replay good for football? Is it good that, between series, quarterbacks can study aerial shots of the plays they just ran and the way the defense lined up against it? Is the camera itself (and the practices engendered by it) good for sports? Is it good for football that when the JumboTron camera pans the crowd, people turn into crazy lunatics? Does the camera have a similar effect on the athletes? Of course it does! Who gets more endorsement contracts—players who are uncomfortable in front of the camera or players who turn into crazy lunatics in front of the camera? But maybe these on-the-field antics aren't crazy at all, but an entirely inevitable and unavoidable response to the presence of so many impossible-to-ignore cameras. Eventually, technology changes everything: how we live our lives, do our jobs, and think about the world we live in.

I don't know if technology is necessarily *ruining* the game of football or *ruining* the game of love, but boy, it sure does change how the games are played. Today, dating is played on a postmodern playing field dominated by Generation Y technology and the conventions and social mores that accompany those technologies. Even if you're a boomer who wants to meet another boomer, or a Generation Xer seeking a fellow Xer, you still have to get with the program, folks. Of course it's preferable to meet people through low-tech channels (school, work, organizations you belong to, family and friends), but when those *actual* social networks don't produce results, and you've been sitting around your house for a month or a year or a decade, then you'll probably turn, as I eventually did, to *virtual* social networks. Be prepared, however, for a culture shock. Just a few months ago, I was walking around thinking, *Oh my God! What if people know I have a profile posted on Match.com!* I'm still a little embarrassed, but not nearly as traumatized as I was.

Recently I did a search on Match for younger men from twenty-five to thirty-two. I'll admit: I felt creepy doing this, virtually robbing the cradle, until I realized that nobody but me really gave a shit. The difference in the profiles astonished me! Here were men who weren't ashamed to be on Match. They smiled broadly and comfortably. Fluent in the communication modes of MySpace and Facebook, these men were able to articulate specifically (in both narrative and list form) who they were, the things they liked, the kind of woman they wanted. I practically jumped out of my chair with excitement. For months, I'd been reading bland profiles written by the modest men of Generation X that told me nothing except that they liked Bill O'Reilly, pizza, and the color blue. Call it Generation Y narcissism if you want, but their impulse to provide too much information helped me (a woman nervously navigating her way through a crowded virtual room) to distinguish what from what.

A few weeks ago I was at a cocktail party surrounded by people my own age and older. Couple A was telling Couple B that they'd met while he was living in one state and she another. "So . . ." said the man in Couple B. "You met. . . ."

"Oh! Not on the Internet!" the woman in Couple A said.

"Oh, no," said her boyfriend. "Of course not."

"*Not* that there's anything wrong with it, of course," said Couple B. Everyone chuckled.

My friend Laura, who was standing nearby, came to my side and placed her hand on my shoulder, a gesture I will never forget. I can hardly blame these couples for this attitude. I carried around the same notions, and it's taken me a long time to shake them. What's helped, I think, is realizing that an online dating profile isn't a lewd personal ad or a self-promoting billboard. It's helpful to see it as the door to your teenage bedroom or your college dorm room, where you affixed pictures of your cultural icons, your favorite quotes, political slogans, funny cartoons, and photographs of yourself doing the things you loved. This door is the gateway between your public self and your private self, a representation of the "real you" that isn't quite the real you, but also sort of is.

Technology breaks down the barrier between our private and public selves, and Generation Y understands that on that spectrum there are many levels of "self," each represented by an avatar, whereas Generation X and older (who don't even know what an avatar is) don't see it as a spectrum at all and get very, very itchy about making the private public. I still remember when one of my students in New Jersey showed me how to use AOL Instant Messenger. Later, I awkwardly IMed with this student for a few minutes, and then his "away message" came up that said he was "in the shower." I gave out a little appalled scream. I didn't want to know this! Later he told me, "Who cares if you know I'm in the shower at that second? It's not like you can see me in the shower. I shower. You shower. We all shower." Still, I stopped using AIM, since the only people to talk to were students I spent too much time with anyway.

What Generation Y understands, and I have been forced to learn, is that the way to use all this privacy-blurring technology to your advantage is to adopt the postmodern pose of many celebrities: the world desperately wants access to the "real you," so you develop an authentic-seeming persona (think Ellen DeGeneres), or in the case of Peyton Manning and his popular commercials, you create a winky, self-aware character, thereby satisfying the public's desire to see the real you without actually having shown it to them.

I'm serious. I think Peyton Manning is a postmodern genius. He doesn't shun the media like Marvin Harrison, who closely guards his privacy. He doesn't showboat like Terrell Owens, who squanders his right to privacy. Peyton is my avatar and my hero because he has figured out how to be "Peyton the Quarterback" and "Peyton the Actor Playing a Quarterback."

Less than twenty-four hours after I kissed Dennis good-bye, I'm driving into Pittsburgh's South Hills to see him again. He calls and gives me detailed instructions about how to get to his house. "Now when you get to the Toyota dealership, get over in the left lane for a while, because idiots will park on the side of the road there. You'll know you're getting close to the turn when you see McDonald's." I hate driving in unfamiliar terrain, and somehow Dennis knows I need these particulars. His voice is kind and calm, and a thought bubbles over my head: *This is how my brother or my dad would give me directions.*

I knock on his front door fifteen minutes later. Upon stepping inside, my first thought is that it doesn't look like the home of a single man but the house of a married couple. The living room is tastefully modern (think Pier 1), and there's a reproduction of Edward Hopper's "Nighthawks" over the fireplace mantel, along with other framed art throughout the house. Dennis shows me the rest of his home, which is when I finally realize that there's not a speck of dust anywhere. No dirty dishes in the sink. No magazine or book lying open on the coffee table. No shoes kicked off by the front door. Panic rises into my chest, and I ask if I can use the bathroom. Sitting on the alabaster toilet, I realize I'm having some sort of PTSD flashback. I had a boyfriend once who got very OCD when he was stressed out (I mean, who doesn't?), but he spent a year "training" me to keep things the way he liked them. I know the signs. The shower, the soap dish are shiny and scumless. Fresh, fluffy towels hang at perfect right angles. I look into the spotless bathroom mirror and tell myself, *Stop it. You're having a* Sleeping with the Enemy *Moment. You don't know for sure.* I walk back into the living room and say cheerily, "Your house is so clean! You're pretty neat," I say.

"I was in the army," Dennis says. "Order and neatness, they get to be a habit."

I am greatly relieved to hear this.

Dennis and I do some Christmas shopping and have dinner at a gourmet pizza place. I think about the e-mail I got from my brother Scott that morning:

> Find out all you can about what he does. Seem interested in it, even though you may not be right now. Be interested in what he does so he feels like he is just as smart as the next guy or even you. He might feel intimidated by what you do and what you know.

So I make an honest attempt to understand what Dennis does for a living, and eventually I come to the conclusion that he is like the voice on those OnStar commercials, the person who runs the computer diagnostic test on very, very large engines and tells the owner of the engine what the problem is. Then Dennis asks me to explain what I do.

"How many hours do you work a week?"

I take a bite of pizza. "One of my friends tried to keep track of it once, in terms of billable hours like how lawyers do, but she couldn't figure out how to account for all her time."

Dennis looks puzzled. "When do you work? What are your hours?"

"Well, I teach my classes on Monday and Tuesday nights and hold my office hours on Tuesday and sometimes also on Wednesdays. Sometimes I have meetings. Sometimes not."

"You work two days a week?" He can't believe it.

"No, I work every day, pretty much. See, in order to teach a class for two and a half hours, I might spend ten hours prepping." He looks at me strangely. "Prepping . . . ah, well, reading and commenting on their stories and papers, rereading a book I'm scheduled to teach, answering their e-mails, office hours. I'm on committees, too." I think for a second. "And then there's writing. Yeah, that's huge. And then there's the time I spend reading. Paying attention to my obsessions. Looking for ideas to bring into the classroom or stuff to write about, you know?"

He doesn't know. He looks at me blankly. I sound like the biggest time-waster in the world, so why do I feel like I'm always too busy, that there's never enough time in the day?

"You get summers off, right?"

"Yes," I say, bristling a bit. Summer is my writing time. When my parents bug me about getting a different career, one that would allow me to work anywhere, I say, "I'll give you four good reasons why I'm a college professor. May, June, July, and August."

"Do you like teaching?" Dennis asks.

"Yes I do. Very, very much. Do you like what you do?"

He shrugs. "It's okay."

I tell him the story about my dad working overtime to put us through college, his advice that we find jobs we love doing. "What do you love doing?" I ask.

Dennis smiles and shrugs. "I don't know."

I decide to drop the subject.

Two days later, Dennis arrives at my house for another date bearing a Christmas card that says how much he's enjoyed meeting me. First, he helps me winterize my outdoor central air-conditioning unit by covering it with a black tarp. Then we go out to eat. It's our third date in four days, and finally the conversation begins to come more easily. We tell funny stories about our families. He laughs at all my dumb jokes. He says, "You're a very nice person," and I almost start crying at the table. When he pulls up in front of my house, Dennis reaches into the back cab of his truck and pulls out a snow-and-ice scraper. "I bought this for you," he says. "I saw the other day you don't have one in your car. You'll need this driving home tomorrow." I'm overcome with thankfulness. I throw my arms around his neck, and we have our first decent kiss. "Call me when you get to Indiana. And be careful," he says as I get out of the truck with my beautiful new ice scraper.

I check my e-mail and there are more messages from Match.com. These days, they come at me in more of a trickle than the initial deluge. One is from a man named Troy who says that he's read my profile a dozen times in the past few weeks and he's finally worked up the nerve to contact me. I consider this situation. If Troy had e-mailed me sooner, I might be dating him right now instead of Dennis. But that's the thing. Dennis didn't wait. He's not unsure. He gave me a card and an ice scraper and said, "You're nice. I like you." That's good enough for me. I log onto Match and hide my profile, which means I'm no longer searchable. I write to Troy: "Thanks for reaching out, but I've met someone."

The next morning, I leave for Indiana before the sun comes up. Five hours later, I'm at my sister Andrea's house so that I can meet baby Daniel, who is two weeks old. Clay keeps kissing the baby's head. My sister asks me what Dennis looks like, so I use her computer to log into Match to show her, but he's hidden his profile, too. "Wow," I say. "We didn't even talk about hiding our profiles. We both just did it."

"I don't understand. Is this a good thing, this hiding?" Andrea asks.

"It means neither of us is looking." Gently, I take the baby from her arms. "I'm very, very glad not to be looking."


On December 18, 2006, the Colts play the Bengals on *Monday Night Football*. I call my brother Scott before the game. "Do you want to watch together?" I ask. He's forty-five minutes away in Batesville.

"Nah," he says. "I gotta work tomorrow. You could come out here if you wanted."

"Mom wants me to help her put up the tree."

For a while we discuss the Colts' recent losing streak. The Cincinnati Bengals are a tough team. What if the Colts lose *three* in a row? Scott thinks this wouldn't be such a bad thing. "Last year, they were too much on the radar, you know? 13–0. Too much pressure. All they need is to make it to playoffs with just a little momentum, and they'll be fine."

"You know, this time next year you'll be in Missouri watching them."

He doesn't say anything for a second. "Yeah, I've been thinking about that a little lately." I hear his voice catch.

My parents are in the living room, so I walk into the bathroom and shut the door. "Scott, seriously, are you sure you're ready for this?"

Even though I can't see him, I hear the hair stand up on his neck. "Yes, Cathy."

"You guys say you want to start a family out there. Do you know how hard that's going to be without either set of parents around?"

His voice is terse. "We can handle it."

"If you move away, it's going to be like when we moved to Aurora and we saw the grandparents and aunts and uncles only a couple of times a year, if that."

"Uh-huh." Scott is tuning me out now.

"And if you move, you're going to have a life like mine."

Thankfully, my brother is kind enough not to say, *No, it won't be like yours. I'm married.* Instead he says, "I really thought you, of all people, would be more supportive." I hear him take a drink of something. "It sounds to me like you don't support our decisions."

Sitting down on the toilet, I let out a long sigh. "No, it's not like that. Look, you go watch the game, okay? We'll talk about it later."

With the game on in the background, Dad puts hooks on all the ornaments while Mom and I hang them on the tree. I'm sure every family has its special holiday ornaments. In my family, there's the one my brother Scott made in nursery school. It's just a circle cut out of red poster board speckled with glitter, a piece of green yarn threaded through a hole-punched hole. But in the middle, there's an adorable picture of my four-year-old brother, sitting at a desk with a goofy grin on his face and a pencil in his hand. Dad walks over and shows it to my mom. Both get tears in their eyes. Mom dangles the ornament from a limb front and center on the tree. The Colts beat the Bengals 34–16, and my dad turns off the television without a word.

Dennis calls me every night. We usually talk for at least half an hour. Once we talk for three hours. "There must be some kind of catch," I say. "There's always a catch. Tell the truth. You're married?"

"Nope."

"You have a prison record?"

"Nope."

"You frequent hookers?"

He's heard my story about Jake the Parachuting Hooker-Lover. "Not lately."

I don't say anything.

"I'm kidding."

"You've fathered twenty children scattered all across the United States?"

He laughs. "Nope."

I can't think of anything else. "You're going to call me tomorrow?"

"Yep."

I catch my dad smoking in the kitchen, huddled by the stove's exhaust fan. He knows he's supposed to smoke outside or in the basement. "Oh, Cathy, I got a lot on my mind. I gotta get organized." He ticks off his list. Scott wants him to run out to Batesville to help him fix something. My sister called and said she needs him to watch Daniel for two hours so she can take Clay to the doctor. His sister in Indianapolis just broke her ankle in three places and her kids, my cousins, want to know if he'll come see her. And before she left for work that morning, my mom gave him a honey-do list. Groceries. Errands. Bills. Make dinner. "I'm not used to this," my dad says, stubbing out his cigarette. "I'm more stressed out than ever since I quit working."

"You know why?" I say, pouring myself a cup of coffee.

"Why?"

"Because now *you're* the wife."

He doesn't think this is funny. So we divvy things up, and between the two of us, we manage to complete half of what my mom used to do all by herself.

My parents have been through two very distinct marriages. Their first marriage is the one I sought to avoid. The second has become my model for what comprises a healthy, hard-won relationship between partners. Marriage number one began in 1967 at the Church of the Brethren in Roann, Indiana. My parents were twenty-one and twenty. Only now that I see my sister caring for Clay and Daniel, born just over a year apart, do I appreciate what my parents (and so many couples of their generation) did: by four years and four months into their marriage, my parents had *three* kids. I'm astounded by this.

Marriage number two started when my mother turned thirty-seven, the same age I was when the events of this book began. One morning in her thirty-seventh year, my mom woke up terribly unhappy with no idea why nor what to do about it, and twenty-one years later, in my thirty-seventh year, I woke up feeling much the same thing. Eventually my mom figured it out: she had a family she loved, but not much fulfillment beyond that, so she went to college. Eventually I figured it out: I had a career I loved but not much fulfillment beyond that. Oh, I wish I could get a PhD to cure what ails me!

Why did I grow up deathly afraid of a conventional woman's life? Um . . . could it be because that life drove my mother a little bit nuts? I grew up in a world where men spent as little time in the house as possible. They worked. They fixed cars. They mowed grass. They played softball. They went fishing. How did I get the message that a conventional woman's life wasn't a worthwhile pursuit? Um . . . could it be because everyone tossed "a woman's work" around like a hot potato? Once I heard my sister Andrea say to her husband John, "I do not want a marriage like the one our parents had. You go to work all day and then on the weekends, you get to have hobbies. Well, I want a hobby, too. If you can go out and race cars every Saturday and leave me home with the kids, then I should be able to go out on Sundays and leave *you* with the kids! But you know what you'd do? You'd take them over to your mom's so you can work on your car!"

You need to know this: I really do like to cook for people. I enjoy laundry and grocery shopping. I love gardens and babies and feelings. But I also love to write. It's not a hobby. It's my dream. Langston Hughes asked: "What happens to a dream deferred?" I know what happened in my family. If my mom hadn't been able—at last, in her forties—to get a higher education and pursue the profession that rounds her life out fully . . . well, I don't like to think about it.

On Christmas Eve my brother calls. "Do you want to come out and watch the Colts @ Texans game at my house?" At my parents' house (which *is* in Indiana, mind you) the only game we can watch is (you guessed it) the Pittsburgh Steelers versus the Baltimore Ravens.

"Nah," I say.

"I thought you were following the Colts this season?" Scott says.

"I was. I am. I just don't feel like driving all the way out there."

"Some fan you are," he mutters. "You've been following them for one season. I've been a fan for *ten years*."

"I never said I was a bigger Colts fan than you." I pause from wrapping the last of my Christmas presents. "I think I just needed a gimmick, a way to trick myself into doing something that scared me."

"So now that you met some guy, you don't care about the Colts anymore?"

Dennis has called me every day since I left Pittsburgh. This is the best Christmas I've had in years. I tell Scott, "Right now? No, I don't."

Scott hangs up on me, but I'm not mad. I know how he feels. Recently, a female writer friend of mine wrote to tell me she'd married a guy she met on Match.com. "Don't hate me," she said in her e-mail, "but he was the first one I went out with." I fumed for the rest of the night.

Three and a half hours later, Scott and Sara show up at my parents'. He's wearing his Peyton Manning jersey. He points to the number 18. "In case you were wondering, the Colts lost," he says.

"They lost *to the Texans*?" I can't believe it. I saw them play each other back in September with Mom and Dad at the RCA Dome. The Colts won that day 43–24. It was a rout. Peyton threw for 400 yards. "This means they've lost four road games in a row." I can tell by his expression that—because I know this stat—my brother is *almost* willing to forgive me for being a fair-weather fan.


It's New Year's Eve, an unseasonably warm Sunday. I'm in Philadelphia for a conference and I've stayed over for a few days. The friend I'm staying with doesn't own a television. I could walk around and try to find a bar in Philly that's showing the Colts versus Dolphins game at 1:00 PM. At 4:15 PM, every bar in Philly will turn on the Eagles versus Falcons game, but at 1:00 PM they'd probably tune in the Colts, if I asked. But I don't feel like asking. I don't feel like hunting down the Colts game. So, I take a nap, wondering if Dennis will call me tonight to wish me a Happy New Year. I haven't seen him since before Christmas.

The Colts win! They defeat the Dolphins 27–22.

I *don't* win. New Year's Eve, New Year's Day, both pass without a phone call from Dennis.

And now, folks, it's time for the playoffs.

# Postseason

I think our basic Midwestern nature here in Indy is that we're nice. And part of that comes from our long-standing—although it's beginning to wane—Indy inferiority complex, that somehow we're not good enough. And we don't want to brag and we don't want to boast because we're afraid it will come back to bite us. Until we've been to a Super Bowl, how much smack can we talk?

—Bill Benner, former *Indianapolis Star* columnist

# WILD-CARD PLAYOFF GAME
## COLTS VS. CHIEFS
### OR
## Someone to Watch the Game With

Late at night on New Year's Day, my plane takes off from Philadelphia, traverses the Keystone State, and touches down in Pittsburgh. Tired, I drive home and greet my lonely cat. My cat-sitter has stacked up all my mail. Tomorrow, I'll do what I do every year at this time: belatedly open Christmas cards, read the third-person holiday newsletters, stick the newest pictures of my friends' children to my refrigerator. In the last few years, I've actually come to dread this ritual, these textual and visual narratives: *Here is our family! Here's what we did this year! We're thinking of you!* Tonight I fight the urge to throw away every single green-and-red envelope. Something dark rises up inside me, so bitter and hateful I'm ashamed of myself, and I push that darkness back down. No, tomorrow, or maybe the day after that, I'll open every card. I'll read every word. I'll open my heart, celebrate my friends' joy, and remind myself that my life is no tragedy. Who am I to complain about a book, a nice job, a good car, a DVR, a fridge full of food, and too much time on my hands? As I get ready for bed, I wonder: Why don't single people send out Christmas newsletters or pictures of themselves sitting alone next to their tree? I make a belated New Year's resolution to do this next year and I fall into a dead sleep.

The next morning I bump up the thermostat to take the chill out of the house. As I'm making coffee, I realize the furnace hasn't kicked on. Flashlight in hand, I venture down into my basement to "investigate," staring at the mysterious metal machine that is my furnace. Actually, I'm sort of glad to have this problem, because now I can call Dennis for a reason other than to ask, "Why haven't I heard from you?"

"I was robbed," he explains. "New Year's Eve. I came home from work and a bunch of kids had broken in through the kitchen door." Dennis says they took his camera, a guitar, his new laptop, some cash out of his sock drawer. They left the TV.

"How do you know it was kids?"

"The TV crew told me."

"TV crew!"

He laughs. A crew from a local news affiliate asked if they could interview him; there'd been a rash of these break-ins, and the robbers were caught with a lot of stolen property. "I watched the news last night, and they had a segment on it. I think I saw my guitar lying on this table with everything else they got."

"Were you on TV?"

"Nah," Dennis says. "I told them I didn't want to be interviewed." Another reason to like Dennis: he turns down the chance to express righteous indignation on the six o'clock news. So this is why he hasn't called. "It's been a little crazy. Cops. And I gotta fix this busted door. How was your trip? Did you have a good New Year?"

I tell him about my furnace. "I've got the day off today. I'll come over and take a look at it." And an hour later, he rings the doorbell. We haven't seen each other in a few weeks, and I'm half expecting to be pinned to the wall of my foyer for a reunion kiss. But that's not what happens. *Oh well,* I think. *It's only eleven in the morning.* He descends into my basement. I find him crouched in front of an open panel. "It's your igniter," he says, brushing off his hands.

I give Dennis a hug. "Thanks," I say. Oh, glory glory hallelujah! To be able to pay for this kind of information with a hug instead of a check.

Later at lunch, I ask him, "What was it like that night, when the police left?"

He looks down at his french fries. "I couldn't sleep for a long time."

But I want to know more. "No, what did you *feel* like?"

Dennis shifts in his seat. He doesn't want to say he was scared, so I touch his hand and smile so he doesn't have to. "Never mind. Hey, I have a reading this Friday. Would you like to come?"

"Sure," he says.

He tags along with me to the grocery store, too. I get a "Personal Shopper," a gun that scans the UPC symbols on the things I buy, which speeds up my checkout. The only catch is that you have to bag your groceries as you shop, so I set a bunch of brown bags in the cart. As we make our way through the store, I notice that Dennis is bagging everything by category: fruits and veggies here, boxed items there, canned goods in this one. "Were you a grocery bagger as a kid?" I ask, teasing him a little.

"No," he says.

In the freezer aisle, I take out a bag of peas and purposely toss it into a bag with cans of cat food. When he thinks I'm not looking, Dennis takes the peas out and sticks them in the bag with my frozen pizza.

Back at my house, Dennis helps me bring in the groceries, and I make some pasta while he installs a wireless thermometer I got for Christmas. *There's someone in my house,* I think, and it feels simultaneously pleasant and incongruous. But I'm glad he's here. Ask anyone who's lived alone for a few years, and they'll tell you: solitude is hard. Sometimes I'll be reading a magazine or watching TV; a thought comes, and most of the time I stop myself from saying it out loud. Unspoken thoughts accumulate in my head. What do I do with them? If a single woman speaks in the woods and no one's there to hear it, does she make a sound? How does she know she exists at all?

Dennis comes into the kitchen, sees me standing by the stove, and flicks on the lights. There's a lamp on my fridge that puts out a pleasant but admittedly very dim light. "I don't like overhead lights," I say.

"But it's dark in here," he says. "How can you see what you're doing?"

I'm stirring pasta. What's there to see? "I can see fine."

Dennis smiles at me, as if to say, "Boy, you sure are funny," and walks into the living room. He leaves the kitchen lights on.

I fight the urge to snap them back off. *You've lived by yourself for too long, Cathy. Just let it go.*

After dinner, I show Dennis the Gist Street Web page on my laptop. I don't think he's been to a reading before, so I figure this is a good idea. Wrong. He points to one of the photographs. "How many people come to this?"

"Maybe a hundred or so."

"Oh, I thought it would be in a bookstore or a coffee shop or something like that."

"No, this is different." I pause. "And I guess I should warn you that a lot of my friends and students will be there."

"Oh."

"I'm just saying this so you don't show up and feel ambushed, like I've pushed you into the spotlight."

Dennis gets his deer-in-the-headlights look.

*Stop it,* I think. *You're making things worse.*

It's getting late and I have class tomorrow, so he gives me a kiss good night. Still no fire. But these days, maybe fire is the last thing I need.

Dennis calls. "Would you care if I didn't go to the reading tonight? I'm really tired."

I keep my voice light. "Oh, please go! This is kind of an important night for me, and I really want you to be there."

Reluctantly he agrees.

It's Friday, January 5, 2007, an unusually warm night in Pittsburgh. The moist air smells like spring, like freshly turned earth. We walk into the studio on Gist Street, and already a large crowd of familiar faces has gathered: my graduate and undergraduate students from Pitt, Philip and Marcus (from the Colts @ Broncos game at Buffalo Blues) and their wives, Janet and Laura and Ben, my neighbors Tom and Rachel. How many months ago was it that I walked into one of these readings feeling sad and disconnected and thought, *How long before I walk into one of these readings and I know more than one person?*

Answer: six months.

An intense period of milling-around ensues in which many people shake my hand and say good luck and ask to be introduced to Dennis. He grips his plastic cup of wine and smiles nervously. I can tell that meeting all these new people at once is very hard for him, so I take his hand and lead him to our seats. "I have to get my thoughts together," I tell everyone. Dennis gives me a look that says, "Thank God."

Eventually I'm introduced. Polite clapping. I walk to the microphone. Courteously, I thank those who have invited me, those who have shown up for this event. I pause for effect. "Tomorrow the NFL playoffs start."

Soft laughter ripples through the audience.

"Last year, my team, the Indianapolis Colts, lost to your team, the Pittsburgh Steelers, in the playoffs. That was a rough day for me. I got no empathy. No understanding. No love."

Laughter. Some applause and cheering.

I take a sip of water. "And here it is, almost exactly a year later, and to-morrow the Colts are taking on the Kansas City Chiefs. And please, I don't want to hear a word about Larry Johnson. Shut up about Larry Johnson, okay? I know he's a great running back. And my God, if I hear one more thing about our run defense, I'm going to scream."

It's amazing what happens when a woman starts talking football. Men you've never met before get this twinkly look in their eyes, while women you've never met before look visibly angry. I can see (and feel) all of this energy as I scan the standing-room audience.

"Dallas Clark is back. And Bob Sanders is back, isn't he?" I point to a young man in the front row, my former student at Pitt, who went to high school with Sanders in Erie, Pennsylvania. "Yes indeed, the playoffs start tomorrow, and um . . . gee . . . I don't think the Steelers made it this year, did they?"

I am assailed by a chorus of boos. I'm in a room full of artsy-fartsy types, but still, this is Pittsburgh. Talking smack is a risky thing to do.

And then I read an essay—the introduction to this book. It's been al-most a year since that Colts versus Steelers game, and so much has changed. A man named Dennis is in the audience, and I like him because being around him feels like being home. I've been seeing him for a month, longer than I've dated anyone in the last five years. At this point I don't know what's going to happen next. Maybe the Colts will beat the Chiefs tomorrow. Maybe *this* is the year they finally go all the way. Maybe it's not. Maybe Dennis is the One, maybe he isn't. Maybe I'm not the one for him. Who knows? The important thing is that it feels really good to be standing here right now. Maybe I'm finally learning to enjoy the journey, to enjoy the small moments of my own life.

After the reading, my friends want to take me out for a drink, but Dennis begs off. "I've got to work in the morning," he says.

I'm realizing that he's not very good at handling social situations on his own, and tonight I'd like to celebrate and have fun. "You're coming over tomorrow for the game, right?"

"Yep."

Dennis gives me a quick kiss and heads down the stairs.


Saturday afternoon, I'm in the Giant Eagle on Centre Avenue in Pittsburgh. I'm buying ingredients to make another pot of Cincinnati-style chili. In the checkout line, I see a young man wearing a Colts hat. Now, I've lived in Pittsburgh for almost two years, and I've never seen another person (besides me) wearing Colts sportswear out in public. Ten feet away is a whole wall of Steelers merchandise, and they aren't even in the playoffs. I walk right up to the Colts fan and tap him on the arm. "Hey," I say, looking around nervously. "Are you a Colts fan?"

He looks around, too, as if we're doing something illegal. "Yeah."

"Me too," I say, lifting my sweater, showing him that underneath I'm wearing blue.

"Oh," he says, relieved. "I thought maybe you were a Steelers fan and you were going to give me a hard time about the hat." He's a tall kid in his mid-twenties wearing a North Face fleece jacket and blue jeans.

"I never see Colts stuff here in Pittsburgh. I just had to say hello!" I'm embarrassed, so I start placing my items behind his on the self-checkout conveyer. He looks at me strangely, and I can tell he's thinking, *Is this chick hitting on me?* I don't know if I am or not. I don't think so. I think I'm just incredibly excited to meet another Hoosier at the grocery store in Pittsburgh the same day the Colts are playing their first game of the playoffs. This seems like a very good omen. "Where are you from?" I ask.

"Indy," he says.

"I'm from Peru. It's a little town north of Indy. North of Kokomo."

"Yeah, I've heard of it." He smiles and swipes his credit card.

"Where did you go to school?"

"IU. Journalism."

"Of course," I say. It's a great journalism school.

I scan my groceries as he slowly bags his. He says, "I work at the *Post-Gazette*."

Hamburger. *Beep.* "Oh, that's great. I work at Pitt."

He nods.

Spaghetti. *Beep.* "Were you here last year when they lost to Pittsburgh?"

"Oh yeah. That was painful."

Cheese. *Beep.* "Funny, isn't it? Just a year ago, you and I were miserable and everyone else here was ecstatic. Now look who's miserable and who's ecstatic!"

He's stealing glances at my face. I think he's trying to decide how old I am, bless his heart. Grabbing his bags in one hand, he walks away with a wave.

Oyster crackers. *Beep.* "Go Colts!"

A few people look up from their carts and fix us in their stare.

He raises his fist. "Go Colts!"


My playoff-watching crew consists of Dennis, Tom, and Rachel. Jersey-born Dennis is actually a Jets fan, and Tom and Rachel like the Steelers. But for today, they are part of Colts Nation. We've just sat down with our plates of Cincinnati-style chili when a Manning pass is intercepted by Kansas City's Ty Law, the same Ty Law who, as a New England Patriot, intercepted three Manning passes in the 2003 AFC Championship game. "Get him, Peyton!" I yell as number 18 tries (not very hard) to tackle Law. Finally, Marvin Harrison brings Law down at the 9-yard line.

We stop eating to see what will happen next. Chiefs quarterback Trent

Green falls down; apparently, one of his own teammates stepped on his foot. The Chiefs can't convert, so their field-goal kicker trots onto the field to boot an easy 23-yard field goal. And . . . he misses.

"Whoo-hoo!" I yell.

Colorman Cris Collinsworth says, "That may be the most expensive step on a foot the Kansas City Chiefs have ever had. The momentum of the game had turned their way, and they simply blew it."

At halftime, the Colts are up 9–0. Halfway through the third quarter, Cris Collinsworth is prompted to note: "Right now in the ball game, the Indianapolis Colts have 22 first downs. The Kansas City Chiefs have 21 *yards*. The Colts have, let's see, over 350 yards to 21 yards. This is unbelievable. I've never seen anything like this, not when the Indy defense is historically bad."

Then the game gets very, very dull, so everyone starts talking. Tom asks Dennis, "So, what did you think about Cathy's reading last night?"

"I liked it," Dennis says. He and I haven't had a chance to talk about it yet.

"I thought the crowd's reaction was very interesting," Tom says. "Some people got really into it, but I could tell there was some . . . how to say it . . . displeasure."

Joseph Addai scores a touchdown. The Colts are up 16–0.

I take a swig of beer. "I looked up and saw people looking at me like I was nuts."

What ensues is a somewhat theoretical conversation about my particular sociocultural influences and the subtle forms of class bias in the world of arts and letters. At some point, the word "hermeneutics" is uttered. I don't know exactly what this word means, but I nod in agreement anyway. Dennis, the only true working-class person in the room, doesn't join in our conversation about class hierarchies, but rather keeps his eyes on the game. It's the end of the third quarter, and Kansas City has just scored a touchdown and gone for the two-point conversion. Score 16–8.

In the fourth quarter, the Colts score again, and it dawns on me that the Colts are actually *not* going to lose their first playoff game (as they did last year). The game grinds down to a slow halt. What's just happened is the exact *opposite* of what everyone predicted. The Chiefs' Larry Johnson, the league's second-leading rusher, was supposed to gallop through the Colts' leaky run defense, the worst in the league. Instead, the Colts' defense held Johnson to a puny 32 yards rushing. The Colts have won, 23–8.

Tom stands up from the couch. "Well, it was nice seeing you again," he says, shaking Dennis's hand.

Wait. What just happened? Watching the game with my friends and Dennis wasn't fun like I thought it would be. At this moment, I'm tense, like I'm trying to put a quiet end to a bad date. "Do you want to stay and watch the Cowboys-Seahawks game?" I ask Tom and Rachel, but secretly, I hope they'll say no.

Rachel shakes her head. "I've got sooo much reading to do."

"See ya," Dennis says.

When they're gone, I clean up the kitchen a little and come back into the living room. I turn off the lamp so the only light comes from my Christmas tree.

Dennis points. "I was going to ask. Why do you still have your tree up?"

I lie down on the couch next to Dennis and put my head on his leg. "I haven't had time to take it down since I got back."

"I'll help you, if you want."

"Maybe I should leave it up," I say. "If the Colts lose, I'll take down the tree, okay?"

Dennis laughs at me. "Okay."

Together, we watch the Seahawks beat the Cowboys, including Tony Romo's botched hold on an easy 19-yard field-goal attempt that would have given the Cowboys the win. Then we watch him have a meltdown. "Poor Tony Romo," I say.

Dennis says, "He screwed up."

I roll over and look up at Dennis. "I don't know if you can point to one player, one play, and pin the entire loss on that." I want to talk about how a football game is sort of like an experiment in quantum physics—with observable macroscopic variables but also almost invisible microscopic variables. Does the universe unfold deterministically or randomly? I know nothing, really, of quantum mechanics, but I received a very good liberal arts education and can fake my way through conversations on any number of subjects. Basically, I like to think out loud with someone willing to think out loud with me. My girlfriends and I do this. Even my mom and I do this. Once Alex and I were driving from Alabama to Indiana and spent three straight hours debating the cultural phenomenon of home-made markers at the sites of fatal car accidents: he assumed the negative stance and I took the affirmative.

Dennis looks down at me on the couch. "Romo flubbed the ball. He cost them the game."

So I change the channel, and together we watch an episode of *Law & Order: SVU.*


After Dennis leaves, a reporter sticks a microphone in my face.

**Reporter:** Cathy, you embarked on this project hoping that the story would end with both you and the Colts getting your long-awaited Super Bowl rings. Well, the Colts just won. Are you on track to reach your goal?

**Me:** I don't know. He's very very nice, but . . .

**Reporter:** Cathy, you've taken me . . . you've taken the viewing audience . . . you've taken *America* on this journey. We're rooting for you! We could care less if the Colts win the Super Bowl or not. We want *you* to win.

**Me:** Thanks, Suzy. That's really nice of you to say.

**Reporter:** So tell us, do you *want* to have someone in your life or not?

**Me** (*Pause.*): Yes, of course I do.

**Reporter:** Do you *want* to win the game of love or don't you?

**Me** (*Pause.*): What do you mean by "win"?

**Reporter:** Oh for Chrissake . . .

> Those who live in the past are cowards and losers.
>
> —Mike Ditka, former NFL coach

---

## AFC DIVISIONAL PLAYOFF
## COLTS @ RAVENS

OR

# Ravenge

---

On the night of March 29, 1984, a cruel, cruel breakup occurred. No, not to me. I'm talking about the way Colts owner Robert Irsay broke up with Baltimore. While the city slept, Irsay ordered up a fleet of Mayflower trucks, packed up the team—tangibles like office furniture, filing cabinets, and blue jerseys and intangibles like the name "Colts," the horseshoe symbol, and over thirty years of history—and left town. He told the hired drivers to head west to Indianapolis. The city of Baltimore awoke to an inconceivable reality: their beloved Colts were gone for good. If you are a sports fan, if you've ever loved your local team, then you don't need an analogy to understand the import of what Robert Irsay did to Baltimore. But if you are *not* a sports fan, let me put it to you this way: have you ever had your heart broken? Has a loved one ever betrayed you, lied to you? Have you ever asked someone, "How can you do this to me after all we've been through together?" I'm not making this analogy; Baltimoreans used these terms to describe what they felt on March 29, 1984.

Robert Irsay and the city had been wrangling about who should pay for a new stadium, who was at fault for the recent underperforming teams and low attendance rates. The day before Irsay skedaddled, the Maryland state legislature passed a law allowing the City of Baltimore to seize the Colts under eminent domain. Irsay's lawyer said his client had to move his team to Indy to protect his interests. Which begs the question: Who did the Colts *belong to?* Technically, of course, they belonged to Robert Irsay and his progeny, in the same way that U.S. Steel belonged to J. P. Morgan and Andrew Carnegie and the first McDonald's franchise belonged to Ray Kroc. But the product Irsay created wasn't steel or hamburgers. He owned a football team—its past, present, and future. He made his money by staging a yearly reality show, a heartwarming saga about a team's quest for an ultimate prize. This story was observed by a large audience which connected with that story in myriad and unique ways.

In a sense, NFL team owners are like movie producers. They fund a form of storytelling. But at least movies have *scripts.* Football seasons are pure, unscripted drama; you can't know how the story will end. And when we become emotionally invested in a story (or team) and that story's characters (the athletes), it becomes "ours" to a certain extent. This is why the people of Baltimore felt that a football team rightly belongs to a *place* and to its citizenry—which is only true of the Green Bay Packers, who do literally belong to their host city.

When a couple divorces, friends often choose sides based on which of the two was more at fault. The same goes for an NFL franchise divorce. When a team leaves a city, fans are forced to decide: my town or my team. Bob Irsay made that choice very easy for Baltimoreans to make. Eventually, they became Ravens fans. Before he died in 2002, Johnny Unitas (the most beloved Baltimore Colt) hung out on the Ravens sideline. Most alumni of the Baltimore Colts who settled down in Baltimore when their playing days were over refused to wear the horseshoe, choosing instead to don the purple, black, and gold of the Ravens. Yet history will record them as—oh the humanity!—"Indianapolis Colts."

We live in a world today where words like "hometown" and "civic pride" sound quaintly anachronistic. But anybody who thinks that place doesn't matter anymore has never been a sports fan.

On Saturday, January 13, 2007, I get up early to clean my house and make Spanish hot dogs. I've invited all my friends over to watch the Colts take on the Ravens in the AFC Divisional playoff game. My brother Scott calls around noon. "Man, I'm nervous," he says.

"Me, too."

"So you're into the Colts again, huh?" he says, teasing. "I thought you said you didn't care, now that you met that guy. What's his name again?"

"Dennis."

"Dennis. Right. How's that going?"

"Good," I say, although I'm not sure if that's the correct answer.


If love is a game, then I'm not very good at taking the big, concussive hits, the kind that knock the wind out of you and land you on ESPN's "Jacked Up." I take Big Hits personally. What I'm supposed to do is shake it off, Johnny, rub some dirt on it, and move on. But I don't. Here's what I do: argue with the guy who just leveled me about why he shouldn't have hit me so hard; yell at the referee (who completely ignores me) about why he didn't throw the yellow flag; plead with my coach not to send me on another route across the middle of the field; and rehash the hit over and over with my teammates until they get tired of listening and wander away to the Gatorade stand. And here's the worst part: the next time I take the field, I'm scared and I play like crap.

Here's a Big Hit I've never forgotten: I'm twenty-two. I'm in graduate school. I've been seeing a boy I'll call Boy. Right before Thanksgiving break, he shows up at my apartment with a two-week growth of beard and a stack of note cards. "My computer crashed," Boy says. "Can I work on my research paper here?" I say sure, come on in. For the next four days, we take turns on the computer. I cook for him. He cooks for me. We cuddle and reassure each other that we aren't total intellectual morons. We read each other's drafts and offer suggestions. To me, those days are pure bliss. The day Boy's paper is due, he shaves off his beard, leaving a lot of little hairs in my bathroom sink. He says, "I'm going to turn this in, go home, and take a nap. I'll call you later." I don't hear from him that night. I leave a message. The next day I call again and leave another message.

Then I start driving past Boy's apartment every four to six hours. His car isn't there.

It's still not there.

Nope. Still not there.

Finally, his roommate calls me. "Cathy, I'm so sorry, but he's in Michigan. He got back together with his ex-girlfriend. He's visiting her right now. I figured you should know that."

I ask his roommate if I can come over and get my things so I don't have to go back into that apartment or talk to Boy ever again. The roommate says, "Of course." He helps me carry bags of stuff to my car. "Wait," he says. "Here, take this." It's a nice wrought-iron plant stand.

"Is this his?"

"No, it's mine," he says, "but I don't really need it."

I use this pity plant stand as a microwave table for the next six years.

The Colts @ Ravens game is scheduled to start at 4:30 PM. It's now three. The phone rings. It's Dennis. "I just got off work," he says, "but I can't come over today."

"Why?" I've been looking forward to introducing him to Janet and Jerry, Laura and Ben. They didn't really get a chance to talk to him at my reading.

"I really want to fix my door," he says.

"Fix your door? The *Colts* are playing the *Ravens*."

Dennis laughs. "I'm sorry. But it's making me nervous not having a secure door."

It's hard to argue with this. "Okay. But couldn't you fix the door tomorrow?"

His voice gets a little stiff. "I want to do it tonight."

"Okay."

"I'll call you tomorrow."

"Okay."

What does a team owe to the city that cheers for it every Sunday for thirty years? What does a business owe to the customer who pays $99 or $1,595 in order to find love? What does a company owe an employee who hurts himself on the job and can never work again? What do we owe the people we love and who love us when we stop loving them?

Here's another Big Hit I've never forgotten. I was twenty-four, and the guy's name was Guy. I dated him for six months or so, but when we broke up, he started dating (and eventually married) a good friend of mine. I'll call her Girl. The day Guy ended our relationship, a hunch made me ask if it had anything to do with Girl, and he said, "No." So I spoke openly to Girl about the breakup. I discovered the truth by accident over a month later. When I confronted Girl, she just looked at me with victory eyes. When I finally confronted Guy, I said, "You owed me more than this. You guys could have at least told me the truth so I didn't have to find out the way I did."

"I don't think you can call it 'seeing' me. I was out of town."

"Did you talk on the phone to each other?"

Guy looked down at his hands in his lap. "Yeah."

"How often? Every day?"

"Pretty much."

I gripped the arms of my chair. "Did you discuss how you felt about each other?"

"Cathy, why do you want to know?"

"I want to know!"

"Then, yes."

"That's called 'seeing' someone. There's an emotional connection. And every time I talked to her about how I felt about you, about our breakup, she betrayed me by listening and saying nothing. You both made a fool of me. Would I knowingly talk to the new girlfriend of the guy that just broke up with me? No."

He listened to all of this with a calm expression. "I don't know, Cathy. When you find someone who makes you really happy, nothing else matters."

"That's not true," I said. "My feelings mattered!"

Guy looked at me like I was nuts. "We love each other," he said.

I took a deep breath, letting those words sink in. "You just waited for me to find out on my own. That was the chickenshit way to handle it."

Guy stared at me. "You think we should have *told you* we were dating?"

"Yeah, I would have respected you more than I do right now."

We argued for two or three hours, and neither of us wavered from our positions. Guy maintained that all is fair in love and war, the ends justify the means, and I maintained that all is *not* fair in love and war, the ends *don't* justify the means. I was twenty-four. I was an idealist. I believed that people should always strive to do right by each other. Literally, I couldn't comprehend what psychological machinations made it possible for someone to rationalize their own bad behavior. Even now, fourteen years later, I'm that same girl, refusing to accept the hard-bitten reality that in this life it's every woman for herself. How could those women at Great Expectations look into my eyes, listen to my story, and still take my money? How could the railroad *railroad* my dad? How can a man say "I will take care of you," and then e-mail a prostitute? And how—once you realize that people do lie, that the world isn't fair—do you go on believing in people? *In anything?* How do you trust anyone again?

I think about this a lot.


At 4:30 PM, everyone arrives and makes themselves a Spanish hot dog—even Ben, who is a vegetarian. The Orioles' Cal Ripken comes onto the field for the coin toss. The game begins! The camera fades in on a montage of Peyton Manning footage, running through the tunnel onto the field. In voice-over Greg Gumbel says, "Like Johnny Unitas in Baltimore, Peyton Manning has been the face of the franchise in Indianapolis, setting record after record in the regular season. Yet, having led the Colts to the postseason six previous times, a cloud of uncertainty hovers overhead."

The camera cuts to slow-motion footage of Peyton on the field. He shields his eyes and looks up into the blue sky, where a black helicopter hovers.

The voice-over continues: "Because all six times he's left frustrated. He's hoping the seventh time is the charm as he again takes his team to the postseason on the strength of his right arm." Cut to Greg Gumbel and Dan Dierdorf sitting in their suits, holding microphones. Behind them is a backdrop of more than 71,000 Ravens fans gathered at M&T Stadium in Baltimore.

"Circumstances beyond the control of any player or coach here today have made this as fierce and heated a rivalry as there is in football," Gumbel says. They cut to footage of Baltimore's old Memorial Stadium, circa 1970. "The last time the Colts were in Baltimore for a playoff game, it was Christmas Eve 1977, and they were *the home team*."

Dierdorf chimes in. "That's right, Greg. If you're past a certain age in Baltimore, you just don't like the Indianapolis Colts."

The Ravens run out onto the field, led by Ray Lewis. The crowd explodes with rage and joy. "Shit," I say. "Why do the Ravens look so much scarier than the Colts?"

"It's their uniforms," Jerry, the former football player, says. "Most teams have dark pants, light jerseys or light jerseys, dark pants. But the Ravens are wearing all dark."

"Ah!" I say. "You know, you gotta love a football team that's named for a poem and still kicks major ass."

"A poem?" Janet says.

"Poe was from Baltimore." I take a bite of hot dog. "Quoth the raven, nevermore."

"Hey! Wait!" Laura says. "Where's Dennis?"

I explain about his door.

Everyone exchanges looks, but they don't say anything.

So here we are in my living room. Janet and Jerry. Laura and Ben. And me. God, I'm really sick of couple, couple, me. Why couldn't Dennis have just come? I wouldn't care if he just sat here the whole time, like last week. No, that's not true. I don't want a blow-up doll just so I can ride in the HOV lane. Sigh.


A reporter says, "Like the Colts' Peyton Manning, Cathy Day has enjoyed a rewarding professional career but has yet to attain her Super Bowl ring. On nine different occasions she's had to watch another woman claim that prize."

The camera cuts to a slow-motion shot of wedding invitations falling like autumn leaves in front of the camera.

She continues: "And like the city of Baltimore, Cathy knows what it means to wake up in the morning and discover that the men you love have skedaddled in the night." The camera cuts to archived photos of Mayflower trucks driving through the snow from Owings Mills, Maryland, to Indianapolis, Indiana, in 1984. Cut to the reporter and me in suits and pumps holding microphones. Behind us is a backdrop of more than 71,000 Ravens fans gathered at M&T Stadium in Baltimore.

**Reporter:** You can feel the pent-up animosity flowing through this stadium tonight. For the citizens of Baltimore, and for Cathy Day, it's payback time!

**Me:** Suzy, I don't know if I can do this . . .

**Reporter** (*Smiles into the camera but covers her microphone.*): You said you'd do the interview. You said you were ready to talk about it.

**Me:** I know, but it's really sort of . . . I don't know—

**Reporter:** How about if I start and you chime in when you can?

**Me:** Would you do that? Oh, that would be great!

**Reporter:** Okay, here goes: This is a story about Cathy and . . . what was his name again?

**Me:** Let's call him Robert Irsay. Bob for short.

**Reporter:** This is a story about Cathy and Bob. They were high school sweethearts—

**Me:** I don't know if *sweethearts* is the right word, exactly. We dated. He was with me when I saw *Hoosiers* for the first time. I remember that.

**Reporter:** —but they parted ways after graduation, when Cathy went off to college and Bob didn't. Eighteen years later, Bob is sitting down to breakfast, reading the morning paper. (*Cut to a black-and-white shot of a man sitting at a kitchen table, drinking coffee. A newspaper rests beside him. Featured on that page is a head shot of a woman with long, dark hair.*) Bob sees Cathy's picture and an article; she's coming to his local library to give a talk! Bob Googles Cathy, finds her Web site, and sends her an e-mail.

**Me:** You know, I didn't like becoming Googleable. I found it very frightening.

**Reporter:** But Cathy is glad to hear from Bob. In truth, she's never forgotten him. Once, before she graduated from college, he went to her grandparents' house and got her phone number from them. (*The camera shifts to a black-and-white handheld shot of a man walking up to a house in the middle of a soybean field and an old couple answering the door with wide smiles.*)

**Me:** My grandparents really liked him.

(*The camera shows the exterior of a sorority house. A phone rings. A voice on an intercom says, "Cathy Day, line one."*)

**Reporter:** Bob called Cathy to say that he was thinking of getting married but that his fiancée had asked, "Is there anyone you still think about?" and he said, "Yes," and she said, "Well, you better figure out what to do about that." So he called Cathy. He wanted to know if she was coming back to Peru after college. Cathy said no, her parents didn't live there anymore anyway, and besides, she was going to graduate school.

**Me:** It was very touching, actually. I told him that if he loved this girl, he should marry her and have a happy life. But every couple of years, my grandma would say, "That boy from high school, he stopped by last fall. He asked how you were getting along."

**Reporter:** Cathy assumed he'd married that woman, but when he resumed contact in 2004 about the upcoming library visit, he didn't mention a wife or anyone else in his e-mails. Yet she wasn't really surprised when he showed up at her reading with his girlfriend, a woman named Yvonne—

**Me:** She wasn't the woman he married.

**Reporter:** —and a little girl who looked exactly like him—

**Me:** Yvonne wasn't the mother, and neither was his ex-wife. It was a little hard to follow.

**Reporter:** What surprised her was that *after* the library event, he kept e-mailing her, saying how he'd never forgotten her, how lucky he was to see her picture in the paper that day, how fate had brought them together again. He looked on her Web site and saw that she was going to be in Indianapolis in December, and he asked if she would meet with him there, and she said yes.

**Me:** Suzy, I know I told you that, but to be honest, it was my idea.

**Reporter:** Oh. Well, thanks for clearing that up.

**Me:** We talked. We had lunch and we talked. He told me he and Yvonne had been arguing for months, that he was leaving her. And I want you and everyone else out there to know that I refused to kiss him good-bye.

**Reporter:** Are you sure? You're not going to change your mind later, are you?

**Me:** No, I'm sure.

**Reporter:** Good. Anyway, before he left, he asked Cathy, "Have you ever seen the movie *The Notebook*? I think you need to watch it." That night in her hotel room, Cathy watched this film, a movie based on the best-selling sappy novel by Nicholas Sparks about two teenage lovers named Allie and Noah who are torn apart by circumstances and reunite years later when Allie sees Noah's picture in the paper.

**Me:** I thought, I ran away from one of the nicest guys I ever dated because I wanted to write a book, and then I write the book, and that's what brings me back to him. Maybe this is the way things were supposed to happen.

**Reporter:** God, that's a good story.

**Me:** I know. Wait. There's more.

If the Colts @ Ravens game is about the City of Baltimore hoping for some long-awaited retribution, it sure doesn't happen in the first half. Twice in the first quarter the Colts can't score in the red zone but trot out their marquee kicker Vinatieri to put them up 6–0. The color analyst Dan Dierdorf tells everyone gathered in my living room, "What's really surprising, I think, is that the Colts find themselves in this position of being below the radar, the decided underdogs. Not very many people think they can win this football game. Most national pundits say the Ravens are far superior."

"Shut your piehole, Dan!" I shout. I've had three beers already.

"I wish Dennis had come," Janet says.

"Me, too." I knock on my end table. "Maybe next week!"

"They gotta get through this game," Jerry says.

"What do you think?" Ben says. "Chargers or Patriots?"

I hit my forehead. "Talk about the lesser of two evils!"

A commercial comes on, so I go out to the kitchen to grab another beer. Laura meets me by the fridge. "How are you?"

"Oh, I'm fine," I say.

"Are you mad he didn't come today?"

I hand her a beer. "A little."

"Ben's been talking about you all week."

I'm taking a sip at that moment, and a little comes out my nose. "What?!"

"He just keeps saying, 'I wonder how Cathy's doing!? This has got to be so exciting for her!' If I didn't know you better, I'd think you guys were having an affair!"

I give her a level look. "Are you crazy?"

She smiles.

I can hear Baltimore roaring for revenge all the way from my kitchen. We walk together back to the living room.

The studio darkens.

**Reporter:** Cathy, let's talk about the events leading up to Valentine's Day 2005. The communication with Bob didn't end, am I right? You kept talking to him, e-mailing, even though you knew he was still living with Yvonne. I need to ask you this: Why?

**Me** (*Long pause.*): When you get lonely enough, you're capable of almost anything. I made up a chickenshit story and convinced myself it was true. I convinced myself that I *deserved* him. I thought about what Guy said. All is fair in love and war, that when you find someone who makes you happy, nothing else matters. I thought about all those Big Hits. I thought about all those years I'd played the game fair and square—and lost. I thought about empty weekends and the years I might still spend alone if I didn't hurry up and find someone. When you're scared, who gives a shit about fair and square? It wasn't like Bob and Yvonne were married. I have quite a few friends who married men who were technically "taken" when they met and began to fall in love. And then there was the whole romantic, *Notebook,* fate-brought-us-together thing. I'm a sucker for that.

**Reporter** (*Wry laugh.*): Who isn't?

**Me:** I think there ought to be a law against movies like that.

**Reporter:** No you don't. You love movies like that.

**Me:** And Bob Irsay was very handsome. I felt good standing next to him. He knew me when I was just . . . me.

**Reporter:** But you did give him a deadline, an ultimatum. You told him you had a reading coming up in Indiana at your alma mater on Valentine's Day.

**Me:** Technically it was the day after Valentine's, the fifteenth.

**Reporter:** Well, thanks for that clarification, but the story is a lot better if it's Valentine's, don't you think? You told him that if he'd left Yvonne by that time, he could come to the reading and see you. And a week before, he left her, right?

**Me:** He called me and said, "I did it!" He gave me the address of his new apartment. He said, "I had to go to Wal-Mart and buy a pillow and a blanket. I'm driving to my apartment. I've just pulled up in the parking lot. I'm unlocking the door. I'm putting the blanket and pillow on the couch, which is where I have to sleep until I get a bed. I'm walking into my kitchen. My fridge is empty. I'm walking into my bedroom, which is full of hangers and garbage bags full of clothes. I'm in my bathroom, brushing my teeth."

**Reporter:** And then what happened?

**Me:** A week later he showed up at my reading. I'd just been offered the job in Pittsburgh, and he told me his company had an office there, that he'd move to Pittsburgh with me. And if the mother of his daughter agreed, he'd bring her, too. We'd be together. A family. After the reading, he gave me a Valentine that said: "I will always support you. I will always be there for you. I'm not going to let you go again. Very few people would bet on you and me, but I think we're going to surprise them."

**Reporter:** You slept with him, didn't you?

**Me:** Oh yeah.

**Reporter:** And then what happened?

**Me:** I didn't realize it then, but that was the last time I'd ever see him.

The great Johnny U, the Golden Arm, the loyal Baltimorean, was born and raised in, of all places, Pittsburgh. He played high school football a mile from where I live today. After college at the University of Louisville, and after being cut (yep, cut) by the Pittsburgh Steelers, Unitas worked construction in the Steel City to support his wife and child; on the weekends he played on a semipro team called the Bloomfield Rams. They played at Dean's Field, located under the Bloomfield Bridge, a few blocks from my house, where I'm sitting in a La-Z-Boy watching the Colts play the Ravens, two teams that both lay claim to Johnny U's legacy.

Halftime's over. The score is 9–3 Colts. So far the game has been a battle between field-goal kickers—the Colts' Adam Vinatieri (three so far) versus the Ravens' Matt Stover (one so far).

The Colts drive 54 yards on their first series but can't get the ball into the end zone, so Vinatieri kicks a 48-yard field goal to put the Colts up 12–3. In the stands, more than 71,000 Baltimoreans scream for blood. They don't want field goals. They're wearing T-shirts that say "Mr. Manning you are no Johnny Unitas!" and "Make Peyton Cry!" and "Ravenge!"

Bring down the lights. Cue the music, those sad but soaring strings.

About a month after Valentine's, I got a call that my grandpa was dying. Coincidentally, my spring break was starting, so I flew to Cincinnati and drove up to Peru with my family. I called Bob and left a message. "I'm coming to Peru for the week. I'll be just twenty miles away from you." I was sad my grandpa was dying, but also I was glad to have a chance to see Bob.

For the next nine hours, we watched my grandpa breathe. And then he stopped breathing.

After, I called Bob. He said he was sorry, that he always liked my grandpa, that he would come to the funeral, but he said he couldn't see me that night. "I have my daughter tonight," he said. "I can't find a babysitter." He said he'd make some calls and get back to me.

Over the next four days, we bought my grandpa a suit and I left Bob a message and we made funeral home arrangements and I left Bob another message and we kept my grandma company and went to the viewing and I stopped leaving Bob messages and we went to the funeral, the burial, the dinner, and gradually, everyone stopped asking me, "Where's Bob?" When it was all over, my family and I went back to our hotel. I curled up on the bed and stared at the curtains. I couldn't move. I couldn't talk. I couldn't even cry. I think I was a little catatonic.

The next day, I rode with my sister and John back to Cincinnati. Andrea was driving. Clay was there, too, a beautiful fist nestled deep in her womb. John turned around in the front seat and said, "Cathy, I'm sorry, but he never really left his girlfriend. You know that, right?"

"Yeah."

"I've seen guys I work with do this. It's easier for them to cheat now that there's cell phones and e-mails. You live in New Jersey, so it's easy for him to fool you. But then you show up here, and that screwed everything up."

"If Grandpa had died a different week, I wouldn't have been able to come back for the funeral, probably. This might have gone on for a long time." I paused. "I don't understand how he could do this to me."

John sighed. "Look, I love your family. I do. But not everybody's like you guys. You think everyone is good and kind and honest, and you're surprised when you find out they aren't. You take it personally."

"Of course I take this personally!" I yelled.

John put his hand on my knee. "But most people look out for themselves, protect themselves and what they want, and they assume that's what everyone else is doing, too."

My sister looked at me in the rearview mirror. We both had tears in our eyes.

There was a box of Kleenex on the backseat, so I blew my nose. "What the hell did he want with me anyway? Why track me down after all these years?"

John gave me a small smile. "To see if he could still get you."

"What? I'm like a mountain that must be climbed? I'm a game that must be won?"

John paused for a second. "Yeah. Pretty much."

"Why don't I know any of this?" I blow my nose again.

"I don't know," John says. "In a way you're lucky you don't."


The Colts stage a 47-yard drive that eats up more than seven minutes. Again the Colts can't get a touchdown, so Vinatieri trots out onto the field again and kicks a field goal—his fifth—to put his team up 15–6 with 23 seconds left.

"Vinatieri was worth every damn penny!" I yell.

"Congratulations," Jerry says.

The camera starts showing the "reaction" shots, the fans' forlorn faces, the Ravens' impassive stares. All that collective hate and bombast deflated. All those silent prayers for payback unanswered.

Then the Colts' Robert Mathis intercepts a Steve McNair pass. Game over. The Colts are going to the AFC Championship. The Ravens are going (or rather staying) home. Laura and Ben put on their coats. The Eagles are playing the Saints in the NFC Divisional playoff, and they want to watch it together at home. "Good luck!" I say. "Go Eagles!"

"What are we going to do if the Super Bowl is Eagles versus Colts?" Janet asks.

Laura and I wave our arms in front of her face. "Stop! Don't say that! You'll jinx it!"


A reporter sticks a microphone in my face.

**Me:** A month after I moved to Pittsburgh, I got an e-mail from Yvonne. We talked on the phone once or twice. Bob left her. And then she met his other girlfriend Violet. And Violet told her about Dina and me. And then Bob ended up with some woman named Ursula. Violet had known about Yvonne and Dina and me, and Dina and I knew about Yvonne, but not Violet nor each other. And Ursula didn't know about any of us. And do you know how he pulled it off? Technology. And the apartment. That night when he narrated his "first night" sleeping there, well, he'd been renting that apartment for a year. Sometimes I say to myself, "I should have known," but Yvonne *lived with* him and she had no clue. But when she found out . . . it was like she drew a time line on a wall of her house. No, two time lines: one for the life she'd lived with him, or thought she was living, and the one that accounted for his whereabouts as he lived his secret life. *So on Easter Sunday 2004, when I thought he was at such-and-such a place, he was really here with so-and-so.* She wanted to know what had been real and what hadn't. God, how horrible that must have been for her!

**Reporter:** Yeah.

**Me:** I told her I hoped she'd find some solace and move on. It's like what Colts' owner Jim Irsay said in an *Indianapolis Star* article I read this morning. "Harboring resentments is not a good thing for any of us, because it turns on you. No matter what the situation is in life, if I forgive you, that frees me. Resentment is bondage. Whatever those feelings are, the cast of characters that existed when my dad was [in Baltimore], and all the things that went on a quarter-century ago, it's a long time ago." He's right.

**Reporter:** Yeah.

**Me:** I still think it was chickenshit, how those guys left me, but I have to move on.

**Reporter:** Yeah.

**Me:** I've been saying that losing the Punter is what started all this. Or losing Alex. But really, I think this was all about Bob Irsay.

**Reporter:** Yeah.

**Me:** You know, Dennis is a nice man. A good man. He's not the least bit Machiavellian. He doesn't think all's fair in love and war. He's like me. He has a good heart.

**Reporter:** Yeah.

**Me:** I should call him.

**Reporter:** Yeah.

**Me:** Um . . . is that all you have to say? Why are you even here?

**Reporter:** Um . . . because your friends and family are worn out from talking this out with you?

**Me:** Yeah.

Being perfect is about being able to look your friends in the eye and know that you didn't let them down because you told them the truth. And that truth is that you did everything you could. There wasn't one more thing that you could've done. Can you live in that moment as best you can, with clear eyes, and love in your heart, with joy in your heart?

—Billy Bob Thornton in *Friday Night Lights* (the movie)

# AFC CHAMPIONSHIP
# COLTS VS. PATRIOTS
## OR
# Exorcising Demons Everywhere

I t's the day after the Colts vanquished the Ravens, and Pittsburgh has been blessed with a January afternoon so mild that I'm not even wearing a coat. Dennis and I sit in a diner booth eating lunch.

"What's your middle name?" I ask.

He tells me.

"Is that your dad's name?"

He tells me.

"What was your grandfather's name?"

He doesn't know.

"How can you not know your grandfather's name?" As soon as I say this, I regret my tone. Too harsh. Too mocking.

Dennis squirms in his seat a little. He tells me his grandfather abandoned his family.

"Oh, I'm so sorry," I say.

"It's okay. I didn't know him." Dennis takes another bite of his sandwich. I tell him about my paternal grandfather and great-grandfather, who were fire chiefs in Peru. I'm in the middle of a story—about a field trip my second-grade class took to the fire station—when I realize that Dennis has never really asked me anything about my family. And why should he, really? I talk enough for both of us. But I decide that for the rest of the day, I'm not going to tell him anything. I'm going to wait for him to ask.

After lunch, I clamber into Dennis's truck. He turns on the radio—the Bears and Seahawks are playing in the NFC Divisional playoffs—and we listen in pleasant silence as he drives from place to place. We go to IKEA so I can buy a rug and wineglasses. We go to furniture stores because I'm in the market for a new living-room chair. We browse. God, it's nice browsing with someone on a Sunday.

It's the third quarter of the Bears versus Seahawks game, and Seattle's Shaun Alexander runs 13 yards for a touchdown, giving his team a lead over the Bears, 23–21. I picture my dad watching this game back in Aurora, Indiana, kicked back in his La-Z-Boy in the living room, a Miller Lite within reach. I think about my brother—in exactly the same pose, drinking the same beer—watching this game in Batesville, Indiana.

I turn to Dennis. "Did I tell you my dad is a big Bears fan?"

"No, you didn't," Dennis says. He smiles.

I could tell him the story about why my dad likes the Bears—but I don't. And he doesn't ask.

Josh Brown's extra point is good. The Seahawks are up 24–21.

I crack the window, filling the cab with the sound of whistling wind.

Later, I'm driving home listening to the Bears game, which is now in overtime. When I enter the Liberty Tunnel, the Bears are lining up to give Robbie Gould a chance to kick a 49-yard field goal. The radio turns to static as I drive through the tubes, and when I emerge, the Bears have won.

It's Wednesday night, and I'm in my office at the Cathedral, grading papers. There's a soft knock on my door. It's Lance, one of my graduate students, returning a borrowed book. He walks in and almost has to stoop;

he's well over six feet tall. He played basketball at Vanderbilt. "Hey, good luck on Sunday," he says. Last Sunday, the New England Patriots defeated the heavily favored San Diego Chargers, and so the AFC Championship will be Colts versus Patriots. Again. Lance says, "I'm not a fan of Peyton, but I'll root for them for your sake."

"How can you *not be* a Peyton Manning fan?"

"I don't know. I guess it's because he's such a perfectionist. It bugs me." Lance leans against the doorframe.

I'm puzzled. "How can you not like someone who *wants* to be perfect? Who wants to be the best he can be?"

Lance sighs. "I don't know. Sometimes having a perfectionist on your team isn't such a good thing." He points at the Colts poster on my office door. "I think it makes him kinda controlling and . . . intolerant . . . when the people around him aren't perfect. Like those comments he made about his offensive line after the Steelers game."

I throw up my hands. "Oh no, not that again!"

Last year, in a postgame press conference after the playoff loss to the Steelers, Peyton was pressed to account for the upsetting loss. The reporters asked twelve different versions of the same question: *Whose fault is it that the Colts lost today?* Peyton didn't say, "Well, it's our idiot kicker's fault." He didn't say, "It's Nick Harper's fault for not running around Ben Roethlisberger, who was falling down anyway." He also didn't say, "Well, it's my fault." Instead he said those words that were repeated over and over again on ESPN: "I'm trying to be a good teammate here, but let's just say we had some problems with protection." Former Steelers quarterback Terry Bradshaw translated Peyton this way: "Of course, it's not *my fault* we lost. It was my offensive line, who didn't protect very well, and thus I was sacked five times."

"Look," Lance says, "hear me out."

And I do, because Lance certainly knows more about being on a team than I do.

"Football is the *one sport* where a single person's perfection makes the *least amount* of difference. There's too many other people playing, too many variables for any player to exert that much control over the outcome of a game."

"True," I say. I remember watching Michael Jordan in the 1996–1997 NBA Finals, playing with the flu because he knew the Chicago Bulls (probably) couldn't beat the Utah Jazz without him.

Lance crosses his arms across his chest. "It's like he thinks that if he could play both offense and defense and kick the field goals—the game would be played *right,* every play, but after each series, he has to take turns and hand the game over to his teammates, and when the Colts lose, he acts like *Hey, I did my part, guys, why didn't YOU?* That would bug the shit out of me." Lance checks his watch; he's on break in an evening seminar. "With a temperament like his, Peyton should really play golf. Maybe box. Not play football."

After he's gone back to his class, I sit in my darkened office letting Lance's words soak in. For the last year or so I've found it comforting to know where Peyton Manning is the week before a big game: in his basement. He's down there studying game film. He's taking notes. He's thinking obsessively. He's trying to crack the code which will reveal the Secret: how to win the game. Then he emerges from the basement and drives to the stadium. Two hours before the big game he walks onto the field with his receivers, and for the next forty minutes they go through their route tree play by play, always in the same order. Their bodies memorize these movements until performing them requires no conscious thought whatsoever, and somehow, magically, the basement-gleaned knowledge flows like electricity from Peyton Manning's brain to his hands and feet. During the game he controls the line of scrimmage, telling everyone else where to be and what to do.

Sometimes when I picture Peyton down in that basement, I feel like he's not down there just for himself or for the Colts but also for the state of Indiana, for everyone, really. He's hunkered down with a horribly complex equation, solving for "x." For the last year or so, I've struggled to solve for "x," to answer one question: *Why am I alone?* I want to solve the equation, crack the code, win the game, and not be alone anymore. I've studied the problem. I've gathered information. I've read books and watched movies and talked to all kinds of experts. I've thought and studied. And I've also challenged myself to put thought into action. I've emerged from my metaphorical basement, driven to the stadium, and run through my routes. My muscles are starting to memorize those routes. I can feel it. I can feel my basement-gleaned knowledge flowing like electricity from my brain to my hands and feet.

But what do I have to really show for all that time in my metaphorical basement? I almost lost two grand to a woman with porn-star lips. I still misread people and situations—all the time. I still miss red flags. What Lance just said fills me with a sudden fear: Are Peyton Manning and I just fooling ourselves? Do we think that because we have filled up notebooks with observations and strategies, we are actually in control or any closer to solving the problem of how to win these games of ours?

If Peyton's perfectionism annoys perfect strangers like Lance, doesn't it annoy the people around him? His wife, Ashley, told *Indianapolis Woman* magazine, "The way I really help Peyton is that I don't demand a lot of his time . . . I think that helps him." His teammates occasionally grumble (anonymously, of course) to the press that their team name should be the Indianapolis Peytons. At a team meeting to discuss restrictions on visitors at their away-game hotel, Peyton will say, "I don't think we should let *anyone* up in the rooms. This is a business trip, and I don't want any distractions. I don't want any crying kids next to me while I'm trying to study."

I think about the number of times I've had a falling-out with a friend, only to hear that friend sigh and say: "I don't think I can live up to what you expect from me, Cathy." I think about my brother-in-law John's words the day after my grandpa's funeral: "Not everyone is like you." I think about the number of times I've heard myself think or say, "I'm so disappointed in [insert name here]." And then I remember Alex—at the end of it all, holding out his hands in a sad gesture I recognize now as defeat. "Cathy, I can't be any different or better than who I am right now." Maybe this—single-mindedness, exasperating conscientiousness—is another thing I have in common with Peyton Manning. Maybe it's also why neither of us has our ring.

My friend Janet knocks softly on my office door. "Are you ready to head home?" A few minutes later we huddle together at the bus stop shelter, waiting for the 54C. We chat about how our classes are going. She calls Jerry on her cell phone to let him know she's on her way home. Our breath billows between us. "Do you know how Peyton Manning met his wife?"

Janet laughs at me. "Do tell!"

"Her parents had these next-door neighbors. This is in Memphis. The man, the neighbor, he just happened to have played football at the University of Tennessee."

Janet looks down Fifth Avenue at the approaching bus. Not ours. "Is the University of Tennessee in Memphis?"

"No, UT is in Knoxville." Janet is from Colorado and can't be expected to know these things. "So this neighbor guy who lives in Memphis introduces Peyton—who is from New Orleans and is gonna go to college in Knoxville—to the daughter of his neighbor, who's gonna go to college at the University of Virginia."

"And this is important why?"

I sigh. "Because if that neighbor hadn't played football for Tennessee, Peyton would never have met his wife, you know? They would have been these two random people at two totally different schools. They never would have met. I'll bet UT never even played Virginia in football while Peyton was there. They're in totally different divisions or whatever."

Another bus stops in front of us. The students shuffle quickly inside, out of the cold. Janet looks at me funny and asks, "Okay, so what's the meaning of that story?"

I look down at my boots. "I just want to know how long before the equivalent of that story happens to me. How long do I have to wait before someone introduces me to the man I never would have met otherwise?"

Standing on the corner of Bigelow and Fifth, Janet gives me a long look. The look is equal parts exasperation, pity, and genuine concern. "So I guess this means things aren't going well with Dennis, huh?"

"I can't talk to him." I pause. "No, that's not right. I can talk enough for both of us. He doesn't talk to me."

"That's a pretty typical complaint women have, you know?"

"I know, I know. Remember that line in *Sleepless in Seattle?* 'Verbal ability is a highly overrated thing in a guy, and it's our pathetic need for it that gets us into so much trouble.'"

"Oh, that Nora Ephron!" Janet chuckles. "But it's true."

"There was this other line. 'You don't want to be in love. You want to be in love in a movie.' That's me," I confess. "That's totally me."

"Isn't that the one that ends with Meg Ryan and Tom Hanks meeting on the top of the Empire State Building?"

"Yeah."

Our bus comes, and we find seats next to each other. Janet continues our conversation, looking straight ahead. "But you know the movie stops there. They hold hands. There's a hint they might fall in love. The elevator doors close. But that's not where the story ends. That's where it begins. Trust me. Or it's where a certain kind of story ends and another begins. Maybe the next day or the next week or the next year, they'll realize they can't stand each other."

I lean my head against the bus window. "What's the difference between 'settling' and 'settling down'?"

The bus rocks to a stop. "I don't know, Cathy. I think it's different for everyone."

On Sunday morning, I go to Giant Eagle. I want to make chili or Spanish hot dogs, like the last two weeks when the Colts won, but I feel bad that I keep making these meat dishes for my football parties, since Ben's a vegetarian. I wander the aisles, reminding myself that ground beef has nothing to do with whether or not the Colts will win this game. Once I have thoroughly convinced myself of this, I head to the produce aisle to buy the ingredients for a vegetarian stew. I scan the customers, looking for a blue hat, looking for the Colts guy I saw in here two weeks ago, but he's not here. Actually, I don't see anyone in Colts gear, but then, I'm not wearing any either. There seem to be a lot of men shopping alone this morning. I see myself reflected in the mirrored produce racks; I look like shit and none of these guys is giving me a second look. And then I wonder, *Wait, why is my cablight on? It's been off for a month.*

A few hours later, the stew is stewing in my Crock-Pot. My brother calls from the road. He's driving to Missouri today to start his new job.

"I can't stand this suspense, Scott. I'm a freaking wreck!"

My brother sighs. "Cathy, I know this is the first year you've really followed the Colts, but try to have some perspective."

I laugh. "Where are you now?"

"I'm on I-465. Just got on the exit for St. Louis."

I know exactly where he is. I can see that exit in my mind. "Imagine that right now you're driving to Missouri and you don't have Sara. That's me. That's my life."

"I can't imagine."

I'm lying on my bed in Pittsburgh watching the snow fall. "You know, there's only one bad thing about growing up in a loving family."

"What's that?"

"Leaving it."

"Yeah."

"Wait. No, two things. Learning how to live without it."


The phone rings. It's Dennis, who for the last month has called me every day even when he doesn't have anything to say. But today—he does. "I'm not coming. I'm sick," he says, and he definitely sounds congested. Sniff. Sniff.

"But do you want to do something later this week?" he asks. "How about a movie on Wednesday night?"

"Sure," I say.

"How are you doing today?" he asks.

I tell him about my brother leaving Indiana and how sad I am.

"You'll get used to it," he says matter-of-factly. "I only see my sister once a year now."

I decide this man doesn't know me at all.

"Dennis, is there anything wrong that I should know about?" I ask, and as soon as I've asked, I realize I should not have.

"No," Dennis says bluntly. "I told you I'm sick."

I can't help myself. I ask again. "Are you sure?"

"Yes."

"Okay. Just checking."

Click.

I go downstairs and stand in front of the TV crying. The Bears are playing the Saints for the NFC Championship at Soldier Field in Chicago. It's the second half, and I watch placidly as the Saints' Reggie Bush runs the ball 88 yards for a touchdown. Who cares? I don't care about this dumb game anymore. Football is dumb. Men are dumb. I'm tired of being disappointed by men and the games they play. I'm tired of working hard, doing everything I can, getting my hopes up, only to lose again and again. I'm sick of losing! I'm going to have to watch this game alone—again! And the Colts are gonna lose—again! Just like they lose every year in the playoffs.

I want a cigarette. I have a beer instead.


It's a half hour before kickoff. Laura calls, and I tell her what happened. "Do you want just girls to come? No husbands? Maybe you need just girls around so you can talk about boys." I'm grateful for this expression of empathy. But I say, "Heck with boys. I'd rather talk about football."


Janet and Jerry arrive first. They look around for Dennis, and I tell them that once again he's not coming. Jerry shakes his head. "I think if he wants to date you, he needs to man up and get his ass over here." Then Ben and Laura arrive, and together the five of us eat stew and watch the game in my living room.

The Patriots score on a fluke, a fumble, when big offensive lineman Logan Mankins falls on the ball in the end zone. Patriots up 7–0.

The Colts drive 56 yards but settle for a Vinatieri field goal. Patriots up 7–3.

On the next drive, the Patriots decide to go for it on fourth down and—of course!—quarterback Tom Brady completes a 27-yard pass.

"I hate Tom Brady," I say.

No one in the room disagrees with me. On the next play, the Patriots score, putting them up 14–3.

Finally the Colts have the ball, but—of course!—Peyton Manning throws an interception to Asante Samuel, who runs the ball for a touchdown, putting the Patriots up 21–3.

My living room grows very quiet. I rock back and forth, back and forth, back and forth. "Oh . . . no . . . oh . . . no . . ."

"It's still early in the game, Cathy," Jerry says.

Ben pats me on the back. "You've still got plenty of time. Plenty of time."

Just then, one of the stats geeks feeds this little tidbit to Phil Simms: No team in conference championship history has *ever* come back from a deficit this big.

The Colts drive again but can't get the touchdown and again they settle for a Vinatieri field goal. Score 21–6.

At halftime my friends all look at me cautiously. "Are you okay?" they ask.

I can't speak. I go into the kitchen and start cleaning. I don't know what else to do with myself. As I empty the dishwasher and sweep and mop the floor, I think, *I know I said I don't care if the Colts win or lose. I know I said I don't care if I win or lose. But I do care! I want the Colts to win! I want to win! Why can't we win? Why don't we ever win? Why? Why? Please, at least let one of us win. Please.*

On the opening drive of the second half, the Colts move downfield and score on a 1-yard surge forward by Peyton himself. Patriots still up, 21–13.

Mojo! The Colts need more mojo! My lucky Christmas tree is pumping out positive white-light energy. "Here," I say, handing out all my Colts paraphernalia. Every single person in this room has a graduate degree, but not one of them thinks this is a silly idea. I give Ben a Colts sweatshirt. I give Jerry some blue-and-silver beads I got at the Texans game in September. I put Laura in charge of my horseshoe necklace that blinks blue neon. "Turn it on when the Colts need more mojo, okay?"

Laura nods. "No problem. I'm on it!"

The Colts force a punt and get the ball back. Tight end Dallas Clark makes a 25-yard reception! Running back Dominic Rhodes runs for 19 yards! Blue beads are rubbed! Blinking necklace is illuminated. Manning throws into the end zone—not to Marvin Harrison or Reggie Wayne, like you might expect—but to big Dan Klecko, a defensive lineman and goal-line fullback. Patriots still up 21–19. Peyton goes for the two-point conversion and finds Marvin Harrison. It's complete! It's a tie ball game, 21–21!

In my living room, we all start murmuring, "Holy shit. Holy shit. Holy shit."

But a few minutes later, the Patriots score again, putting them up 28–21.

At the beginning of the fourth quarter, the Colts get their turn to score on a fluke, a fumble, when center Jeff Saturday falls on the ball in the end zone. It's a tie game again! 28–28.

Holy shits! Blue beads! Blinking necklace!

New England gets a field goal. Drat! Patriots up 31–28.

Indianapolis gets a field goal, too! Tie game again! 31–31.

Holy shits! Blue beads! Blinking necklace!

New England gets a field goal. Patriots up 34–31. To win the game, the Colts have to go 80 yards. Time remaining: 2:17.

I fall on the floor and roll around like I'm in physical pain. I actually do feel pain. My whole body aches. "Oh, my God, this is too much, I can't take this anymore!" I grab a pillow and put it over my head except for a half-inch slit through which I can still see the television. For some reason, this makes me feel better, and it's in this position that I witness the next two minutes and seventeen seconds of the game, the most amazing two minutes and seventeen seconds of my life. So far, at least.

It goes like this:

Peyton completes a pass to Reggie Wayne. Eleven-yard gain. First down.

A pass to tight end Bryan Fletcher falls incomplete.

Fletcher tells Manning to try him again, and he does, completing a 32-yard pass. First down!

Holy shits! Blue beads! Blinking necklace!

This time, Peyton throws to Reggie Wayne. The ball flies up out of his hands, out of control.

A muffled cry rises up from within my pillow. "Nooooooooooooooooo oooooooooooo!"

But luckily, none of the Patriots sees the loose ball, and Wayne regains control for a 14-yard gain that's transformed into an amazing 26-yard gain because a Patriot made contact with Peyton's helmet.

Running play. Joseph Addai for 5 yards.

Another running play. Addai again for 3 yards.

Holy shits! Blue beads! Blinking necklace!

This is the moment that Peyton Manning, the man with the laser-rocket arm, has been waiting for all his life. Does Peyton throw a glorious pass? No, he does not! It's another running play, to Addai again! Touchdown! The Colts have the lead 38–34!

Peyton takes a seat on the bench. These are the moments between series when he studies aerial photographs or calls his quarterback coach on the phone. But tonight there's no way to play the game any better than he just did. The camera watches him sitting there head down, unable to watch the last minute.

I can't watch either.

Instead, I writhe around on the floor moaning. Sure, it's improbable that New England can come back and win. They need a touchdown with just a minute left on the clock. But these are the Patriots! That's Bill Belichick! They have two time-outs left! Wouldn't it be just like this stinking, unfair life for Tom Brady to throw a Hail Mary and win the game? Isn't that the way it always happens?

But this time—this game, this season—that's *not* the way it happens.

A few minutes later, Colts' safety Marlin Jackson intercepts Brady and falls to the ground, clutching the ball in his arms. There are 17 seconds left on the clock. My living room explodes, but I still refuse to believe the Colts have won until I see the team run out onto the field. It's true! They did it! A local Colts announcer screams, "WE'RE GOING TO THE SUPER BOWL! WE'RE GOING TO THE SUPER BOWL! MARLIN JACKSON WITH THE INTERCEPTION! WHAT A COMEBACK! WHAT AN EFFORT! THE COLTS ARE HEADED TO THE SUPER BOWL, EXORCISING DEMONS EVERYWHERE!"

Peyton hugs his father, Archie! Tony Dungy smiles his freckled grin! Oh, the drama! Oh, the blue-and-white confetti! Oh, Indiana! I love you! *This* is why we keep playing (and watching) the game even though it so often breaks our hearts. Because when it *doesn't* break our hearts, when we finally finally finally win, it feels so extraordinarily and amazingly and overpoweringly *wonderful*.

My friends give me hugs and gather their coats. It's been snowing hard during the game, and I tell them to drive home safely. As I wave good-bye, I think briefly about how much I wanted to have a man with me here to-night, someone to share this moment with. I just spent a year working as hard as I possibly could to make that dream a reality, to *force* it into being, if need be, and the Colts just beat the Patriots in the AFC Championship, and I'm still alone. Isn't that just like this life? Isn't that the way it always happens?

But you know what? I don't feel alone. In fact, on this particular night, I feel more loved and more connected to the world than I've felt in a long, long time. My brother calls from his hotel room in Missouri. "Go Colts!" he yells. My sister calls from Harrison, Ohio, and she hands the phone to Clay. "Go Coats! Go Coats!" he says. Mom and Dad call from Peru. They watched the game with a couple they've been friends with since high school. "We've got Colts Band-Aids stuck all over us!" Mom says, and then e-mails me the pictures to prove it. But then my phone keeps ringing and beeping. My computer keeps dinging with new mes-sages. I'm not alone at all. So many people—friends and family, students and strangers—reach out to me from all over the United States.

Congratulations! I was thinking about you tonight.

What a game! What a nail-biter! What a comeback!

I'm a die-hard Steelers fan, but I still love an underdog.

That was the best game I've ever seen! Holy crap!

You don't know me, but I heard you read your essay about being a Colts fan. As much as it pains me, because Peyton Manning will now be in every single commercial on television, congrats to you and your Colts.

Wow!!!!!!! What a game!!!!!!!!!!!!! You must be in Colts heaven!!!!

In the small hours of the night, Jillian e-mails me. "Hey, wasn't there a big game tonight? Did the Colts win?" she asks. "Did you?"

And I tell her, "Yes."

> People who work together will win,
> whether it be against complex football defenses
> or the problems of modern society.
>
> —Vince Lombardi

---

# SUPER BOWL XLI
# COLTS VS. BEARS
## OR
# On the Road to the Super Bowl

---

I t's a week before the Super Bowl, and Dennis calls, checking in like he does almost every night. He talks for five minutes or so about his tires. He needs new tires. They will be expensive, and he doesn't have a lot of time to drive around pricing tires.

"Dennis, why do you like me? Why do you call me every day?"

"Oh gee," he says.

"Why?"

"I . . . feel really on the spot."

"Okay. Think about it and call me tomorrow."

He doesn't call the next night. But he does call the night after that, three days before the Super Bowl. Dennis has bought new tires.

"Dennis, why don't you come over when I'm with my friends?"

He sighs. "I'm just not comfortable."

I try to convince him that my friends are really very nice, normal people—only with PhDs. But I see his point, too. "I know what you mean. My family has said the same thing to me. Hell, sometimes I feel like a dumb-ass compared to my friends." He chuckles. "Do *I* make you feel uncomfortable?"

Dennis doesn't answer for a second. "No, not really."

I sit down on my bed and put my head in my hand. "You like Indiana Cathy, but you know, I'm Pittsburgh Cathy, too."

"What?"

"Nothing. Look, Dennis, I think you need to look for a different girl."

"Oh."

"It's nice to have someone to do things with. But I don't think we're really crazy about each other."

Dennis sighs. "I don't even think I can do that anymore."

I smile to hear him say that. "Did you *ever* feel it?"

"A long time ago."

My cat jumps up on my bed, and I stroke his head. "You know, I haven't felt it in a long time either, but I still want it. I think you deserve it. We both do."

"Yeah."

"But if we keep hanging out, we'd just be settling because we're bored. And lonely."

"Yeah."

"You're a good man, Dennis." I really mean this.

"Thanks," he says. "Bye."


My brother Scott calls. He's on the road driving from Missouri back to Indiana to watch the Super Bowl with the family. "Hey, aren't you coming home to watch the game with us?"

I'm in the basement, doing laundry. "No, I'm going to watch it here with my friends."

I hear him take a sip of what I know is Mountain Dew. "Are you going to watch the game with Dennis?" I tell him we aren't dating anymore. "Cath, don't take this the wrong way, but I think that's good. I know you had this big plan to find love by the end of the season and everything, but you know what I think? That's just too much pressure. You were trying so hard there for a while, it's like you wanted to write a man into the story of your life. But that's not how life happens."

I look above my head at the pipe. That stupid pipe! "I don't know what the hell I was thinking."

"Well, would you rather you hadn't done it?"

I consider this question. I stand back and look at what the last few months would have been like if I hadn't transformed them into "a season." No feeling vulnerable. No Match.com. No information about me zipping around cyberspace. No Max saying "Thanks, but no thanks." No letters from Great Expectations. No Erica or Polly or Gidgie. No Rick or Stan. No Starbucks. No screaming on the phone with customer-service representatives. No Jake the Parachuting Hooker-Lover. No explaining to my lawyer how I got ripped off. No Pennsylvania Bureau of Consumer Protection. No logging into Chemistry with Chris the Rocker sitting in my office. No strange, sometimes creepy online hellos. No sudden, mysterious online good-byes.

But also, no quitting smoking. No Dennis for Christmas. No Quinn reminding me that marriage isn't a ticket to happiness. No Broncos and Buffalo Blues. No Buzz Bissinger. No Janet and Jerry, Ben and Laura, Tom and Rachel. No Spanish hot dogs and chili on Sundays. Last fall would have passed like so many other falls: teach my classes, then go home, sit by myself, chain-smoke, and wonder why I'm lonely. I got out of my house and met real, actual people rather than staying inside and making them all up.

"No, you're right," I tell my brother. "I'm glad I did it."

"I think *this* is the point you needed to get to," Scott says, "the point of *not caring.*"

"Well, I care . . ."

"Sure you do, but it's different now. *You're* different now."


In the weeks leading up to the Super Bowl, the sports media monster must be fed a steady diet of stories, and one of my favorites is this: Jim Irsay owns *On the Road*. At a 2001 public auction, the Colts' owner purchased the original manuscript, which literary aficionados know as "the roll," a continuous 120-foot scroll of paper upon which Jack Kerouac banged out his legendary novel. Oh, the metaphor of the road! On the road, the road not taken, standing at the crossroads. It implies the geographical, metaphorical, and temporal. The road is both an actual physical object and an intangible idea. Sports commentators might say, "For the Indianapolis Colts, it's been a long road to the Super Bowl." But what does that mean literally? To make sense of it, get a huge map the size of a football field. Now consider each player on the Colts' roster—everyone from Peyton Manning to the players you might not have heard of, like wide receiver John Standeford or defensive end Ryan LaCasse. Look up each player's biography, readily available on the Internet via a Google search, or you can just go to the team's Web site. It's all there: where he was born, where he went to high school, where he attended college, and in some cases, what other NFL teams he's played for.

Let's start with Peyton Manning. Pick a color for his road. UT orange? Or Colts blue? Whatever. Draw a line that starts in New Orleans and goes to Knoxville, and then follow it to Indianapolis. Then continue that line to Miami, Florida, the end of the road, the site of Super Bowl XLI. Now do this for the other fifty-two members of the team. Each of those lines represents a lifetime of perseverance and two-a-day practices. A lake full of Gatorade and sweat. Each road represents a dream from origin to fruition.

And the coaches—getting to the Super Bowl is their dream, too. Before he became head coach of the Indianapolis Colts, Tony Dungy was the head coach of the Tampa Bay Buccaneers, before that, the defensive coordinator for the Minnesota Vikings, before that, the defensive backs coach of the Kansas City Chiefs, before that, defensive coordinator of the Pittsburgh Steelers, before that, the defensive backs coach at the University of Minnesota, and before that, a player for the Steelers and the 49ers.

Tony Dungy is married to a lovely woman named Lauren. Next to almost every football coach in America is a Lauren Dungy. It's not easy to be married to a football coach. In fact, it's so difficult that the wives of football coaches have discussion boards where they swap encouragement and advice. I found one of their Web sites and I printed out a few pages of their words of wisdom. And I got this crazy idea. *Cathy, stop with the whole big map and the fifty-three markers thing. Pretend that the life of a female executive, lawyer, scientist, editor, actress, doctor, professor, politician, artist, business owner, et cetera, is a lot like the life of a football coach. Just rewrite what the football coaches' wives said but change the pronouns.* So that's what I did.

## Advice for the Husbands of Football Coaches

- Don't miss her games. She needs to know you support her. Smile big when she looks up from the sidelines and finds you sitting in the stands. Win or lose, make sure you're the first person she sees when she comes out of the locker room. Always say you're proud of her, no matter the final score.
- Tell her you love her every single day. Don't get caught up in what you're giving up, and yes, it's a lot. She really does understand what she's missing at home and she really does feel guilt about this. She needs to know that you're okay with it so she can do her job well. A lot of people depend on her to do that job well.
- Support the career path your wife has chosen. You knew coaching was an important part of who she was when you married her. She must pay her dues. Help her pay them.
- Realize that a coach must move frequently. You will make friends at each school, in each town, and those relationships and memories can be carried with you.
- Understand: you will raise the children. Raising children is a joy and privilege.
- Make up several meals before training camp begins and freeze them. It's one less thing you have to do.
- What makes your sacrifice worth it? When one of your wife's players gets a scholarship or a good job. When parents come up to say what an impact she made in their child's life. Make sure you tell your children their mother is making a difference in the world.
- Remember: no marriage is easy.

A reporter sticks a microphone in my face.

**Reporter:** That was so funny.
**Me:** Yeah, we only recognize the value of what women do when we try to imagine asking a man to do the same thing.

**Reporter:** No, I meant that it's ridiculous to picture a man doing that stuff.

**Me:** Why does it have to be ridiculous? My mom says the world would be a better place and marriages would be a lot happier if more men were capable of doing even some of what's on that list.

**Reporter:** I knew it! You want a male wife. That's why you're still single.

**Me:** How many times do I have to say this? I want a man who's willing to be *a partner,* and I want to be a good partner in return.

**Reporter:** Honey, you need to know this. Deep, deep down, men want to marry a woman who will put him first. Consciously or unconsciously, he'll pick her over you every time.

**Me** (*Sigh.*): And so a young woman—consciously or unconsciously—won't let herself dream because she's still—still!—afraid a man won't pick her. God, I've seen it happen so many times. Something crosses before her eyes, like a cloud passing before the sun. A little flame of fear blooms inside her, inside all of us, and we wonder, "Will I end up alone if I'm *like that?*"

**Reporter:** Like what?

**Me:** Like the way I'm being *right now.* You know, I'm beginning to think that there's only one way for our daughters to have a shot at both personal and professional dreams: we have to teach *our sons* how to love and support them. I know the women who came before me fought for my professional opportunities. I have a college education, a great job, a published book. But now it's hearts and minds time. We've got a real social dilemma on our hands. We've raised a generation or two of brilliant, ambitious women who perhaps can't expect to marry.

**Reporter:** Cathy, that's not a social dilemma—

**Me:** You're right. *Dilemma* is too weak a word. It's *unjust.*

**Reporter:** Oh, for Chrissake, you're calling your inability to get a man a social injustice. That's rich.

**Me:** "Get a man"? Listen to yourself. Think about it historically. Our country believes in dreams, right? Seventy-five years ago, if an African-American, male or female, said, "My dream is to be a professional athlete," people would have said, "You need to accept that it's not possible." And then it became possible. Thirty years ago, if a black athlete, male or female said, "I don't want to just play the game. I want to coach, too," people would have said, "You need to accept that it's not possible." And look at this Super Bowl. Two African-American head coaches.

**Reporter:** My husband says they're making too big a deal about that.

**Me:** Maybe your husband is just used to seeing people who look like him doing important work in this world.

**Reporter:** Hey, leave my husband out of this.

**Me:** You brought him up. (*Deep breath.*) Anyway, what I was trying to say is this: we can scarcely imagine a time when to be born not white meant you literally couldn't dream big, and yet we tell women all the time to accept this. Women tell *each other* to accept this.

**Reporter:** Honestly, Cathy, didn't anybody ever warn you about all this?

**Me:** No! (*Pause.*) Actually, yeah, someone did. My freshman year of college, a professor of mine made the class talk about it. . . .

**Reporter:** Well, let's get her over here. Professor? Do you have a minute?

**Professor** (*Walks in the door with a canvas tote bag.*): Of course. (*Sees Cathy.*) So you were my student?

**Me:** A really long time ago. You made us talk about our career and family plans, but I forget why.

**Professor:** Well, we were reading Plato's *Republic* in which he's trying to define "justice" by setting up an ideal society. He says that a just society requires that the leaders, whom he calls "guardians," be given the best possible educations. I always point out that the students in the room are the future guardians of our society.

**Reporter:** Do you remember this, Cathy?

**Me:** I remember now! I thought, *Yeah, that's who I am—a guardian!*

**Professor:** I'm just glad you remember it!

**Me:** I know what you mean. Sometimes I wonder if anything I say really gets through to the little buggers.

**Professor:** Plato argues that since women can be guardians, too, it would be unjust to expect guardian women to do housework and take care of children while simultaneously holding important leadership positions. He suggests some very dramatic changes in how marriages should work, how society should work so that all guardians can have children. Basically, he suggests sharing the responsibility of raising children with men and the community.

**Reporter:** So what did you say, Cathy?

**Me:** I don't remember. Professor, do you remember?

**Professor:** That was twenty years ago. I have no idea.

**Me:** I do remember that *all* of the men in the class wanted career and family, but none of them wanted to modify their career plans to have that family. *That* should have told me something right there. There was one guy who said he didn't mind "letting" his wife work. And you [I point to the professor] were the only one who really got on him for saying that.

**Professor** (*Sighs.*): I know.

**Me:** All of the women wanted a career, too, but only until they started having kids. I remember this one woman—Jessica?—who was really confident. I think she wanted to be a lawyer. Someone asked her, "Who is going to take care of your kids?" and she said, "What's wrong with day care? What's wrong with my husband helping out?" And everyone looked at her like she was nutso.

**Professor** (*Sighs.*): I know.

**Me:** I wonder if *she* ever got married? I hope so. She knew exactly what she wanted, even then.

**Reporter:** What did you want, Cathy?

**Me:** I didn't have the slightest idea. I couldn't wrap my head around what the professor was saying. I think I remember thinking—man, that's pretty vague—*By the time I have to deal with this, the world will be different.*

**Professor:** I don't think there's any perfect choice for any of us. Men or women. Back then, Plato was merely speculating, pretending, thinking outside the box, but his suggestions aren't really that outrageous anymore. The thing is that if we want justice for smart women, something has to give. Something has to change. Someone might have to suffer a little. But who should it be: men, women, or children?

**Reporter:** Well, you've certainly given us some interesting food for thought!

**Me:** That's putting it mildly.

**Professor:** Thanks for inviting me. (*The professor shakes my hand, but then decides to give me a hug, and then she leaves.*)

**Reporter:** Okay, I'm lost now. What did that have to do with dating?

**Me:** It had *everything* to do with dating. Ever since I was a little girl, I've been told that the only way for a woman to play the game of love is to accept that the rules aren't fair. Lie about your age. Lie about what you do for a living. Assume a submissive posture. Flirt. Flatter. Don't make him feel anything less than absolutely manly. Don't talk too much. Don't be weird. Be vanilla. Or pretend to be vanilla. And I'm not talking about *Rules* girls either. I can't tell you the number of well-educated, socially progressive women—the kind who wear Che Guevara T-shirts, the kind who berate you if you say "freshmen" rather than "first-year students"—who've looked me straight in the eye and effectively said, "You're not willing to do what it takes to get and keep a man." But I want to be loved for who I *am,* not some seemingly younger, less threatening, less unique version of myself.

**Reporter:** You realize you're doing this the hard way, don't you?

**Me** (*Sigh.*): I know.

**Reporter:** Damn it, Cathy! Why can't you just make it work with Dennis?

**Me:** He's nice, but he doesn't really get me, Suzy. And, um, there's not much chemistry.

**Reporter:** You realize everyone's going to say, "Well, no wonder she didn't get a man. No wonder she's single."

**Me:** I know. They should be ashamed of themselves for saying that. But yeah, I know.

**Reporter:** Oh, sweetie! Well, I think this interview is over.

**Me:** What? You're leaving?

**Reporter:** Yeah. It's time. I think I've served my purpose.

(*A big hug.*)

**Me:** This reminds me of that scene in *Cast Away,* when the volleyball was floating away. "Wilson! Wilson! I'm sorry, Wilson!"

**Reporter:** God, I cried. Did you cry? I'm thinking, *You swim out there! He was your friend!*

**Me:** Yeah, me, too. (*Pause.*) Suzy! Suzy! Thank you, Suzy! Good-bye! (*Backing away into the tunnel, the Reporter keeps waving until she steps from sunlight into darkness and disappears.*)


The week before the Super Bowl, ESPN.com's Wright Thompson writes, "It's taken a while, but Manning seems to have found some Zen during the football season. He's trying to run his own race, not to measure himself against others. . . . The arm and brain were never the problem. He just wanted it so bad that his teammates could sense the desperation." His father, Archie Manning, says he's noticed that his son seems to be "enjoying the journey" more. In the huddle before the Super Bowl, Peyton Manning tells his teammates: "We're playing for a lot of people tonight, all right? Our families. Our coach. Let's play for each other, all right? Play for each other. Stick together. I love every one of you guys. Let's bring this championship home tonight."

The whole world gathers around televisions to see if Peyton Manning will finally get his ring—93 million Americans, according to Nielsen Media Research. It will become the third-most-watched TV program in U.S. history, behind Super Bowl XXX (Cowboys versus Steelers in 1996) and the final episode of *M\*A\*S\*H*. In Aurora, Indiana, my entire family is gathered in the living room, waiting anxiously for the kickoff. In Pittsburgh it's snowing outside and the windchill is below zero. Janet and Jerry are hosting a Super Bowl party; they just bought a huge plasma TV. Tom and Rachel arrive, along with Ben and Laura. I tell my friends, "Thanks for being here, guys." We raise our beers in salute.

"We should chest bump!" Janet says. Everyone laughs.

In Miami, the Colts kick off and flashbulbs strobe the stadium. The Bears punt return man, Devin Hester, carries the opening kickoff 92 yards for a touchdown, the first time this has happened in Super Bowl history. It's already 7–0 Bears, and the Colts haven't even taken the field yet. My friends give me concerned looks. But all through the sloppy first quarter—the missed routes, the turnovers, false-start penalties, an interception—I feel strangely calm. *I know* the Colts are going to win this game. It's their time. It's our time. Three-plus hours later, the Colts have beaten the Bears 29–17. What message has the universe just delivered to me courtesy of the Indianapolis Colts? That's easy: if Peyton Manning can work hard year after year, lose and try again, lose and try again, lose and try again, and then finally, *finally* realize his dream, then there's hope for all of us.

Fans, for the past two weeks you have been reading about the bad break I got. Yet today I consider myself the luckiest man on the face of this earth. . . . I may have had a tough break, but I have an awful lot to live for.

—Lou Gehrig, July 4, 1939

---

## A POSTGAME LOCKER-ROOM SPEECH

### OR

## After the Super Bowl Comes Valentine's Day

---

The Super Bowl is over, the Pro Bowl is over. For football fans everywhere, the yearly withdrawal symptoms begin: aimless Sundays, empty Mondays, a weeklong melancholy, like you have nothing to look forward to anymore. There's a particular rhythm to the football season that exists in no other sport. It's one game, once a week, a slow build of tension that's released on Sundays. Each football game is a story with a beginning, middle, and end, but the season as a whole has a narrative arc, too, like a novel unfolding chapter by chapter. Baseball, basketball, hockey—their seasons are structured in terms of the series, in clusters, a narrative form that imprints itself in different but still profound ways. More than any other sport, the football season resembles a TV series. The 2006 Colts season was my favorite show this year; I cherished every episode. But now my show is on hiatus, and I'll have to find something else to get excited about for the next few months.

Wait! It's not over! Peyton Manning is going to be a guest on *David Letterman*! Oh, thank God.

As you may or may not know, David Letterman is a Hoosier and an avid Colts fan. On February 13, 2007, Letterman drops some (but not all) of his ironic swagger and asks Peyton Manning the question that's been on my mind ever since the Colts beat the Patriots on January 21: Did you feel vindicated after that game? Peyton says:

> People said, "Well that's the drive he needed to have." But what if [the Patriots had] returned the kickoff after that for a touchdown? Does that mean all of a sudden I didn't have a great drive? That I'm all of a sudden the bum I've always been? I always believed that eventually we would win a Super Bowl—once we got the right team and the breaks went our way. And this year, it happened.

For a long time, I think about Peyton's words. Would he still have said this if the Patriots *had* returned the kickoff for a touchdown? Wait, in that case, would he be on *Letterman*? No, Tom Brady would be on *Letterman*. Or maybe Rex Grossman or Brian Urlacher. That's why it's so hard to believe the old adage: it's not whether you win or lose; it's whether you did your best. Because winning is what gets you on *Letterman,* not losing. Americans don't want to hear, "We'll get 'em next year." Americans console themselves with these words all the time. America wants happy endings. Not this: it's the night before Valentine's Day, and I'm alone, watching Super Bowl MVP Peyton Manning philosophize about the vagaries of fate. Why couldn't my story end happily, like a Hollywood movie? The Colts win the Super Bowl, and I watch the game with a man I love and who loves me. Why is any ending other than that unacceptable, even to me?

Normally, the only acceptable ending to a narrative like this (part sports story, part love story) is a happy one. There must be a victory, a wedding or a championship celebration, a big kiss or at least a hug, a declaration of love, a foaming champagne bottle, fireworks spilling into the sky. But the truth is: life is not a movie. Nobody needed to learn that more than me. Sports movies, I'm convinced, aren't macho at all. They're really just chick flicks with helmets so men won't feel silly caring about love. Even though he loses to Apollo Creed in a split decision, Rocky Balboa wins in *Rocky* because he and Adrian fall in love. For whatever reason, they *get* each other. And that's all anybody wants—not to get a man or get the girl, but to *be gotten.*

But I must face this undeniable truth: there might not be a lot of men out there who can really get a girl like me. I mean, look at my family. They've known me for almost forty years, and they're just now starting to catch on. So how do I find my needle in the male haystack? After *Letterman,* I sit down with my laptop and revise my Match.com profile again. I want to cut down the number of responses, not increase them. I write something that I hope will bring me the kind of man I'm looking for:

> Why am I still single? Maybe it's because I'm an optimist and idealistic. I'm holding out for Mr. Amazing. Or at least Mr. Great. Too many people settle for Mr./Miss Kinda Sorta Okay because they don't want to be alone. And that's a shame. Maybe it's because I'm very driven. My career has kept me very busy and on the move. Maybe it's because in the last ten years I've moved five times. I've made it statistically difficult for myself to meet anyone and—when I have met someone—difficult to maintain the relationship. Maybe there is no "reason." Maybe this is just the weird way life works out for some people. Anyway, what should be fairly obvious to you by now is that I think a lot. About you: you're comfortable in a variety of social situations—at a cocktail party talking about *American Idol* or the latest Malcolm Gladwell book, or on a barstool arguing about whether the Chargers should have fired Marty or who's the bigger genius: Thom Yorke, Jack White, or Beck.

And you know what? It works. I get fewer responses, but the ones I do get are from smart men who get all (or most) of those varied references. But a few days later, I also get this message:

> your kiding me right! if you been holding out that long you might as well invest in singles persons retirement home read books they say if you were never maried at your age there is something wrong upstairs!!!!

I sit there for a few minutes, trying to comprehend why a man would take the time to write this to me. The next day, his profile is gone, and I can only assume that he was at the end of a long and difficult journey, and he lashed out. I just happened to be the woman (virtually) standing there when he did. Man, I wish this game had referees to throw yellow flags, but it doesn't. Don't forget to wear your helmet and shoulder pads.

I used to think that winning—at sports and at love—was a product of magic or fate or some such nonsense. For a while this year, I started to think that winning was a numbers game, a matter of statistics and probability, purely mathematical. But now I think that love is nothing more than two compatible people finding each other and being ready for each other at exactly the same time. And this in itself is a minor miracle. A touchdown is the unfolding of a thousand fortuitous events, toppling like dominos. Winning the game on Sunday? A million dominos. A Super Bowl victory? Oh my, it's infinite. Billions and trillions of tiny choices (conscious and unconscious) that accumulate softly and unpredictably over the course of a season, and there's absolutely no way to predict what any more than a handful of these might be. The truth is, we can't control how anything ends. We can work hard, sacrifice and sweat, stack the odds in our favor, do everything right, and we still might lose. It's damn hard to cope with this fact, and every single day I struggle to accept it.

The universe unfolds softly and unpredictably, and on those occasions when it actually unfolds in our favor—on the field of love or football—we must marvel at the wonder, at the joy of this blessing. The hardest thing in this world is waiting for and preparing for that blessing. The next hardest thing is letting yourself love and be loved by another human being. That's what I learned this year, and strange as it sounds, I learned it by watching football.

# Acknowledgments

For their support, the author wishes to thank: Isaac Bower, Jim Collins, Eugene Cross, Jessica Enoch, Shannon Firth, Rich Gegick, Eric Johnson, Hannah Johnson, Dara Kinney, Kristen Laine, Anna Redcay, Catie Rosemurgy, David Walton, and Scott Wible. For the gift of time, she thanks the English Department at the University of Pittsburgh. She'd also like to thank her students, her lawyer, her doctor, her acupuncturist, her hairstylist, her health coach, her shrink, and her gynecologist. The author is grateful to the men she met during her comeback season; each taught her something quite valuable. Thanks to Lou Harry at *Indy Men's* magazine and B. J. Schecter at SI.com for publishing her early musings on this subject. In the beginning, her agent, Peter Steinberg, asked, "So you're writing this book because you want to marry Peyton Manning, right?" She thanks him for not getting it, because explaining to (and arguing with) him on the page and in her head helped her figure out exactly why she was writing this book. She thanks her first editor, veteran quarterback Liz Stein, and her amazing backup QB, Wylie O'Sullivan, who finished the game like a Super Bowl champ. The author couldn't have written this book without the unwavering love of her family. They are great material, and they are good sports about being great material. For this and many other reasons, she is the luckiest woman on the face of this earth.

# About the Author

**Cathy Day** is the author of *The Circus in Winter,* a finalist for the Story Prize, the Great Lakes Book Award, and the GLCA New Writers' Award. Her work has appeared on NPR's *Selected Shorts* and in *New Stories from the South, Story, Antioch Review, Southern Review, Shenandoah,* and SI.com. She teaches fiction in the Writing Program at the University of Pittsburgh.